Fleming, Martha H.
The Late Medieval Pope Prophecies:
The "Genus Nequam" Group
MR 204 / 86698-246-9

Catalog: $25, £22
(discount 20%) $20, £18
Display copy (discount 50%) $12.50, £11

Name _____

(must pay before signing)

The Late Medieval Pope Prophecies:

The *Genus nequam* Group

Medieval and Renaissance
Texts and Studies

Volume 204

The Late Medieval Pope Prophecies

The *Genus nequam* Group

Edited by

MARTHA H. FLEMING

Arizona Center for Medieval and Renaissance Studies
Tempe, Arizona
1999

Library of Congress Cataloging-in-Publication Data

The late medieval Pope prophecies : the Genus nequam group / edited by
Martha H. Fleming.
    p. cm. — (Medieval & Renaissance texts & studies ; v. 204)
    Includes bibliographical references and index.
    ISBN 0-86698-246-9 (alk. paper)
    1. Popes—Prophecies—Manuscripts. I. Fleming, Martha H. II. Series:
Medieval & Renaissance Texts & Studies (Series) ; v. 204.
BX958.P75L38 1999
262'.13–dc21   99–39578
                                                 CIP

Table of Contents

Acknowledgements   vii
List of Abbreviations   viii
List of Illustrations   ix

INTRODUCTION

The Prophecies   1
General Principles   12
Archetype and Copy Text: Text and Image   18
Relation of Manuscripts   27
Description of Manuscripts

   A.   Vatican Library, MS Vat. lat. 3822, fols. 6^r, 5^v 40
   C.   Cambridge, Corpus Christi College, MS 404, fols. 88^r–95^r 44
   D.   Oxford, Bodleian Library, MS Douce 88, fols. 140^r–146^v 51
   F.   Florence, Biblioteca Riccardiana, MS 1222B, fols. 1^r–8^v 56
   L.   Lunel, Bibliothèque de Louis Médard à la Bibliothèque
       Municipale, MS 7, fols. 4^r–19^r, 22^v 62
   M.   Yale, University Library, T. E. Marston MS 225,
       fols. 15^r–22^r 70
   N.   Paris, Archives Nationales, MS JJ 28, fols. 285^r–291^v 78
   P.   Monreale, Biblioteca Comunale, MS XXV.F.17,
       fols. 1^r–17^r 80
   V.   Vatican Library, MS Vat. lat. 3819, fols. 147^r–149^r 87

The Picture Tradition   94
Figures 1–21   115
Bibliography: Works Cited   137

The *Genus nequam* Prophecies   148
Notes to the Edition   189

Index   201

Acknowledgements

This book has been a long time in the making. I wish to thank Harold Lee, Morton Bloomfield, and Bernard McGinn for support and encouragement early on. I thank my colleagues at the University at Albany, SUNY: Mary Beth Winn and John Monfasani, John in particular for all his help on matters paleographical. I am indebted to Robert E. Lerner for his meticulous reading of an earlier version of this work, for bibliographic pointers, and helpful suggestions regarding the manuscript at various stages. Above all, I thank Marjorie Reeves for her wise advice and her helpful and generous-spirited reading of numerous drafts. I owe her a great deal.

I owe a debt to numerous institutions and organizations for the use of their research facilities and to all the librarians who supplied me with photocopies, microfilms, photographs, and information. I am grateful to them all, as I trust acknowledgements elsewhere in this book will demonstrate. I thank too the editors at Medieval and Renaissance Texts and Studies (MRTS) who helped turn manuscript into book.

I had support for this research in the form of fellowships and awards from the Newberry Library, the National Endowment for the Humanities, Union College, the University at Albany, SUNY, and United University Professions. A National Endowment for the Humanities Summer Seminar at Cornell, directed by Robert G. Calkins, opened my eyes to new ways of looking at manuscript illumination. Thanks too go to my family, Jim and Matthew, and to my mother, Ella M. H. Hitchcock, to whose memory this book is dedicated.

List of Abbreviations

AFH	*Archivum Franciscanum Historicum*
HJ	*Historisches Jahrbuch*
MGH	*Monumenta Germaniae Historica*
NA	*Neues Archiv der Gesellschaft für ältere deutsche Geschichtskunde*
PG	*Patrologiae cursus completus ... series graeca*, ed. J.-P. Migne (Paris, 1857–1876)
ZRVI	*Zbornik Radova Vizantoloskog Instituta*

List of Illustrations

Figure 1:   *Vaticinium I:* pope, bear, and nursing cubs. Oxford, Bodleian Library, MS Douce 88, fol. 140^r. Reproduced with permission of the Bodleian Library, Oxford.

Figure 2:   *Vaticinium II:* pope, serpents, and birds. Cambridge, Corpus Christi College, MS 404, fol. 88^v. Reproduced with permission of the Master and Fellows of Corpus Christi College, Cambridge.

Figure 3:   *Vaticinium II:* pope, tree with birds and serpent, kneeling figure. Yale, University Library, T. E. Marston MS 225, fol. 15^v. Reproduced with permission of the Beinecke Library, Yale University.

Figure 4:   *Vaticinium II:* (lower register) pope, bird on standard, dragon. Vatican Library, MS Vat. lat. 3819, fol. 147^r. Reproduced with permission of the Biblioteca Vaticana.

Figure 5:   *Vaticinium IV:* vessel or font and head. Florence, Biblioteca Riccardiana, MS 1222B, fol. 2^v. Reproduced with permission of the Biblioteca Riccardiana, Florence—Ricc.1222.B.

Figure 6:   *Vaticinia IV–V:* sickle-bearer. Cambridge, Corpus Christi College, MS 404, fol. 89^v. Reproduced with permission of the Master and Fellows of Corpus Christi College, Cambridge.

Figure 7:   *Vaticinium IV:* columns, heads, scimitar. Yale, University Library, T. E. Marston MS 225, fol. 16^v. Reproduced with permission of the Beinecke Library, Yale University.

Figure 8:   *Vaticinium V:* sickle-bearer (monk with cowl, small figure). Yale, University Library, T. E. Marston 225, fol. 17^r. Reproduced with permission of the Beinecke Library, Yale University.

Figure 9:   *Vaticinium V:* sickle-bearer (pope). Pasquilino Regiselmo, *Vaticinia sive Prophetiae Abbatis Joachimi et Anselmi Episcopi Marsicani* (Venice, 1589), unpaged, *Vaticinium XX.*

Figure 10:   *Vaticinium VIII:* cityscape or fortress under siege. Florence, Biblioteca Riccardiana, MS 1222B, fol. 4ᵛ. Reproduced with permission of the Biblioteca Riccardiana, Florence—Ricc. 1222.B.

Figure 11:   *Vaticinium VIII:* (third register) arches (fortress) with soldiers. Vatican Library, MS Vat. lat. 3819, fol. 148ʳ. Reproduced with permission of the Biblioteca Vaticana.

Figure 12:   *Vaticinium IX:* pope, crossed standards or banners, fox. Monreale, Biblioteca Comunale, MS XXV.F.17, fol. 10ʳ. Reproduced with permission of the Biblioteca Comunale di Monreale.

Figure 13:   *Vaticinium X:* empty throne. Cambridge, Corpus Christi College, MS 404, fol. 92ʳ. Reproduced with permission of the Master and Fellows of Corpus Christi College, Cambridge.

Figure 14:   *Vaticinium XI:* figure on rock (hermit summoned forth). Yale, University Library, T. E. Marston 225, fol. 20ʳ. Reproduced with permission of the Beinecke Library, Yale University.

Figure 15:   *Vaticinium XI:* figure on sarcophagus (hermit summoned forth). Oxford, Bodleian Library, MS Douce 88, fol. 144ᵛ. Reproduced with permission of the Bodleian Library, Oxford.

Figure 16:   *Vaticinium XI:* naked figure emerging from rock (hermit summoned forth). Florence, Biblioteca Riccardiana, MS 1222B, fol. 6ʳ. Reproduced with permission of the Biblioteca Riccardiana, Florence—Ricc.1222.B.

Figure 17:   *Vaticinium XI:* seated figure (hermit summoned forth). Monreale, Biblioteca Comunale, MS XXV.F.17, fol. 12ʳ. Reproduced with permission of the Biblioteca Comunale di Monreale.

Figure 18:   *Vaticinium XII:* angel holding papal tiara born aloft by animals. Cambridge, Corpus Christi College, MS 404, fol. 93ʳ. Reproduced by permission of the Master and Fellows of Corpus Christi College, Cambridge.

Figure 19:   *Vaticinium XII:* angel holding papal tiara, sarcophagus, arcs with animal heads. Florence, Biblioteca Riccardiana, MS 1222B, fol. 6ᵛ. Reproduced with permission of the Biblioteca Riccardiana, Florence—Ricc.1222.B.

Figure 20:   *Vaticinium XV:* pope, beast with human face. Florence, Biblioteca Riccardiana, MS 1222B, fol. 8ʳ. Reproduced with permission of the Biblioteca Riccardiana, Florence—Ricc.1222.B.

Figure 21: *Vaticinium XV:* pope, beast with human face. Pasquilino Regiselmo, *Vaticinia sive Prophetiae Abbatis Joachimi et Anselmi Episcopi Marsicani* (Venice, 1589), unpaged, *Vaticinium XXX.*

Pictures I–XVI: *Vaticinia I–XVI.* Lunel, Bibliothèque de Louis Médard à la Bibliothèque Municipale, MS 7, fols. 4ʳ–22ᵛ. Reproduced with permission of the Bibliothèque Louis Médard à la Bibliothèque municipale de la ville de Lunel.

INTRODUCTION

The Prophecies

The *Genus nequam* prophecies[1] are the earliest group of late medieval Latin pope prophecies that describe the progress of the Church from Nicholas III (1277–1280) to the final pontiff. Besides Nicholas and the last angelic pope, in these fifteen prophecies we see depicted Martin IV (1281–1285), Honorius IV (1285–1287), Nicholas IV (1288–1292), Celestine V (July–December 1294), Boniface VIII (1294–1303), and Benedict XI (1303–1304).[2]

The prophecies, ascribed to Joachim of Fiore but linked historically with the fortunes of the Italian Spiritual Franciscans in the late thirteenth century, were an attempt to interpret the events of the times within a larger framework of meaning, one provided by the rhetoric of eschatology. Marjorie Reeves and others suggest that the prophecies were intended as a vehicle of both propaganda and reform, concluding that the authors not only wished to influence the outcome of contemporary events including

---

[1] The early work on these prophecies was done by Herbert Grundmann, "Die Papstprophetien des Mittelalters," *Archiv für Kulturgeschichte* 19 (1929): 77–138, reprinted in *Ausgewählte Aufsätze, 2: Joachim von Fiore,* MGH, Schriften 25, 2 (Hanover, 1977), 1–57; Marjorie Reeves, *The Influence of Prophecy in the Later Middle Ages* (Oxford, 1969), 393–462; eadem, "Some Popular Prophecies from the Fourteenth to the Seventeenth Centuries," in *Popular Belief and Practice,* G. J. Cuming and Derek Baker, eds., *Studies in Church History* 8 (1972), 107–134. More recent studies include Bernard McGinn, "Angel Pope and Papal Antichrist," *Church History* 47 (1978): 115–173, and " 'Pastor Angelicus': Apocalyptic Myth and Political Hope in the Fourteenth Century," a paper presented in Assisi, October 1987, and reprinted in *Santi e santità nel secolo XIV,* 221–251 (Perugia, 1989); and Robert E. Lerner, "Ursprung, Verbreitung und Ausstrahlung der Papstprophetien des Mittelalters" in Robert E. Lerner and Robert Moynihan, *Weissagungen über die Päpste: Vat. Ross. 374* (Stuttgart, 1985); also Lerner, "On the Origins of the Earliest Latin Pope Prophecies: A Reconsideration," *Fälschungen im Mittelalter,* MGH, Schriften 33, 5 (Hanover, 1988), 611–635.

[2] There is some disagreement on this point. Robert E. Lerner maintains, and Bernard McGinn agrees, that in the early form there was no reference to Benedict XI. I won't rehearse the arguments here, but see McGinn, " 'Pastor Angelicus'," 235, and Lerner, *Weissagungen über die Päpste,* 33; see also below n. 36.

perhaps the papal election of 1304, but also wished to inspire a reform and *renovatio* in a larger context—that of the church and society as a whole.[3]

Bernard McGinn calls the pope prophecies a new literary genre.[4] Certainly it was a genre which quickly became a "best seller," as the range of nine extant manuscripts indicates: they are of Italian, French, English, and possibly German provenance. In an expanded verson of thirty prophecies, they appear in numerous manuscripts of the later fourteenth and fifteenth centuries and in a substantial number of printed editions of the Renaissance. Moreover they were widely imitated.

There are other indications of the prophecies' popularity and influence, as can be seen by examining some of the references to these prophecies in the first two decades of the fourteenth century. One of the first explicit references to the *Genus nequam* prophecies is that by Francesco Pipini who was working on his chronicle as late as 1317.[5] He refers to the first nine prophecies only (although describing only eight of them, omitting number eight), associating the prophecies with popes beginning with Nicholas III and ending with Clement V.

Another witness, Hugh of Novocastro in his *Tractatus de Victoria Christi contra Antichristum* (1314–1316), makes reference to this group of prophecies, although not by the *incipit, Genus nequam*.[6] His interest is in the group of prophecies following that for Clement V and particularly in the final five units of the set, and he counts seven popes between Clement V and the terrible beast.

The evidence of a third witness, Bernard Délicieux, is of even greater interest. He also seems to have possessed a *libellus* containing the *Genus nequam* prophecies. At the time of his arrest in 1317, as Reeves and others have noted, Délicieux spoke of a "papalarius," i.e., a set of papal prophecies, attributed by him to Joachim of Fiore, "in which past and future

---

[3] Reeves, *Influence of Prophecy*, 401–403.

[4] Bernard McGinn, *Visions of the End: Apocalyptic Traditions in the Middle Ages* (New York, 1979), 188.

[5] Francesco Pipini, *Chronicon*, in L. Muratori, *Rerum Italicarum Scriptores*, OS 9 (Milan, 1721), cols. 724, 726, 727, 728, 736, 741, 747, 751. Pipini was writing some time before 1317 (for dating, see Lerner, "On the Origins," 620, n. 21).

[6] Hugh of Novocastro, *Tractatus de victoria Christi contra Antichristum* (Nuremberg, 1471, unpaginated), Lib. II. cap. 28. See Reeves, "Some Popular Prophecies," 116 and Lerner, "On the Origins," 623, n. 27; Robert Lerner, *The Powers of Prophecy: The Cedar of Lebanon Vision from the Mongol Onslaught to the Dawn of Enlightenment* (Berkeley, 1983), 55–56, n. 36. dates the *Tractatus* to 1315. The *Tractatus* reads: ". . . libello in quo Romanorum Pontificum figure describuntur ab ultimo pontifice qui obiit A.d. MCCCXIIII usque ad nudum pontificem renuentemque coronam dignitatis pontificalis, et consequenter usque ad bestiam, nonnissi pauci, vii videlicet, intermedii fieri computantur."

popes were represented in pictures."[7] Alan Friedlander in his recent work on Délicieux has brought to light the testimony of two witnesses, Raimond Curti and Arnaude de Nogarède, testimony which confirms that this "papalarius" was indeed the *Genus nequam* sequence.[8]

By the mid-fourteenth century, the *Genus nequam* prophecies were circulating widely. By this time references to the prophecies were often included with—or on occasion conflated with—references to the *Horoscopus* and the *Liber de Flore* and their respective commentaries, by, for instance, Gentile of Foligno in 1345[9] and the Franciscan Joachite, John of Roquetaillade, in 1356.[10]

The *Horoscopus* is dated to 1303–1304 and the commentary to ca. 1307, and it traces the papacy from Nicholas III through a future angelic pope.[11] The commentary on the *Horoscopus* has been studied in some detail by Robert Lerner in his quest to identify the compiler of the *Genus nequam* prophecies as one Rabanus Anglicus: the commentary identifies Rabanus Anglicus with the *Genus nequam* prophecies, citing Rabanus, along with Cyril, Joachim, and Hildegard, as privileged sources of revelation. As Lerner has put it, quoting in part from the commentary, ". . . the prophetic truth communicated to Rabanus was 'the progress of the church as seen in the figures of the Roman popes from Nicholas III to the final pontiff,' a patent description of the earliest Latin pope prophecies."[12]

The *Liber de Flore*, known also as the *Liber de Flore sive de summis*

---

[7] Reeves, "Some Popular Prophecies," 117. On Délicieux, see Michel de Dmitrewski, "Fr. Bernard Délicieux, O.F.M., sa lutte contra l'Inquisition de Carcassonne et d'Albi, son procès, 1297–1319," *AFH* 17 (1924): 183–218, 313–337, 457–488, 18 (1925): 3–22; and more recently Alan Friedlander, "Jean XXII et les Spirituels: le cas de Bernard Délicieux," in *La papauté d'Avignon et le Languedoc 1316–1342,* Cahiers de Fanjeaux 26 (Toulouse, 1991), 221–236.

[8] Friedlander, "Délicieux," 228–230 citing B.N. Lat. 4270, fols. 260ᵛ–261ʳ. See also Orit Schwartz and Robert E. Lerner, "Illuminated Propaganda: The Origins of the *Ascende calve* Pope Prophecies," *Journal of Medieval History* 20 (1994): 157–191, here 183, notes 46 and 47 for precisions on the way his copy looked.

[9] A commentary on the prophecy "Ve mundo in centum annis," ascribed to a Gentile of Foligno, links or conflates the *Genus nequam* prophecies with the prophecies of a sequence of angelic popes in the *Liber de Flore*: for this text see Heinrich Finke, *Aus den Tagen Bonifaz VIII* (Münster, 1902), 220–221, n. 12; also Reeves, *Influence of Prophecy*, 252–253.

[10] Jean de Roquetaillade, *Liber Ostensor*, Vat. Ross. MS lat. 753, fols. 52ᵛ, 78ᵛ, quotes from both the *Liber de Flore* and the *Genus nequam* prophecies. On Roquetaillade, see also Jeanne Bignami-Odier, *Études sur Jean de Roquetaillade* (Paris, 1952), 142–156, 243–244; for revised edition see *Histoire littéraire de la France* vol. 41 (Paris, 1981), 75–284. For the most recent work, see *Johannes de Rupescissa, Liber secretorum eventuum,* ed. and trans. (into French) by Christine Morerod-Fattebert, Historical Introduction by Robert E. Lerner (Freiburg, 1994).

[11] Lerner, "On the Origins," 624, n. 31.

[12] Lerner, "On the Origins," 635; see also 629–630, n. 44 for connections between this commentary and Arnold of Villanova.

pontificibus, consists apparently of a base text and a commentary designed to explain it.[13] It has been assumed that the author of the text knew the *Genus nequam* prophecies, as it begins with descriptions of historical popes (with Gregory IX, 1227–1241, rather than with Nicholas III as do the *Genus nequam* prophecies). The *Liber de Flore*, however, quotes only from prophecies eleven and twelve of the *Genus nequam* group (referring to the first of the angelic popes).[14] In addition, there are references to Martin IV as the "man of blood" and the identification of Nicholas III with the words "Principium malorum," both references thought to be to the *Genus nequam* prophecies. What distinguishes the *Liber de Flore* from the *Genus nequam* prophecies is the political program identified in the descriptions of the angelic pope and his three successors.[15]

Despite the manifest importance of these prophecies, they have never been edited. For a long time they were known to scholars from the pioneering work of Herbert Grundmann and later of Marjorie Reeves under the title *Vaticinia de summis pontificibus* or Pope Prophecies. Now we recognize that this title, in fact, signified three quite different productions.

The earliest version of pope prophecies (*Inc. Genus nequam*), probably circulating ca. 1304, consisted of fifteen pictures with accompanying texts and captions or mottoes—picture, text, and caption together constituting each "prophecy." The fifteen units describe a series of popes, beginning with Nicholas III (1277–1280). In its early form, the *post eventum* series continued certainly through Boniface VIII (1294–1303) and possibly through Benedict XI (1303–1304). The final five units, that is, eleven through fifteen, describe the coming of an angelic pope, the progress of his papacy and/or those of his three successors. Text and image alike were subject to continual emendation and change. This set of fifteen prophecies was ascribed in the fourteenth century most frequently, although quite erroneously, to Joachim of Fiore, and, until recent challenges, was thought to have been put together by someone within a group of Franciscan Spiri-

---

[13] For a partial edition of the text, see Herbert Grundmann, " 'Liber de Flore.' Eine Schrift der Franziskaner-Spiritualen aus dem Anfang des 14. Jahrhunderts," *HJ* 49 (1929): 33–91; see more recently McGinn, " 'Pastor Angelicus'," 239–246. The copy of the *Liber de Flore* I have consulted is Nuremberg, Stadtbibliothek, MS Cent. IV.32, fols. 46ʳ–70ᵛ. For other manuscript copies of the *Liber de Flore*, see McGinn, " 'Pastor Angelicus'," 239, n. 351.

[14] Nuremberg, Stadtbibliothek, MS Cent. IV.32, fols. 57ʳ, 59ᵛ.

[15] See McGinn, " 'Pastor Angelicus'," 242–246 for discussion of this program. As McGinn and others note, the work that gave the widest possible distribution of this sequence of prophecies was the *Liber de magnis tribulationibus et de statu ecclesiae* ascribed to Telesphorus of Cosenza. For bibliography on Telesphorus, see McGinn, " 'Pastor Angelicus'," 249, n. 84.

tuals in Perugia ca. 1304.[16] It had its origins in the so-called Leo Oracles, a series of prophecies concerning the fortunes of the Byzantine empire in the twelfth century, the central feature of which was the portrayal of a savior-emperor who would restore unity to the empire.[17]

Sometime in the mid-fourteenth century, perhaps as early as ca. 1328, a second set of pope prophecies appeared (*Inc. Ascende calve*), in the same format as the first.[18] This set began as well with Nicholas III but ended with an image of the dragon of the Apocalypse, and, as a discrete set, seems to have had more limited circulation than the earlier set, as well as a more overtly "propagandistic intention."[19] Recent research has demonstrated the close connection between several manuscripts of the *Genus nequam* group with the *Ascende calve* prophecies.[20] By the first quarter of the fifteenth century at the latest, the two sets were joined.[21] The second set came first, typically ending with an image of the Antichrist. The earlier set now constituted prophecies sixteen through thirty in the combined edition. It is in this form that the prophecies were known in the many fifteenth-century manuscript copies and in the sixteenth-century printed editions.[22]

---

[16] Reeves, "Some Popular Prophecies," 107, and n. 2. Recently both authorship and dating were challenged by Robert Lerner, "On the Origins," (see above n. 1); for further discussion see Marjorie Reeves, "The *Vaticinia de Summis Pontificibus*: A Question of Authority" [for "Authorship"] in *Intellectual Life in the Middle Ages: Essays Presented to Margaret Gibson*, Lesley Smith and Benedicta Ward, eds. (London, 1992), 145–156; the work of Andreas Rehberg as well as that of Hélène Millet and Dominique Rigaux (see below n. 23); Robert E. Lerner, "Recent Work on the Origins of the *Genus nequam* Prophecies," *Florensia: Bollettino del Centro Internazionale di Studi Gioachimiti* 7 (1993): 141–157.

[17] For the Oracles, see the edition by P. Lambecius in PG, ed. J.-P. Migne (Paris, 1857–1876), 107:1121–1168; See also Grundmann, "Die Papstprophetien," 107; Cyril Mango, "The Legend of Leo the Wise," *ZRVI* 6 (1960): 59–63; Paul Alexander, *The Byzantine Apocalyptic Tradition*, ed. Dorothy deF. Abrahamse (Berkeley, 1985); Antonio Rigo, *Oracula Leonis: Tre manoscritti greco-veneziani degli oracoli attribuiti all' imperatore bizantino Leone il Saggio (Bodl. Baroc. 170, Marc. gr. VII.22, Marc. gr. VII.3)* (Venice, 1988); most recently the as yet unpublished edition of the Leo Oracles which has been prepared by Dr. Jeanne Basquin-Vereecken of Ghent. Although the Leo Oracles MSS as we have them postdate the Latin pope prophecy MSS, the Oracles existed in the late twelfth century, as they were known to Nicetas Choniates. The question of how the East-to-West transmission took place remains a puzzle.

[18] On dating, see Reeves, "Some Popular Prophecies," 117–118; Lerner, *Powers of Prophecy*, 96–97, n. 28; on the prophecies, see Lerner, *Weissagungen*; also Hélène Millet and Dominique Rigaux, "*Ascende calve*: Quand l'historien joue au prophète," *Studi Medievali* 33 (1992): 695–720 and "Un puzzle prophétique dans le manuscrit 6213 de la Biblioteca Nacional de Madrid," *Revue Mabillon* n.s. 3 (=64) (1992): 139–177; Schwartz and Lerner, "Illuminated Propaganda," who argue "they were created between c.1318 and c.1340, more likely between 1328 and 1330," 157.

[19] Schwartz and Lerner, "Illuminated Propaganda," 170–178.

[20] Schwartz and Lerner, "Illuminated Propaganda," 178–182.

[21] Lerner, *Weissagungen*, dates the combined version to the pontificate of John XXIII (1410–1415), but see also Reeves, "Some Popular Prophecies," 119.

[22] Pasqualino Regiselmo, *Vaticinia sive Prophetiae Abbatis Joachimi et Anselmi Episcopi Marsicani*

The full history of these prophecies has yet to be written, but its outline is beginning to take shape. Robert Lerner argues that the time has come to reserve the name *Vaticinia de summis pontificibus* for the full set of thirty prophecies and that the title "Pope Prophecies" may not be appropriate for the first set usually known by that name, suggesting that this set might best be known by the *incipit* of the first prophecy, *Genus nequam*. That this group of prophecies did become identified with a series of popes is uncontested; however, recent research by Andreas Rehberg as well as by Hélène Millet and Dominique Rigaux also makes it clear that a very early version, perhaps the earliest, of the *Genus nequam* prophecies referred to a series of cardinals rather than to a series of popes.[23] The number of units in this version remains open to question; however, the work of Rehberg, Millet and Rigaux, and most recently Samantha Kelly, makes it clear that the first six or eight units of the *Genus nequam* prophecies were in circulation possibly as early as 1287 but certainly by 1292.[24] Thus arises the problem of nomenclature. The first six or eight prophecies of the *Genus nequam* group had a life as cardinal prophecies and a life as pope prophecies, as well as a common history in their relation to the Byzantine Leo Oracles. It seems useful therefore to distinguish between the cardinal prophecies and the pope prophecies, and, among the pope prophecies, to distinguish three sets: the *Genus nequam* prophecies, the *Ascende calve* prophecies, and the combined set, the *Vatinicina de summis pontificibus*. The *Genus nequam* set alone remains unedited.

Questions of authorship, authorial intention, and dating raise vexing issues. Until recently the creation or compilation of the prophecies was connected to the activities of the Italian Spiritual Franciscans and their attempt to influence the outcome of the papal election of 1304. Recent

---

(Venice, 1589; repr. Leipzig, 1972), unpaged in Latin and Italian. In this edition, the earlier fifteen prophecies, circulating ca. 1304, and which here are numbered 16–30, are attributed to the mythical bishop Anselm of Marsico, and the later set, composed mid-fourteenth century, and here numbered 1–15, are ascribed to Joachim of Fiore.

[23] Andreas Rehberg, "Der 'Kardinalsorakel'-Kommentar in der 'Colonna'-Handschrift Vat. lat. 3819 und die Entstehungsumstände der Papstvatizinien," *Florensia: Bollettino del Centro Internazionale di Studi Gioachimiti* 5 (1991): 45–112, here 50–58; Hélène Millet and Dominique Rigaux, "Aux origines du succès des *Vaticinia de summis pontificibus*," in *Fin du monde et signes des temps: visionnaires et prophètes en France méridionale (fin XIIIᵉ-début XVᵉ siècle)*, Cahiers de Fanjeaux 27 (Toulouse, 1992), 129–156, here 144.

[24] Rehberg dates the commentary to the first half of 1287 and a revision to ca. 1297 (" 'Kardinalsorakel'," 70–81); Millet and Rigaux date the commentary to 1285–1287 ("Aux origines," 143–144). See also Lerner, "Recent Work," 149–156. For the 1292 date, see Samantha Kelly, "The *Visio Fratris Johannis*: Prophecy and Politics in Late-Thirteenth-Century Italy," *Florensia: Bollettino del Centro Internazionale di Studi Gioachimiti* 8–9 (1994–1995): 7–42.

research however would appear to push back the date to at least 1292 and possibly earlier, and, in addition, to call into question previously held assumptions about authorship and intention.[25]

It is Samantha Kelly's work on the *Visio Fratris Johannis* that establishes the 1292 date. She has demonstrated close connections between the *Visio* and the first eight units of the *Genus nequam* prophecies, and if she is correct in dating the *Visio* to the summer of 1292, the *Genus nequam* prophecies, in some form, must have been in circulation by that time.[26] The prophecies might then have been created or compiled immediately after the death of Nicholas IV in April of 1292, during what was to turn out to be an interregnum of twenty-seven months, or, more likely, some time during the pontificate of Nicholas IV (1288–1292).

The chief difficulty regarding dating and authorship stems from the relationship between the cardinal prophecies and the early versions of the pope prophecies. The existence of the cardinal prophecies as a separate group depends on the evidence of the commentary on these prophecies identified by Rehberg and Millet and Rigaux.[27] The commentary quotes from these prophecies and explicates the text, making it clear that at least the first six units of the *Genus nequam* prophecies were not originally designed to be pope prophecies, "... and that the first six units were originally meant to apply to five Orsini cardinals." The commentary appears in a Vatican manuscript (Vat. lat. 3819) dated by Rehberg to 1331–1334, and follows a copy of the full fifteen units of the *Genus nequam* prophecies, separated only by a short prophetic text apparently unconnected to the *Genus nequam* prophecies, and by a list of popes from Nicholas III to John XXII. Lerner makes the point, well worth re-stating: "It must be emphasized that the text of the prophecies copied in [this Vatican manuscript] is different from the text used as a basis for the commentary, the latter representing an early level in the transmission, the former a later one."[28] Lerner dates the commentary to sometime between 1280 and early 1305, Rehberg to between 1285 and 1287.[29] (Rehberg also suggests a revised and an unrevised version of the commentary.) Lerner also argues that the "... prophecies were invented in Italy by an enemy of the Orsini family who was well-informed about curial politics."[30]

---

[25] See above n. 16.
[26] Kelly, "Visio," 24–26.
[27] See above n. 23.
[28] Lerner, "Recent Work," 147, n. 14.
[29] Lerner, "Recent Work," 149–156.
[30] Lerner, "Recent Work," 155.

Now comes the rub. The *Genus nequam* prophecies exist in nine extant manuscripts. One of these, among the earliest,[31] records the text of the first eight units only; in the adjacent space are either directions to the painter of the miniatures (never executed) or brief descriptions of the miniatures in the exemplar. The question remains: did the "inventor" of the cardinal prophecies have before him a series of six units, of eight units, or of fifteen units? Analysis of textual and iconographic evidence (as will be discussed in some detail below) suggests close connections between three of the extant copies of the *Genus nequam* prophecies (that in the Vatican manuscript noted above and the version recorded in two English manuscripts)[32] and the text of cardinal prophecies, as it is represented in the commentary; but questions do remain. Much hinges on the assumption that the original intention of the creator of the *Genus nequam* prophecies coincides with that of the interpreter in the cardinal or Orsini commentary. It is on the basis of this assumption that Rehberg as well as Millet and Rigaux argue that the original version of the prophecies must have been only eight units long (as represented by the Vatican manuscript), an argument reinforced by the work of Kelly.[33]

Lerner, on the other hand, argues that the earliest version must be closer to that represented in the two English manuscripts (i.e., fourteen/fifteen units), and that the Vatican scribe simply ran out of space. The other possibility is of course that the compiler of the version represented by the two English manuscripts returned to the Leo Oracles for further inspiration, a scenario Lerner finds unlikely.[34]

It remains clear, however, that the version of the prophecies referred to in the commentary is not always the closest to that of the Leo Oracles.[35] The arguments then, are strong, if not conclusive, that the first version of the *Genus nequam* prophecies must have been fourteen or fifteen units long, with a cumulative effect, however, that must have been different from that of the cardinal prophecies. Thus the dating for the creation or compilation of the full set of fifteen units must remain open, ranging from as early as

---

[31] Vatican Library, MS Vat. lat. 3822, fols. 6^r, 5^v.

[32] Cambridge, Corpus Christi College, MS 404, fols. 88^r–95^r and Oxford, Bodleian, MS Douce 88, fols. 140^r–147^r.

[33] The commentary explicates only the first six units of the *Genus nequam* series, but Rehberg argues that the original version must have contained eight units (" 'Kardinalsorakel'," 100–101) as do Millet and Rigaux, "Aux origines," 134; Kelly, "Visio," 26, argues that the author of the Visio borrows from the eighth unit of the *Genus nequam* series as well as selectively from earlier units.

[34] Lerner, "Recent Work," 154, n. 29.

[35] Lerner, "Recent Work," 149, n. 17.

1280 to as late as early 1305. Even though it is clear that the first six or eight units of the *Genus nequam* prophecies were in circulation by 1292 or possibly earlier, there is no conclusive evidence for the circulation of the full fifteen units by that date.[36]

Tacitly acknowledging the difference in cumulative effect between the six or eight units of the cardinal prophecies and that of the fifteen units of the *Genus nequam* prophecies, Lerner sums up the matter of intention as it currently stands: "To portray the author as primarily a political propagandist ignores the fact that his prophecies led up to a supernaturally-guided transformation in the government of the Church and the crowning of popes by angels." On the other hand, even though no one would argue that the *Genus nequam* prophecies came to be identified with the fortunes of the Spiritual Franciscans, ". . . to portray [the author] as a Joachimist or Spiritual Franciscan ignores the fact that distinctively Joachimist or Franciscan points of view are absent in the earliest level of the evidence."[37]

A final point to be considered here is the relation between image and text. Recent interest in the manuscript as artifact has led to renewed and newly focused discussions of the relation between text and image, as well as on a more theoretical level, between visual representation and language.[38] Images on the page can serve ornamental, memorial, illustrative, or explanatory functions: they can highlight or enhance the text or provide an alternative to the text. The problem here is to find the language that best describes the relation between text and image in the *Genus nequam* prophecies.

No one to my knowledge disputes the assumption that the images were part of the original conception of the prophecies. It is beyond doubt that the *Genus nequam* prophecies had their origins in the so-called Greek Leo Oracles, each unit of which also consisted of image, text, and caption or motto. In some instances, units of the *Genus nequam* series are very faithful to their counterparts in the Leo Oracles in both the language of the text and details of the images. Contemporary witnesses identified the prophecies with the images as often as with the texts. Délicieux, as noted above, spoke

---

[36] None of the extant nine MSS can be dated conclusively to before the election of Clement V in June of 1305; Lerner, "Recent Work," 156, n. 33.

[37] Lerner, "Recent Work," 156.

[38] The literature on this topic is considerable, beginning with Kurt Weitzmann's pioneering work *Illustrations in Roll and Codex: A Study of the Origin and Method of Text Illustration* (Princeton, 1947), but see especially W. J. T. Mitchell, *Picture Theory: Essays on Verbal and Visual Representation* (Chicago and London, 1994); Robert G. Calkins, *Illuminated Books of the Middle Ages* (Ithaca, New York, 1983); Michael Camille, *The Gothic Idol: Ideology and Image-Making in Medieval Art* (Cambridge, 1989).

in 1317 of a "papalarius," or pope prophecies, "in which past and future popes were represented in pictures." Pipini, writing no later than 1317, is interested only in the pictures and identifying pictures with popes, perhaps finding the text too obscure.[39]

It is clear as well that these images serve more than a simple illustrative function, but how much more, and how is this added function to be described? Certainly the total effect of picture plus text (and motto) is greater than that of either component alone. Additionally, each provides a means of understanding, even decoding, the other. Habits of mind give primacy to text, a logocentric bias, as it were, but in this instance the images are more accessible than the text, often providing a referent in time and space that the text lacks. The text of unit one, after all, does not refer explicitly to a pope; it is the image that does so.

It is not possible to go so far as to say that each component requires the other for meaning to be produced; yet the three parts of each unit, text, image, and motto, mutually elucidate one another.[40] Page organization illustrates this point. Units of the prophecies are carefully delineated, one from the other, often one unit to a page, even when the text is very short. Some witnesses give the text on one page, the image on the facing page. When the units are arranged one to a page, the image takes up two-thirds of the space. Mottoes precede the text, set apart from it in some way, either as headings or *tituli*, or by rubrication.[41] Identifications of historical popes, when they are made, are written above the image or sometimes above the motto. Nothing about the page organization suggests the primacy of one component over the other, and everything points to a special kind of complementarity between text and image.

Yet, this complementarity or movement between text and image is anything but straightforward. Pipini, for instance, knew the series was to begin

---

[39] There are of course some contemporary references to the *Genus nequam* prophecies that appear to be to the text alone or to a combination of motto and text. The *Liber de Flore* quotes from units eleven and twelve and makes no explicit reference to the images.

[40] The captions or mottoes appear in a short form as well as in a (later) long form. Two MSS record the short form; of the remaining MSS, one gives both short and long forms, distinguishing between them, five give the long form, and two omit captions altogether. Recently there has been some discussion as to what to call these "captions" or "mottoes" (Lerner, "Recent Work," 151–152, n. 20); often they are referred to as "mottoes;" Millet and Rigaux term them "rubrics." The verb used to refer to them in the commentary on the cardinal prophecies is *intitulatur*; Pipini refers to *superscriptiones*; I will use "motto" or "caption" interchangeably. Some MS witnesses add a fourth element, the identification of an historical pope.

[41] On the use of *tituli* and parallels between this use and the planned integration of text and image, see Daniel S. Russell, *Emblematic Structures in Renaissance French Culture*, (Toronto and Buffalo, 1995), 17–20.

with Nicholas III, and therefore identified the pope in the second unit of the series as Martin IV. The image in unit two, in at least four of the witnesses, shows a pope and to his side a snake-like serpent attacked by two crows. Pipini, in an effort to fit the iconography to Martin IV, describes the "serpent" as an "anguilla" or "eel," and elsewhere in the passage refers to Martin IV's fondness for eels. The snake-like serpent attacked by two crows, however, comes directly from the parent image in the Leo Oracles[42] where clearly it had quite a different referent. The writer of the commentary on the cardinal prophecies identifies this "flying serpent" as Cardinal Matteo Rossi Orsini and the crows as anti-Orsini forces. In probably the latest of the witnesses, the copy in Vat. lat. 3819, the element of opposition has been retained, but the details are quite different: here the pope stands with a book in his left hand, and holds with his right hand a standard with a large bird perched atop, beak open. To the pope's left is a large dragon figure. The dragon and bird thus face each other, separated by the pope, who, because he holds the standard, is to be aligned with the bird. The significance of these particular changes is lost to us. All we can say is that no change in the text precipitated these changes in the image, yet the changes in the image have the potential at least for altering the reading of the text.

---

[42] PG 107:1151, Figure 1.

General Principles

Recent work in textual editing and in manuscript studies has made editors acutely aware of the problems inherent in the editing particularly of so-called non-canonical texts like the *Genus nequam* prophecies. The traditional philological approach which requires the establishment of an ideal or Ur-text is challenged by those editors who give priority to the reading of a single manuscript. Two features of the *Genus nequam* prophecies are important here. First, the texts from their earliest circulation lent themselves to emendation, correction, and adaptation to the changing circumstances of history, thus calling into question the very notion of *auteur*. Second, each of the fifteen units of the *Genus nequam* prophecies consists of image, text, and motto; in other words there exists a special kind of complementarity between text and image that goes beyond simple illustration of text. Both these features present special if not unique problems for the editor.

The *Genus nequam* prophecies may be called a "fluid" text, but in a special sense. The term has recently been applied to *trouvère*, where, it is recognized, poetry orally performed resulted in a variety of texts, all valid versions of a song which was always changing.[1] It was constantly a "text in the process of becoming,"[2] undergoing mutations through performance,

---

[1] See Rupert Pickens, *The Songs of Jaufré Rudel* (Toronto, 1978). For a text closer to the *Genus nequam* prophecies, see Robert Lerner's edition of the "generations" of the Cedar of Lebanon Vision in *Powers of Prophecy*. A review article by Joseph J. Duggan, "Editing Medieval Texts: How to Do It," in *University Publishing* 9 (Summer, 1980): 12, 17, gives an excellent overview of the state of textual editing, particularly as it applies to medieval texts. See also Alfred Foulet and Mary Blakely Speer, *On Editing Old French Texts* (Lawrence, Kansas, 1979), 1–39. More recently the debate has quickened in the light of contemporary literary theory. Here a good starting point is Jerome J. McCann, *A Critique of Modern Textual Criticism* (Chicago, 1983), and G. Thomas Tanselle, *A Rationale of Textual Criticism* (Philadelphia, 1989); see also David F. Hult, "Reading It Right: The Ideology of Text Editing," in *The New Medievalism*, ed. Marina S. Brownlee, Kevin Brownlee, and Stephen G. Nichols (Baltimore, 1991), 113–130. For the conservative view, see J. B. Hall's review article "The Editing and Emendation of Medieval Latin Texts: Two Case Histories," *Studi Medievali* 3rd ser. 19.1 (1978): 443–466.

[2] This is a loose translation of Paul Zumthor's term *mouvance*: Paul Zumthor, *Toward a Medieval Poetics*, trans. Philip Bennett (Minneapolis, 1992), 47.

oral transmission, scribal revision, and the intentional spinning of new versions. Obviously the *Genus nequam* prophecies were not such poetry in the making, changing in each performance. They derive from a single text, the Leo Oracles, and therefore—unless one posits the independent adaptation of this by several different authors—there must have been an archetype. Yet there is a sense in which these prophecies form a living text. Their "matter" was a subject of immediate and vital contemporary concern, while the original text was gnomic enough to leave open the door to varying interpretations or "creative readings."[3] Hence from their first circulation, the prophecies lent themselves to emendation, correction, and adaptation. Traditional guidelines on the editing of texts tend to rule out any consideration of this fluid quality and concentrate wholly on the establishment, as near as possible, of the archetype, and thus access to authorial intention. But popular prophecy, like popular poetry, invites another approach, although this raises its own problems.

This can be illustrated by examples from some manuscript witnesses. Text C (a Cambridge MS) preserves a different reading from text A (a Vatican MS which also has a relatively "pure" text); this may be either a corruption or a new reading, i.e., a deliberate substitution in order to adapt the material to slightly different circumstances. The simplest form of this type of emendation is an updating by change of tense or date, thus renewing the prophecy. In such a case, there is a point of reference outside the text, and it can be regarded as a new original. On the other hand, if no such reason is apparent, the alteration may simply be a corruption, a misreading, or a grammatical or orthographical emendation, or a word substitution which seeks to make better sense.

The versions of the prophecies in a Florentine MS (F) and a Yale MS (M) well illustrate the general problem. These witnesses of all the fourteenth-century examples contain the greatest number of idiosyncratic and/ or unique readings. In a number of important instances, each stands alone

---

[3] For recent work on the reading of such gnomic texts, see Walter J. Ong, *Orality and Literacy: The Technologizing of the Word* (London, 1982), and Frank Kermode, *An Appetite for Poetry* (Cambridge, Mass., 1989), and *Poetry, Narrative, History* (Oxford, 1990). See also Lee Patterson, "The Logic of Textual Criticism and the Way of Genius," in *Negotiating the Past: The Historical Understanding of Medieval Literature* (Madison, Wisc., 1987), 77–113 and, in particular, his distinction between a rhetorical poetics and a symbolist poetics, the latter one "in which language is not transparent but dense and even opaque, by definition overdetermined and furnishing an abundance of signification" (96). An examination of the commentary on the cardinal prophecies from this perspective would provide a case in point as to how such texts were read.

against the readings of all the other witnesses. The traditional conclusion is that these texts must be the most corrupt; yet that is not necessarily the case. In the Florentine MS, the reader can see the scribe at work, trying to interpret what he records, following a particularly baffling phrase with a *vel* and seven or eight words of interpretation or an alternative explanatory sentence. (It is also possible, of course, that the explanatory sentences were included in the scribe's exemplar.) The scribe apparently identified the popes through Benedict XI (1303–1304) and perhaps through Clement V (1305–1314), although there is evidence of erasure; in addition there are a number of enigmatic abbreviations above some of the images, and in several instances descriptions of or references to the images. Above picture thirteen is "papa coronatus ab angelo," which does not correspond to the picture represented below. Discrepancies between image and description can be explained in several ways: the scribe either knew of or was looking at a different picture than the one drawn below this text, or else this confusion was also incorporated in his exemplar. The argument for scribal intervention is strengthened by the fact that in the other witnesses under discussion *vel* signals an alternative reading rather than an explanation. On the other hand, the discrepancies between the images and the descriptions provide contrary evidence. The images show few signs of having been executed by a professional illuminator, and thus we might well have expected reconciliation of these discrepancies by the scribe. The most likely explanation is that this witness records both instances of scribal intervention and evidence of early contamination and confusion.

The Yale MS version of the prophecies is of particular interest on two counts: first, it, like the Florentine witness, contains a high number of idiosyncratic or unique readings, and second, it is unique among the fourteenth-century witnesses in that the prophecies are part of an anthology apparently organized around a specific theme. In this instance, the large number of unique readings and the many variations of the text suggest less the deliberate alteration of the text for a particular purpose than that the Yale version is a conservative copy of a presently unknown text. A number of features point to a conservative scribe. There are a fair number of *lacunae* in the Yale record, as well as annotations in the margins making corrections, additions, and filling in the *lacunae*. The marginal annotations are all in the same hand, probably a second later hand. The presence of the *lacunae* suggests a conservative scribe, even if the glossator and the scribe were the same person.

Because it is an anthology, the Yale manuscript provides important clues to the way the text was read by the anthologizer as well as clues to the purpose he or they thought the texts could serve.[4] The body of the manuscript is in a single hand, and the anthology is organized around a specific theme, that of savior-emperor. In addition it presents an early example of the convergence of two motifs, last world emperor and angelic pope, a combination which was to become popular in prophetic programs of the later fourteenth and fifteenth centuries. Of particular interest in this anthology is the Latin version of the Greek Anonymous Paraphrase of the Leo Oracles or "Cento of the True Emperor," as Paul Alexander has called it,[5] the prophecy of a great pauper-king, the *imperator*. This is the only instance in which this text follows the text of the *Genus nequam* prophecies,[6] although in the Greek texts of the Leo Oracles, the Greek Paraphrase often followed the text of the Oracles, as it does in the edition of Lambecius, reproduced in Migne. The Yale anthology, then, provides a context for reading the *Genus nequam* prophecies, a context that is generally lacking in the other witnesses.

Thus it is clear that the variants are as interesting as any possible "established" text. Neither a reconstituted nor a purified text would have the validity or the immediacy of individual witnesses. But to print each version would be impossibly cumbersome. The text presented here therefore represents a compromise, and this compromise needs some explanation.

Since Lachmann it has been assumed that a critical edition of any work presupposes a single authorial version, one from which all other versions descend in varying degrees of correctness. This assumes a stable text, or rather a text that should be stable. The *Genus nequam* prophecies are not such a text, yet it is clear that they did circulate in some consistently recognizable form, certainly very shortly after their production. It seems likely that the very earliest version of the prophecies had but a brief life as a discrete version and was very quickly turned into what can now be seen as a relatively consistent and recognizable version.[7] A very early version, that found in Vatican Library, MS Vat. lat. 3822, is incomplete, for it gives only the first eight prophecies and descriptions of pictures rather than the pictures themselves, or it is a complete text in the sense that what the scribe wrote down

---

[4] See Stephen G. Nichols and Siegfried Wenzel, *The Whole Book: Cultural Perspectives on the Medieval Miscellany* (Ann Arbor, Mich., 1996), 1–7 on the single manuscript as historical artifact, and in particular, on the miscellany and/or anthology. For a list of contents of the Yale anthology, see below, "Descriptions of Manuscripts."

[5] Alexander, *Byzantine Apocalyptic Tradition,* 130–136.

[6] I have discovered one additional instance: see London, British Library, MS Add. 39660, fols. 16^r–17^v.

[7] On the life of the cardinal prophecies, see Rehberg, " 'Kardinalsorakel'," 92.

is all he thought there was.[8] Either way, it is a version which has to be read, must have been read, differently from the somewhat later versions, for its cumulative effect is different. The same point, with some reservations, can be made about the copies in Cambridge, Corpus Christi College, MS 404 (C) and Oxford, Bodleian Library, Douce MS 88 (D), both of which present the prophecies with distinct variations in the pictures and with distinct aberrations of order within the series. The version in these two manuscripts, very similar but not quite identical, again, must be read a bit differently from the later versions, even though they preserve a pristine version of the text; regardless of what the scribe and artist thought they were doing, the resulting version generates a different response.

The text presented here therefore represents an attempt to come as close as possible to the version of the *Genus nequam* prophecies that corresponds to the version of the prophecies recognized as pope prophecies in the early decades of the fourteenth century. In other words, I have not tried to reconstruct the version of the text which must have been circulating as early as 1292, i.e., the version referred to by the author of the commentary on the cardinal prophecies or the author of the *Visio Fratris Johannis*. Rather, I am focusing on that version of the text that was recognizable as a series of pope prophecies, circulating ca. 1304–1305. I have tried to reconstruct its archetype, but not necessarily the Ur-text itself.

Although a critical edition traditionally focuses on text alone, the special kind of complementarity between text and image characteristic of the *Genus nequam* prophecies requires a different approach. The interplay among text, image, and motto or caption raises a number of interesting questions. Are the texts more stable than the images? Are the variations in the text paralleled by variations in the images? What in the images or in the texts generates a particularly figurative or a particularly historical reading? What kind of movement was there between these readings? And particularly as far as the images are concerned, what is the tension between the iconographic content—and its variations—in any given image and the accumulated iconographic build-up generated by the series of images? Does examination of the manuscripts themselves, not simply as vehicles for the transmissions of these particular texts, but as productions made in a specific time for a specific occasion or audience and with a specific program, reveal evidence not obtained by other means of analysis? And does the production of a

---

[8] There is some debate on this point: see Rehberg, " 'Kardinalsorakel'," 100–101, and Lerner, "Recent Work," 154, n. 29.

critical edition of a text like the *Genus nequam* prophecies to some extent blur these distinctions?

These questions cannot be answered in full at this point. What can be said, however, is that any edition of the *Genus nequam* prophecies would be incomplete if it were not accompanied by the corresponding set of images. The special kind of complementarity between image and text noted earlier requires that the reader be able to take in text, image, and motto as a unit. Thus the images cannot be placed in a clutch at the end of the edition; they must be part of the edition.

Unfortunately it is not possible to construct an adequate apparatus for an "edition" of the images similar to that for the text, and certainly it is not possible to construct a composite image or an emended image. The compromise I have effected is this: image, text, and motto will be presented as a unit for each of the fifteen units of the series. Below each image will be a brief recapitulaton of the significant variations among the images. The description of each manuscript will include a discussion of those questions iterated above that are particularly relevant to it. Description of the Yale manuscript, for instance, requires a discussion of the anthology of which it is a part. The Lunel record shows evidence of an accumulated inconographic build-up not characteristic of the other records under consideration. In addition, a separate section will be given over to a discussion of the picture tradition.

Archetype and Copy Text: Text and Image

There are nine important manuscripts of the fourteenth century containing the *Genus nequam* prophecies. Many later manuscripts contain the combined version of the *Genus nequam* prophecies and the *Ascende calve* prophecies, but this edition is limited to an examination of those manuscripts of the fourteenth century that record versions of the *Genus nequam* prophecies before they were combined routinely with the later set.

THE MANUSCRIPTS

A   Vatican Library, MS Vat. lat. 3822, fols. 6^r, 5^v

C   Cambridge, Corpus Christi College, MS 404, fols. 88^r–95^r

D   Oxford, Bodleian Library, MS Douce 88, fols. 140^r–146^v

F   Florence, Biblioteca Riccardiana, MS 1222B, fols. 1^r–8^v

L   Lunel, Bibliothèque de Louis Médard à la Bibliothèque Municipale, MS 7, fols. 4^r–19^r, 22^v

M   Yale, University Library, T. E. Marston MS 225, fols. 15^r–22^r

N   Paris, Archives Nationales, MS JJ 28, fols. 285^r–291^v

P   Monreale, Biblioteca Comunale, MS XXV. F.17, fols. 1^r–17^r

V   Vatican Library, MS Vat. lat. 3819, fols. 147^r–149^r

The *Genus nequam* prophecies derive from the Leo Oracles; thus, the simplest view suggests that the archetype of these prophecies must be that extant or reconstructed version which is closest to the Leo Oracles. Yet the problem of identifying this archetype is the more difficult because all the manuscripts of the *Genus nequam* prophecies under consideration are earlier than any manuscript witness of the Leo Oracles, and, even more importantly, they are not Latin translations of the Greek Leo Oracles but are adaptations of these Oracles.[1]

---

[1] Here, as elsewhere, the reference is to the Lambecius edition of the Leo Oracles as printed in PG 107:1121–1168.

Textual and iconographic analysis of the *Genus nequam* prophecies in the manuscripts under consideration, as well as comparison of these versions with that adduced from the commentary on the cardinal prophecies, distinguish three recensions of the text. The first recension is one for which there is no manuscript witness except the text as it can be adduced from the commentary on the cardinal prophecies. This is a very early version and one close to the Leo Oracles.[2] The commentary makes reference to the pictures and quotes liberally from the first six texts of the *Genus nequam* prophecies.[3] The second group consists of the Cambridge and Oxford manuscripts and represents another version of the *Genus nequam* prophecies. A Vatican manuscript, Vat. lat. 3822, although it gives only eight of the fifteen prophecies, giving only descriptions of the pictures, belongs to this group as far as its text is concerned but seems to represent a slightly different picture tradition. The largest group, consisting of the Lunel, Paris, and Monreale manuscripts, together with MS Vat. lat. 3819, represents what can be called the established reading of the text; when contemporary writers refer to the *Genus nequam* prophecies, both text and pictures, they seem to be referring to the version of the prophecies found in this group.[4] Closely allied to this group of four manuscripts are two other continental examples, the Florentine and Yale codices. Each has a number of unique features, both textual and iconographic, which set it somewhat apart from the others.

Although the three recensions have much in common, each does in fact represent a separate production, compiled in different circumstances and for different purposes, and certainly read differently. The version referred to in the commentary on the cardinal prophecies corresponds in a number of ways to the version represented in the Cambridge and Oxford manuscripts and particularly to that represented by the Vatican 3822 and Florentine manuscripts, but the line of descent is not a straightforward one. The three recensions are not simply three stages in the transmission of a single text but rather three productions or versions which are related to one another in very clear ways but also are in a very real sense independent productions. If the version of the prophecies referred to in the commentary on the cardinal

---

[2] Rehberg calls this commentary the "Cardinal Commentary;" Millet and Rigaux refer to the commentary as the "Orsini Commentary." For reservations as to the proximity to the Leo Oracles, see Lerner, "Recent Work," 149, n. 17.

[3] See Rehberg, " 'Kardinalsorakel'," 107–112 for transcription of the commentary as it appears in MS Vat. lat. 3819, fols. 149ᵛ–150ᵛ.

[4] I.e., Pipini, Hugh of Novocastro, Bernard Délicieux, Gentile of Foligno, and John of Roquetaillade and the references in the *Liber de Flore,* the *Horoscopus* and their respective commentaries.

prophecies did consist of only six texts and pictures, then it is clear that the
compiler of the version represented by the Cambridge and Oxford manuscripts not only was dependent on this first version but also returned to the
texts and pictures of the Leo Oracles.[5] This sort of relationship among
recensions and between the recensions and the Leo Oracles calls into
question the whole notion of archetype as far as these prophecies are
concerned.

How then to put the construction of the edition on a sound footing,
and how to determine the appropriate base text? How to accommodate the
evidence of the three recensions without losing sight of the fact that each
represents a different version—particularly in its cumulative effect—of the
prophecies?

The characteristics of the first recension can only be adduced from the
references to it in the commentary on the cardinal prophecies found in MS.
Vat. lat. 3819, fols. 149[v]–150[v] (and the fragment of this same commentary
found in Arras, Bibliothèque Municipale, MS 171, fol. 81[r], recently identified by Hélène Millet and Dominique Rigaux). Its cumulative effect is
clear: it refers to the series of five Orsini cardinals, the first of whom is
Giovanni Gaetano Orsini (Pope Nicholas III).[6] Given the pattern of quotations in the commentary, several generalizations about the text of the oracle
itself can be adduced. First, there is no version of the *Genus nequam* prophecies among the manuscripts under consideration that corresponds in all
particulars to the text adduced from the commentary. Although the textual
similarities between this recension and the other two outweigh the differences, there are nonetheless some striking differences. Again, given the
pattern of quotations in the commentary, it seems quite clear that the first
unit of the cardinal oracle did not include the second paragraph (*Inc. Serpens
autem omnes*) found in later versions of the *Genus nequam* prophecies. Substantial textual differences occur in the opening words or lines of units
three, five, and six; what is interesting is how much remains in later versions of the opening words of the other units, particularly when it is clear

---

[5] One very obvious example: the second paragraph of prophecy one (*Inc. Serpens autem
omnes*), as it appears in Vat. lat. 3822, is combined in the Cambridge and Oxford manuscripts
with prophecy number two, and unlike the rest of prophecy one, is drawn from the Leo
Oracles. The commentary on the cardinal prophecies contains no references to this paragraph.
Rehberg suggests the original version of the *Genus nequam* prophecies had only eight units (as
in Vat. lat. 3822), but see Lerner, "Recent Work," 154, n. 29 who finds it "hard to imagine
someone between the phase of [A] and [C and D] 'reinventing' prophecies to the extent of
going back to the Leo Oracles," and accounts for the fact of only eight units in the Vatican MS
"on the grounds of lack of space."

[6] Rehberg, " 'Kardinalsorakel'," 49–61 ; Millet and Rigaux, "Aux origines," 144–146.

from the identifications of prophecies with popes that the referent has changed.[7]

The manuscripts of the second recension, including the Vatican manuscript (Vat. lat. 3822) provide a pristine version of the text: one measure of pristinity is that each has a very small number of type one variations, that is, readings in which one manuscript stands alone against all other versions (e.g., A:CDFLMNPV). The Vatican manuscript (A) has the fewest type one and type two variations, i.e., instances in which A stands alone or in which A and one other stand against the rest (e.g., AC:DFLMNPV). The version in Vat. lat. 3822 is, however, incomplete, giving only prophecies one through eight, omitting the so-called angelic series, and substituting brief descriptions for the pictures. The descriptions of the pictures contain a number of anomalies, anomalies which separate this version from all the others.[8]

The Cambridge and Oxford manuscripts (C and D) share sufficient similarities both textual and iconographic to indicate that, although neither is a copy of the other, both stem from a common ancestor. Both have two instances of a combination of texts, an anomaly that runs counter to the general tradition of the *Genus nequam* prophecies and in particular to the Vatican manuscript (A).[9] The second instance, the combination of prophecies four and five and their pictures, points to the very outlook and purpose which might well have inspired the work, for it omits any reference to Celestine V. Most scholars have assumed that the prophecies were from the beginning conceived in apocalyptic terms, as a juxtaposition of the worldly papacy to the true angelic papacy of the future. Marjorie Reeves and others have seen in the juxtaposition of the saintly Celestine V (unit five) to Boniface VIII (unit six) evidence not only of a Joachimist resonance in the prophecies but also evidence of Spiritual Franciscan provenance.[10]

---

[7] Note for instance the beginning of prophecy two: there are differences between the two versions, but the text apparently accommodates reference either to a cardinal (Matteo Rosso Orsini) or a pope (in this case Martin IV who, unlike Nicholas III and Honorius IV, was not one of the five cubs noted in unit one).

[8] See below, "Relation of Manuscripts," for comparisons between the text as represented in Vat. lat. 3822 and that adduced from the commentary on the cardinal prophecies, and for comparison of iconographic features.

[9] On the first combination of texts, see above n. 5.

[10] Reeves, "A Question of Authority," 146–149, 151. I am unwilling to jettison the assumption that the version of the prophecies represented in the Cambridge and Oxford manuscripts refers to a set of popes, in spite of the fact that the pictures identified with prophecies four/five and seven do not show popes. As noted elsewhere, the cumulative effect of this set is different from that of the third recension, but it is also clear that at least Henry of Kirkestede (see below, "Description of MSS") identified the prophecies with a series of popes. See below,

The textual differences between C and D are small. A look at the type one variations for C and D shows that many of the differences are minor: one has an ablative case, the other accusative, where either would do; some are clear errors. Others are more interesting in that they show how risky it is to label variations errors. In the sentence from the text of unit one, "Sicut autem bene manens canes nutris novas et habeas istos sicut adiutores in media tempestatum," CD omits "sicut adiutores," AFMNPV's reading.[11] D however adds at the end of the sentence, after "tempestatum," "sicut adulatores." Both readings make sense; "adulatores" is simply pejorative where "adiutores" is not directly so. The sixteenth-century Regiselmo edition omits the phrase; the sense of the corresponding lines in the Leo Oracles (1–3) would not be violated by either word. What, then, is the reading of C and D's ancestor? Since C omits the phrase altogether, to call both errors, one of omission, the other a reading of *iu* as *ul*, not the most likely of confusions, but certainly not an unlikely one, means that the scribe had to have made two errors, one in the placement of the phrase in the sentence, another in the word itself. Or, the scribe, having realized his omission, in tacking the phrase on the end of the sentence, saw an opportunity for embellishing the comparison. D's reading may be an error or it may be simply an idiosyncrasy. All that can be said is that the probability is that "sicut adiutores" is the "archetype's" reading and that it, as well, became the established reading. Such a hypothesis would be supported by the evidence of the commentary on the cardinal prophecies.[12]

A cannot be a direct intermediary between the archetype and CD, first because it is incomplete, and second because of the considerable difference between the pictures described in A and the pictures as represented in CD, although neither identifies the figure of Celestine V. A and C give the short form of the captions; D gives both short and long forms, distinguishing between them.[13] Yet A, C, and D do show remarkable textual agreement:

"Relation of Manuscripts," for comparison of the prophecies as they appear in the Cambridge and Oxford manuscripts with the version adduced from the commentary on the cardinal prophecies.

[11] For "sicut adiutores," the Lunel manuscript (L) reads "sicut adultores"; given the pattern of errors or misreadings in L, it is possible the L scribe read the *iu* as *ul*. In one instance, the captions in D and L show an unusual correspondence: both read *gule* for *castrimargie* in the caption for unit number five.

[12] The commentary on the cardinal prophecies reads "adiutores" (I: 29); see also Rehberg, " 'Kardinalsorakel'," 107. All citations are to Rehberg's transcription by unit and line number, " 'Kardinalsorakel'," 107–112.

[13] The longer version possibly may have been added later; see below, "Description of MSS," for discussion of the captions in the Oxford MS.

there are no instances of either AC or AD as a separate group, apart from the captions. There are very few clues to determine which manuscript of the three records the earliest version of the first eight texts, apart from the evidence of the captions. One variation, again from prophecy one, is of interest in this connection. The last sentence of the first paragraph and the sentence immediately following the one quoted above reads in ACD "Sed *tempus* manifestabit cogitationes" (italics mine). FLMNPV read "Sed *Christus* manifestabit cogitationes." A, however, has an interlinear addition above "tempus" which reads "vel Christus." A number of explanations are possible: the scribe was uncertain about the abbreviation in his copy text and gave both possibilities (and there are other internal corrections in the A text), or he knew of the alternative reading of "Christus" for "tempus," or he was interpreting what was meant by "tempus." The third seems the least likely: the A text shows signs of haste; it is arranged in an irregular fashion on the page, there are other corrections within the text, one of a long eyeskip. The Leo Oracle text has "tempus" in the corresponding sentence, but the sense of the sentence is different; the Regiselmo edition has "Christus" with no indication that "tempus" might have been an alternative reading. Assuming "tempus" to be the earlier reading because of the agreement among A–CD, clearly very soon "Christus" became the preferred reading. The commentary on the cardinal prophecies is no help in resolving this reading, as there is no reference to this sentence.

In summary, this group of three manuscripts, A–CD, represents a very early version of the text, although D adds the later version of the captions. A omits the series of angelic popes, and A, like CD, omits any reference to Celestine V in unit five; in fact, the description of this picture refers to the figure as "juvenis." Certain iconographic features in CD link the images in these manuscripts with those of the Leo Oracles, i.e., a king in picture number seven rather than the usual pope. (A also describes a king in number seven.) While each of these manuscripts is undoubtedly closer to the archetype than is any one of the remaining manuscripts, it is clear that the version represented by these three manuscripts was written with a different purpose than the others and clearly must be read differently.

Of the remaining manuscripts, those constituting what can be called the "Vulgate" version, the Florentine and Yale manuscripts (F and M) have the greatest number of type one readings, many of which cannot be accounted errors. Of the group LNPV, that is, the Lunel, Paris, Monreale, and Vatican 3819 manuscripts, the Lunel manuscript shows the greatest number of type one readings, most of which can be accounted errors or omissions in transcription. The type one readings in the Monreale manuscript tend to be concentrated in several prophecies rather than spread throughout the work. The version in the Paris manuscript, a fine copy by a professional scribe, also has some unique readings, although a good percentage can be accounted errors; it however lacks the pictures. The second Vatican manuscript, Vat. lat. 3819 (V), has relatively few type one variations and shares a number of textual features with the Lunel, Monreale, and Paris versions and iconographic features with the Lunel and Monreale versions.

Several generalizations can be made about the captions. F and M consistently omit them. The others (DLNPV) record the longer version of the caption, with many variations among them. The Leo Oracles in the Lambecius edition all have the short versions of the captions.[14] One might expect the captions to have fewer variations than the text itself, but such is not the case: even though in the group A–CD, A and C agree (short caption), this agreement is always in the context of a complex variation, that is, a variation with more than two groups.

Considering then the evidence of text, captions, and iconography, it seems clear that while a reconstruction of the archetype would produce a text that would be similar to that referred to in the commentary on the cardinal prophecies, at least for the first six units, as well as to the text of A–CD, it would at the same time result in a version that might well have been read quite differently. In other words, the cumulative effect of the prophecies as they are presented in CD, as well as in A, is different from the response generated by the recension represented by the Florentine, Lunel, Paris, Monreale, Yale, and Vat. lat. 3819 manuscripts.

The evidence of contemporary references to the *Genus nequam* prophecies in the first two decades of the fourteenth century, in particular, those by Pipini ca. 1317 and by Délicieux as early as 1314 noted above, supports this grouping of manuscripts. It also makes it clear that the third recension of the *Genus nequam* prophecies provides the basis for the mainstream or established version of the text.

The edition presented here then is an archetype of sorts, that is, a version which attempts to reconstruct the version of the *Genus nequam* prophecies, corresponding to that version generally referred to in contemporary accounts in the first decades of the fourteenth century. The base text of this edition is, with the exceptions noted below, that of the Lunel manuscript (L), although in fact this version of the text does not differ greatly from the version represented in A–CD and F.[15] All variant readings witnessed by

---

[14] The commentary on the cardinal prophecies as well refers only to the short captions.

[15] The Lunel MS does have a good many unique readings, almost all of which however can

the fourteenth-century record, including variations in spelling (with exceptions noted below), are recorded in the footnotes; testimony from the commentary on the cardinal prophecies is introduced when appropriate, but in the supporting notes rather than in the textual apparatus itself.

The exceptions to the use of the Lunel manuscript are as follows:

1. In the presentation of the text, the short caption is on the first line, the expanded version (long form) on the second line. Readings of the individual witnesses are recorded in the apparatus.
2. Scribal errors in the Lunel manuscript are corrected by readings from other manuscripts and cited in the notes. To resolve the disagreement evidenced by complex variations, that is, a variation with more than two groups, weight has been given to the group containing readings from both groups, A–CD and FLMNPV. There are only a handful of truly problematic readings where ACDF is one group and LMNPV the other; in these instances the rationale for decisions has been presented in the notes.
3. The orthography of the Lunel manuscript has been modified by eliminating a number of double consonants and by adopting a consistent spelling for words ending in *ci* or *ti*; these two modifications are not cited in the footnotes. (All other variant spellings, including those of proper names, are cited in the footnotes.)
4. Punctuation, paragraphing and capitalization have been modernized.
5. Abbreviations have been resolved in conformity with forms established in Adriano Cappelli's *Dizionario di abbreviature latine ed italiane* (Milan, 1961) and the *Supplément* to Capelli, Auguste Pelzer, *Abbréviations latines médiévales* (Louvain and Paris, 1966).

The pictures facing the text are from the Lunel manuscript as well because this set has the fewest unique features and at the same time represents an early and complete version. The pictures in the Lunel, Monreale, and Vat. lat. 3819 manuscripts are all closely related, but the Monreale manuscript has one or two altered pictures, and the Vatican manuscript has a number of unique features. The cumulative effect of text and pictures in the Cambridge and Oxford manuscripts is different from that of the larger

---

be attributed to scribal error. The pattern of errors suggests that the scribe showed little inclination to tamper with the text, for many of the errors reveal the scribe's propensity to copy without regard for sense. See below, "Description of MSS," for the connections between the Lunel and Oxford copies, also Millet and Rigaux, "Aux origines," 137–138, on the importance of the Lunel witness. The Lunel copy is the only copy to mark the end of the sequence with an *Explicit*.

group FLMPV. The argument for using the pictures in the Florentine manuscript is stronger, for the pictures represent an early version and the cumulative effect is similar to that of LMPV. The chief objection to using this set stems from the inconsistencies between the description of the pictures (in the scribal notes following some of the texts) and the pictures themselves. Thus, since the Paris manuscript has no pictures, the Lunel pictures seemed the best choice. Although a critical edition traditionally focuses on the text alone, in this case the "text" is a combination of picture, text, and caption. Presenting the three together in an edition which is close to the actual witness of the Lunel manuscript preserves, as much as it is possible to do, the "sense of the book" of this sequence of prophecies without abdicating the responsibilities of an editor.

Relation of Manuscripts

The *Genus nequam* pope prophecies consist of mottoes (or captions), texts, and pictures. The pictures are not decorative additions to the text; rather, picture, caption, and text constitute the "text." Thus in establishing the relations of the manuscripts, evidence of text, caption, and picture has to be taken into consideration, and one would expect the evidence of one to reinforce the evidence of the others, unless scribe and artist are assumed to have drawn on different exemplars.[1]

As will be seen, evidence of mottoes, texts, and iconography confirms the groupings of A–CD, LNPV, and F and M as not consistently aligned with either of the two main groups, but in their cumulative effect clearly aligned with LNPV rather than with A–CD. Not only are there distinctive variations characterizing the two main groups, there is also considerable variation within each of the two main groups. Analysis of these variations helps to determine the relation of manuscripts within each of the groups and underscores, as well, the importance of each manuscript witness as a source of clues to the ways in which the prophecies were perceived and received.

TEXTUAL EVIDENCE

An analysis of the mottoes or captions shows F and M omit them, A and C give the short form, and DLNPV give the long form. In addition, D shows knowledge of the mottoes in both short and long forms.[2] Except for

---

[1] In some instances, scribe and artist may have been the same person; in others, the miniatures may have been supplied separately. The scribe of the Paris MS (N), for instance, executed the text and the caption, leaving blank a space for the artist to decorate the first initial of each text. Neither decorated initial nor picture was added. Errors in the first word of unit one in the Yale and Vat. lat. MSS (MV), ("Senus") for "Genus," can be attributed to the rubricator rather than to the scribe.

[2] See below, "Description of MSS": the longer form of the caption in the Oxford manuscript might well have been added later. The commentary on the cardinal prophecies refers only to the short form of the captions.

the first motto, A and C's versions show only minor variations; there are many variations, however, in the group DLNPV, although NPV is a group more often than not. For some texts L has two sets of mottoes, one at the head of the text executed by the scribe and one within the miniature, presumably executed by the artist, and the two sets of mottoes are by no means identical.

Overall, textual analysis shows A–CD as a group, CD a distinct subgroup sharing substantial common anomalies in the arrangement of texts one/two and texts and pictures four/five; F and M are separate "groups" of one, each with many idiosyncratic readings. When the readings divide into groups of two, F is most frequently aligned with A–CD and M with LNPV. Although N has a good many unique readings, it also shares significant additions, omissions, and errors with P. L is clearly related to P and V, but it does not share the additions and omissions of P nor the additions to text of V. L could be an intermediary between NPV and their ancestors, but the contrary is highly unlikely.

It is useful to look at the textual evidence in two parts, first the evidence for units one through eight and then the evidence for units nine through fifteen. The Cambridge, Oxford, and Florentine manuscripts (CDF), along with the Vat. lat. 3822 witness (A), present early versions of the text. At least for the first six units of the series, the commentary on the cardinal prophecies sheds considerable light on the relations among these early witnesses. Rehberg, in his analysis of the commentary, suggests that the commentator's exemplar must have been close to the text as it is presented in the English group, that is, C and D, and especially close to the Italian group, that is, Vat. lat. 3822 and the Florentine witness.[3] A detailed examination of the correspondences between these two groups of manuscripts and the version referred to in the commentary helps to determine the relation between the English and Italian groups and reinforces the distinctions already made between the Oxford, Cambridge, and Vat. lat. 3822 manuscripts and the rest of the manuscripts under consideration.

One particularly interesting correspondence occurs in line one of unit four: the commentary (IV:82) reads "Iste collateralis quartus ..." corresponding to the reading in the Florentine manuscript. The other witnesses read "collis" or "collus" for "collateralis." The "collateralis" reading makes good sense in the commentary (apparently referring to Latino Mala-

---

[3] Rehberg, " 'Kardinalsorakel'," 65; Rehberg here refers to the combination of textual and iconographic evidence.

branca),[4] whereas the "collus" or "collis" makes no particular sense in the other witnesses, and, to be sure, the "collateralis" reading in the Florentine manuscript no longer has the same referent the word had in the commentary. If "collateralis" were abbreviated in some form in the exemplar, as Millet and Rigaux suggest, it is easy to see how "collateralis" became "collis" or "collus," especially since the referent was no longer obvious.

The instances in which the readings from the commentary aid in resolving differences between the readings of the Vatican manuscript and the two English manuscripts are less striking. As noted earlier, a problematic reading in unit one of the two English MSS ("sicut adiutores") is resolved in favor of the reading in the Vatican manuscript on the basis of evidence from the commentary. As Rehberg has pointed out, there are a number of instances where the reading in the Florentine manuscript is closer to that of the commentary than are the readings in the two English manuscripts; often these readings occur in the context of complex variations and the reading from the commentary does help in the resolution. It is essential to note, however, that often early readings seem to have been retained even when the referent has changed and the reading no longer makes any sense. In unit four, for instance, the abbreviation "La. M." has been retained in some form in all the witnesses, even though the subject of the prophecy is no longer Latino Malabranca but Pope Nicholas IV.

One particularly striking difference between the text as represented in the commentary and that of the other witnesses occurs in unit one. The commentary makes no reference to the second half of unit one (beginning "Serpens autem omnes") and in fact omits reference to the previous sentence ("Sed Christus ..."). The references in the commentary on unit one are (with the exception of the last quotation) to that part of the text which clearly can be assigned to the originator of the prophecies, as it is not found in the Leo Oracles. This omission, the pattern of references to the cardinal oracle, the idiosyncratic use of "etc." to indicate omission of words, sentences, or, on one occasion at least, a single word, all make it very difficult to reconstruct with any certainty the "original" text. As has been noted elsewhere, the commentary customarily would have followed the text it was explicating, and thus the quotations from the text served primarily as reference points.

For the last five units of the sequence, eleven through fifteen, textual evidence suggests the same groupings of manuscripts, although the pattern of variations is somewhat different. An examination of the variations in the

---

[4] Lerner, "Recent Work," 148, n. 15.

opening line of prophecy eleven, the prophecy of the angelic pope, illustrates rather clearly both the relations and the problems of determining the relations among the manuscripts. The text begins, according to the reading of C, "Et revelabitur *unctus*": F reads "untus" [sic], DLM "virtus," NV either "vinctus" or "iunctus," and P reads "unitus" (for "unitas"). The word in the corresponding line in the Leo Oracles reads "unctus."[5] In what may be a reference to this line in the *Liber de Flore,* the phrase reads "Et revelabitur *virtus.*"[6] Which, then, is the earliest reading? Which is the established reading?

The Cambridge, Oxford, and Florentine (CDF) manuscripts all represent early versions of the text; the disagreement in this reading is one of the very few important differences between C and D, for otherwise they are remarkably similar. "Unctus" is probably the earlier reading, for in addition to the testimony of C and F is the testimony of the Leo Oracles. Furthermore "unctus" marks the legitimate, that is, the duly consecrated, king or emperor, anointed as he is with holy oil. In the "Cento of the True Emperor," as given in the Yale manuscript (folio 23^r), the emperor is referred to as "de laudato paupere et electo imperatore," and further on as "unctus futurus." When Roquetaillade quotes the opening lines of the "Cento," the word "emperor" has been changed to "pope."[7] (He does not quote the "unctus futurus" phrase.)

---

[5] PG 107:1137–1138.

[6] Rehberg (" 'Kardinalsorakel'," 91) makes this same assumption. The copy of the *Liber de Flore* I have consulted is Nuremberg, Stadtbibliothek, MS Cent. IV 32, fols. 46^r–70^v, here fol. 54^r. (A superscript, however, in the Nuremberg MS reads "Benedictus," which means at least one reader saw these lines as referring to an historical person.) The *Liber de Flore* quotes only fragments (fols. 57^r, 59^v) from prophecies eleven and twelve of the *Genus nequam* prophecies. Another, later, fourteenth-century copy of the *Liber de Flore*, Arras, Bibliothèque Municipale, MS 138, fols. 85^r–106^v, reads "revelabitur unctus": see Grundmann, " 'Liber de Flore'," 82. The sixteenth-century printed edition of the pope prophecies edited by Pasqualino Regiselmo, *Vaticinia sive Prophetiae Abbatis Joachimi et Anselmi Episcopi Marsicani* (as above, "The Prophecies," n. 22) reads "elevabitur unctus" with "virtus" given as a variant reading. Of the eight manuscripts under consideration, only the Florentine manuscript (F) reads "*elevabitur* unc[t]us" (italics mine). There are a number of other prophecies of holy popes, among them the *Visio fratris Johannis*: for references to this and similar texts, see Reeves, *Influence of Prophecy*, 401–415; Lerner, "On the Origins," 618, n. 15; and McGinn, " 'Pastor Angelicus'." On the *Visio*, the most recent work is that of Samantha Kelly (see above, "The Prophecies," n. 24).

[7] Jean de Roquetaillade, *Liber Ostensor*, Vatican, Ross. MS lat. 753, fols. 52^v, 78^v; see Bignami-Odier, *Études sur Jean de Roquetaillade*, 142–156, 243–244. Those in holy orders are anointed as well; perhaps the reason why fifteenth- and sixteenth-century versions read "unctus" reflects the distinction between the Avignon and Roman papal lines, and at one point, between these two and the Pisan line. Or "unctus" in the later versions may simply represent a return to the more general term. (A reference to the Messiah, i.e., Christ, the "Lord's Anointed," seems less likely.) See also Lerner, "Historical Introduction," in Lerner and Morerod-Fattebert, eds., *Rupescissa, Liber secretorum*, 69–70, on the angelic pope, "anointed by God" in Roquetaillade (*Liber secretorum*, #20), noting that in the pope prophecies the angelic pope is anointed by an angel.

The complexity of the evidence is inarguable. A reasonable hypothesis is that "unctus" is probably the reading of the archetype, but that "virtus" is the better reading for *Genus nequam* pope prophecies as they must have circulated in the early decades of the fourteenth century. It seems unlikely that the many variations are a result of error, for this phrase represents the opening lines of a key prophecy and, together with the next four, is often quoted in contemporary sources, as in the *Liber de Flore,* where none of the earlier prophecies is quoted. I would argue that the readings of NPV represent a somewhat different emphasis than those of DLM, pointing to a pope whose function would be "to make one" or "to join."

As for the group LNPV, textual analysis shows a close connection between N and P, the Paris and Monreale witnesses: both, for instance, record a sixteenth unit, a short text and caption which in later versions are combined with the text of the fifteenth unit. On the other hand the Monreale record shares with the Vat. lat. 3819 witness (V) but not with N the addition of five lines to the text of the fifteenth unit, although in the instance of the Monreale witness, in a different and perhaps later hand. This same Vatican witness (V) adds two lines to the text of unit ten (from Dan. 8:14 with some modification). The Lunel witness is clearly related to NPV but lacks the additions to units ten and fifteen found in V, as well as the text of a sixteenth unit found in N and P.

ICONOGRAPHIC EVIDENCE

It is useful to look at the iconographic evidence in two parts as well, first the evidence for pictures one through six (and seven–eight), and then the evidence for pictures nine through twelve. Here the evidence is drawn from eight manuscripts rather than nine, as the pictures in the Paris manuscript were never added. To this evidence is added the weight of Pipini's descriptions,[8] and more importantly for determining the relations of the Oxford, Cambridge, Florentine and Vatican 3822 MSS, one to the other, the evidence of the commentary on the cardinal prophecies. Analysis of the iconographic evidence of the first eight pictures shows that A–CD form a group, CD a sub-group; LPV are a group, F and M have clear affinities with LPV, but each differs from LPV in several important instances. No

---

[8] *Chronicon,* cols. 4, 726, 727, 728, 736, 741, 747, 751. As noted above, Pipini's description in the main corresponds with those pictures found in the LMPV group rather than with A–CD, particularly as far as pictures one, four, five, and seven are concerned (i.e., different arrangement of bears in number one, columns in number four, clear identification with Celestine V in number four, and a pope rather than a king in number seven).

two versions are identical iconographically (although the Cambridge and Oxford versions are very close); each manuscript has some feature or features that are unique to it; the groupings represent constellations of important similarities.

The first unit of the commentary refers to the "*primus filius,* id est primus ex quinque cardinalibus. ...." (I:8). Rehberg suggests that the picture must have been that of a bear with five cubs but perhaps not the figure of Nicholas III, who is both one of the five cubs and pope.[9] The Vatican manuscript omits a description of this picture (but gives the long version of this prophecy). The Oxford manuscript shows a bear with five cubs, the Cambridge one a bear with four cubs, the Florentine manuscript a bear with multiple young (the corner of this folio is damaged); the latter three show a pope as the main figure, identified as Nicholas III in the Oxford and Florentine copies. The Oxford and Cambridge copies give the short version of the prophecy, corresponding to that alluded to in the commentary (although both include the remainder of the prophecy as part of the second unit).

The second unit of the commentary refers to a "flying serpent," and ravens attacking its eyes, features found in all four of the manuscripts under consideration. Rehberg identifies the subject of this prophecy as Matteo Rosso Orsini, made cardinal in 1262 and instrumental in the election of Giovanni Gaetano Orsini as Nicholas III.[10] The description in the Vatican manuscript reads "hic fiat ymago unius diaconi ... cum bitortu in capite" (fol. 6[r]), and Rehberg argues that the *diaconus* in question (wearing a mitre) might well be a cardinal, linking this version more closely to that represented by the commentary.[11] The Oxford and Florentine manuscripts show a pope, identified in the Florentine manuscript as Martin IV.

The third unit of the commentary again provides a connection between the text referred to in the commentary and the record in the Vatican manuscript, for the Vatican manuscript refers to an "ymago similis priori

---

[9] Rehberg notes that the pictures are not described in any detail in the commentary because it can be assumed the commentary followed a copy of text and pictures and thus the description was not necessary. The introduction to the commentary (Rehberg, " 'Kardinalsorakel'," 107) suggests Nicholas III is identified as the first of the cubs by the rubrics: "Et hec rubricella alludit principali, id est Gaietani, quasi iam tenebat guai, id est mala." The Arras copy reads, "Et hec rubricella alluditur nomini primi catuli, scilicet J. Gaietani, quasi iam tenebit quay. id est mala." (See Lerner, "Recent Work," 150, n. 19.) Neither the portion of prophecy not alluded to in the commentary (with the exception of the final quotation) nor the image associated with it in the *Genus nequam* prophecies appears in the corresponding unit of the Leo Oracles in the Lambecius edition. See below, "Picture Tradition," for further discussion of this point.

[10] Rehberg, " 'Kardinalsorakel'," 52–54.

[11] Rehberg, " 'Kardinalsorakel'," 67.

cum corona sancti . . ." (fol. 6^r), an indication of why Rehberg suggests that the originator of the description in the Vatican manuscript was aware that the reference was to either a pope or a cardinal, in this instance, Jacopo Savelli (Honorius IV, 1285–1287).[12] The commentary also refers to an eagle, a unicorn and a "knight" (*eques*). The first two elements are found in all versions; as for the *eques,* the Vatican 3822 copy refers to a *puer* as the second figure which more closely corresponds to all versions except the Florentine copy.

The evidence of unit four of the commentary is particularly interesting, for Rehberg argues that units four and five of the commentary refer to a single cardinal, Latino Malabranca, made cardinal by Nicholas III in 1278, and one who saw himself as a maker of popes.[13] If this is is the case, then the origins of the combined pictures associated with prophecies four and five in the Oxford and Cambridge manuscripts become more understandable and less attributable to error, although it is true that both the commentary and the Vatican manuscript represent units four and five as discrete units. The commentary for unit four refers to a severed head and a sickle in the picture; the Vatican manuscript has no description for number four; the Oxford and Cambridge manuscripts show the severed head and sickle in the picture which combines prophecies four and five; the Florentine manuscript shows a head, a bust rather than a severed head, in a vessel or on a capital with a curved "element" encompassing it which could be a crude version of a sickle. (The Florentine manuscript also identifies this figure with Nicholas IV.)

Unit five of the commentary describes the main figure as holding a sickle in one hand and a rose in the other, again, as noted above, referring to Latino Malabranca. This image corresponds to that in the Leo Oracles (although the image in the Leo Oracles also shows an angel). The identification of this figure in the Oxford, Cambridge and the Vatican manuscripts is more problematic. The description in the Vatican manuscript refers to a "juvenis" (fol. 6^r), holding a sickle and a rose; the Oxford and Cambridge manuscripts show a barefoot figure (of uncertain age), not tonsured but in simple dress, holding a sickle in one hand and an angel in the other (as well as medallions with a crowned head in each, again, all part of the combined

---

[12] Rehberg, " 'Kardinalsorakel'," 68, also n. 92 for a discussion of the image in the Florentine MS where the second figure wears what may well be a crown.

[13] Rehberg, " 'Kardinalsorakel'," 56–58, but on this point, see also Lerner, "Recent Work," 152–155.

picture for prophecies four and five). The Florentine manuscript shows a monk (identified as Celestine V) holding a sickle and a rose and with an angel at his shoulder.

The last unit of the commentary refers to a pope, a cow, and two crowned heads. The first two elements are found in all the versions; the crowned heads are heads with mitres in the Florentine mansucript, and the two crowned heads are part of the previous image in the Oxford and Cambridge manuscripts. The text of the commentary refers to the fifth son of the bear, that is Giordano Orsini, although Rehberg argues that the text must have been subject to interpolation, for he finds the reference to Giordano oblique at best.[14]

What this analysis suggests is that the version of the *Genus nequam* prophecies represented by this group of manuscripts is very close to that referred to in the commentary on the cardinal prophecies. Textual and iconographic evidence in particular link the Vatican and Florentine versions to that referred to in the commentary, but questions do remain. First, it is impossible to know for certain the number of units in the commentator's exemplar: the exemplar could have contained as few as six units, as many as fifteen.

Samantha Kelly's work on the *Visio Fratris Johannis* demonstrates parallels in language between units one, two, five, six, and eight of the *Genus nequam* series and the *Visio*, thus strengthening the argument that at least eight units of the *Genus nequam* series must have been in circulation circa 1292.[15] In addition, the pattern of borrowings in the *Visio* illustrates how free, even eclectic, were these borrowings. Certainly the author of the *Visio* was not constrained by his source. The commentary on the cardinal prophecies, on the other hand, explicates the first six units of the source, paralleling the sequence of the first six-unit sequence quite carefully. The pattern of citation in the commentary and the testimony of A (MS Vat. lat. 3822) led Rehberg as well as Millet and Rigaux to conclude that the exemplar must have been eight units long.[16] Yet Lerner's point, noted earlier, that it is unlikely that the author of the full fifteen units of the *Genus nequam* series then would have returned to the Leo Oracles for further inspiration seems a reasonable one, however unprovable. A final point: if either of these exemplars were in fact fifteen units long, clearly it had an

---

[14] Rehberg, " 'Kardinalsorakel'," 59–61; Rehberg argues that it is only the later version which refers to the events surrounding the papacies of Celestine V and Boniface VIII.

[15] Kelly, *Visio*, 26.

[16] Rehberg, " 'Kardinalsorakel'," 100–101; Lerner, "Recent Work," 154, n. 29.

agenda different from that evidenced by the *Visio* or by the pattern of references in the commentary on the cardinal prophecies.

The arguments are strong, then, if not conclusive, that the first version of the *Genus nequam* pope prophecies must have been fourteen or fifteen units long, must have contained both parts of prophecy one (the commentary on the cardinal prophecies makes no reference to the second half of unit one), and quite likely contained elements in the pictures derived from the those in the Leo Oracles but not mentioned in the commentary. The version of the prophecies in the Vatican manuscript is closest to that referred to in the commentary, in that the sequence does not refer to a series of popes and may well refer to cardinals, particularly in the descriptions for units two and three. The sequence in the Florentine manuscript clearly does refer to a series of popes (and with a different cumulative effect than that of CD), but it shows as well striking affinities with the version of text and pictures referred to in the commentary. In addition the evidence of the commentary helps to account for what heretofore seemed anomalies in the Cambridge and Oxford copies.

Of the first eight pictures, numbers one, four, five, and seven are critical. As noted above, A omits the description for picture one, CDF are a group, and LMPV are a group (the number of bears has been reduced to three and none shows a bear with nursing cubs). For picture number four, A omits the description, CD is a group, LPV is a group and F and M, although varying from LPV, are clearly aligned with LPV and not with CD (LMPV show three columns). For picture number five, A–CD form a group, and FLMPV form a group, in all instances with some variations. Pipini identifies the pope as Celestine V, aligning his description here as elsewhere with FLMPV; the Leo Oracle picture shows a king with sickle and rose, and an angel. For picture number seven, all witnesses show a pope, bear and nursing young, except for A–CD which substitute a king for the pope.

For pictures nine through twelve, there is no longer the evidence of A, and Pipini stops with picture number nine. For this group of pictures, numbers ten and twelve are key ones, and to a lesser degree, numbers eleven and fifteen–sixteen, and once again, analysis of the evidence reinforces the pattern of groupings. For picture number ten, CD show an empty throne. FMLPV show a cityscape or fortress. For picture twelve, CD and F all show a marked affinity with the Leo picture of a mummified emperor held aloft on the backs of four animals and ministered to by an angel. LV show a pope (MP an angel) holding a tiara over four animals. In picture eleven CD again have a strong affinity with the Leo picture which shows a figure seated on a sarcophagus. CDF show a star as does the cor-responding Leo picture. For picture fifteen, F adds an awkwardly drawn animal with a human face and a headdress-crown of horns, labelled on its flank "antichristus."[17] LPV show an animal with a human face and crown as picture number sixteen; only P includes a prophecy; L has a sentence at the bottom of picture fifteen indicating that with this prophecy the series ends. As noted elsewhere, C adds a crudely drawn "beaver" on the page following the fifteenth text and picture.[18] There are, as well, a good many other minor differences among the miniatures in the series as a whole.

The general pattern, then, remains the same. C and D constitute a group. F, like C and D, shows clear affinities with pictures in the Leo Ora-cles as printed in the Lambecius edition (i.e., picture 12), yet in pictures eleven and fifteen, F shares features with LMPV (11) and LPV (15), and the cumulative effect of F is closer to that of LPV than to CD. LPV are a group with M standing somewhat apart from it, but closer to it than to CD, and LV form a sub-group.

Two groupings emerge, then, from the combined evidence of mottoes, texts, and iconography: one, A–CD and the other LNPV, with F and M not consistently aligned with either of the two main groups, but in their cumulative effect clearly aligned with LNPV rather than with A–CD. CD is a group except for the captions, where AC have the short form, FM omit the captions, and DLNPV have the longer form. The longer form of the cap-tions, of course, includes the short form, and, in D, the divisions are clearly marked. In several instances L shares with D readings that otherwise would be unique to D, and there are many variations within the DLNPV group.

Within each recension, there is considerable variation, and analysis of these variations helps to determine the relation of manuscripts within each group. Details of iconography in the Cambridge, Oxford, and Florentine manuscripts suggest that at first the last five prophecies in the series were read as the progress of a single pope.[19] Some of these details are missing or

---

[17] Following the text of unit fifteen are the words "papa cum libro in manu et cum metria." This description does not coincide with the image, which shows the pope holding a staff terminating in the episcopal cross; more importantly, the description makes no mention of the human-faced animal.

[18] See below, "Description of Manuscripts: C." Since there is no background decoration in the drawing, the animal could have been added at another time.

[19] M. Fleming, "Metaphors of Apocalypse and Revolution in Some Fourteenth-Century Popular Prophecies," in *The High Middle Ages*, ed. Penelope Mayo, ACTA 8 (Binghamton, 1980): 131–146; see also Friedrich Baethgen, *Der Engelpapst* (Leipzig, 1943), 101 [27], n. 2. (I thank David Heffner for supplying the Baethgen reference.) Hugh of Novocastro, writing in 1315, "reads" the group as a series.

are changed in the Lunel, Monreale, and the second Vatican manuscript (V), suggesting that the group was now seen as a series: an angelic pope followed by three successors, similar to the program found in the *Liber de Flore*.

Analysis of variants both textual and iconographic not only helps to establish relations among the manuscripts but also calls attention to the ways in which each witness yields valuable evidence of its own. The Lunel manuscript, Lunel, Bibliothèque de Louis Médard, 7, a manuscript re-discovered only a few years ago in a small municipal library in southern France, provides an interesting illustration of how some of the changes in emphasis may have come about.

One change, perhaps the major change, which distinguishes the two groups A–CD and FMNLPV is a new emphasis on the connections between pictures five and eleven, tying together the image identified with Celestine V and that of a future angelic pope.[20] For many, but especially for the Franciscan Spirituals, Celestine V came to represent the prototype of the angelic pope. In time, the controversy over the validity of his resignation was convenient ammunition for the political opponents of Boniface VIII, and for Philip the Fair in particular.[21] This emphasis can be seen very clearly in the Lunel manuscript, where a series of five wide borders decorated with hybrids and three-faced heads acts as a kind of underlining of the stages by which these two features came to be connected and a special kind of decorative build-up "pointing" to the angelic pope in unit eleven. Images one, two, four, five, and eleven have these borders. A three-faced head wearing a crown connects the beginning of the series (unit one) with the image of the angelic pope in unit eleven. The borders as well call attention to the connection between units one, five, and eleven. This particular "program" of borders may well help date the manuscript to 1310 or 1311 just before the Council of Vienne.[22]

---

[20] FLP explicitly identify prophecy five with Celestine V; the Monreale manuscript (P) has, above the text of prophecy five, the line "pius papa," and the Florentine scribe identifies this pope as Celestine V; on Celestine *redivivus*, see Lerner, "Historical Introduction," in Lerner and Morerod-Fattebert, eds., *Rupescissa, Liber secretorum*, 69–70.

[21] Rehberg (" 'Kardinalsorakel'," 76–79) notes that the later version of the commentary (ca. 1297) does reflect the controversy surrounding the papacies of Celestine V and Boniface VIII, and while this version makes reference to Celestine V, it does not highlight his papacy in the manner of the Franciscan Spirituals.

[22] "Three topics of discussion were listed in the bull of convocation *Regnans in excelsis* (12 August 1308): the affair of the Order of the Templars, the recovery of the Holy Land, and the reform of the Church" (Sylvia Schein, *Fidelis Crucis: The Papacy, the West, and the Recovery of the Holy Land 1274–1314* [Oxford, 1991], here 239, on the Council of Vienne, 239–257); see below, "Picture Tradition," n. 43.

The particulars of picture eleven also underwent change as the connection between Celestine V and the angelic pope was worked out in greater detail. This change is illustrated in the Lunel manuscript as well as in the earlier Florentine manuscript. In the earlier version of the prophecies represented by the Cambridge and Oxford manuscripts, this figure, always half naked, almost always with the same gestures (one hand to his head as if in sleep, being awakened or summoned forth by an angel) is seated on a sarcophagus or tomb. In both these manuscripts there is no indication that the compiler meant any reference to Celestine V. In the Lunel manuscript, as in others of its recension, a rock or cave has been substituted for the sarcophagus. While the language of the text changes only slightly, it is clear that it was now read differently. The text is full of references to a general messianic expectation, and language that could be seen as recalling the circumstances of Celestine's election (called forth as he was from his rocky hermitage), as well as language that came to have a particularly Franciscan resonance. It is not by chance that this figure is described elsewhere, as in the Florentine manuscript, as "papa nudus," for "nudus" was a code word in the ongoing debate on poverty in the Franciscan order: for the Spirituals it meant simplicity, literal poverty, innocence, and the imitation of Christ.[23] Thus, while the language of the text changes only slightly, the shift in the details of the picture provokes a different reading, that is, one that sees Celestine V as a precursor of the angelic pope.

The prophecies end on a note of both triumph and submission, and again there were a number of changes in the specifics of the ending. In what seems to be the earliest version, the angelic pope is surrendering his tiara at death.[24] In later versions, this ending was made more explicit or was adjusted to the "program" of other prophecies circulating at the time, and the end of this pope's reign is identified with the Last Things and the advent of an Antichrist, if not the great Antichrist.[25] The picture tradition

---

[23] See Grundmann, " 'Liber de Flore'," 67: the words "simplex," "benignus," "sanctus," "pius," "rectus," "verus" are applied to Celestine V and "perversus," "obliquus," "pseudo," "impius," and "iniquus" to Boniface VIII. For "Franciscan resonance," see Fleming, "Metaphors," 145–146, notes 38 and 39. On "nudus," see especially John Patrick Oakley, "John XXII, the Franciscans, and the Natural Right to Property" (Ph.D. diss., Cornell University, 1987), 143–144. On Celestine V, see Peter Herde, Cölestin V (1294): der Engelpapst (Stuttgart, 1981).

[24] McGinn, " 'Pastor Angelicus'," interprets the final scene "as the abdication of the pope before the coming of Antichrist, a parallel to the similar abdication found in the imperial myths" (239, n. 49). For further discussion, see below, "Picture Tradition."

[25] As in the programs of the Liber de Flore and the Libellus of Telesphorus: for a summary and discussion of these programs, see Reeves, The Influence of Prophecy, 325–331, 342–345, 370–372, 406; also McGinn, " 'Pastor Angelicus'," 239–245, 249–250.

supports this interpretation and the arrangement of texts and pictures in the Lunel manuscript gives clues as to how this may have happened.

The fifteenth unit in the Lunel manuscript concludes with the words: *Explicit liber ymaginum papalium* and an image of a pope holding a book in one hand and the papal tiara in the other. This image coincides with that of the early versions as represented by the Cambridge and Oxford witnesses, as well as the Yale witness. The later versions represented by the Monreale and Vatican 3819 manuscripts show the beast with a human face alone as a sixteenth unit or in combination with the pope, with distinctive additions to the text. The Lunel version makes it clear that the series ended with unit fifteen; a sixteenth unit, however, is appended to the series. The image shows a beast identical with that found in the sixteenth units of the Monreale and Vatican 3819 witnesses, but the image is not accompanied by the usual texts but rather by a series of five prophecies from quite different sources.[26] Thus, the Lunel manuscript is a key one in the transmission of the prophecies, and moreover its version of the prophecies suggests how changes in the cumulative effect of the sequence came about.

---

[26] Including the pseudo-Hildegard prophecy, *inc.* "In die illa elevabitur draco repletus," and several Joachite prophecies. See below, "Description of Manuscripts: L."

Description of Manuscripts

The descriptions of the individual manuscripts are more elaborate than is usual, for the manuscripts are viewed not simply as vehicles for the transmission of the texts, but as productions made in a specific time for a specific occasion or audience and with a specific program. Thus analysis of the manuscript as artifact can sometimes reveal evidence not obtained by other means of analysis.

A. VATICAN LIBRARY, MS VAT. LAT. 3822, FOLS. 6ᴿ, 5ᵛ

Description: O. Holder-Egger, "Italienische Prophetieen des 13. Jahrhunderts III," *NA* 33 (1908): 97–187; J. Bignami-Odier, "Notes sur deux manuscrits de la Bibliothèque du Vatican," *Mélanges d'archéologie et d'histoire de l'École française de Rome* 54 (1937): 211–241; M. Reeves and B. Hirsch-Reich, "The *Figurae* of Joachim of Fiore: Genuine and Spurious Collections," *Medieval and Renaissance Studies* 3 (1954): 170–199, here 177–179 and *passim;* Reeves, *Influence of Prophecy*, Appendix C, 534–535 for list of contents.

The manuscript is vellum, in octavo format, measures 27 x 17 centimeters, and is bound in red leather. It is written in a number of hands of the thirteenth, late thirteenth-early fourteenth, and fourteenth centuries, in, for the most part, two columns. According to Holder-Egger the manuscript is most certainly of Italian origin; he posits Rome and a Franciscan provenance.[1] The manuscript is an anthology of prophecies, "a typical Joachimist textbook,"[2] with two main divisions.

Folios five and six were bound in separately and did not originally belong to this manuscript. The *Genus nequam* prophecies, texts without pic-

---

[1] Holder-Egger, "Italienische Prophetieen," 97.
[2] Reeves and Hirsch-Reich, "The *Figurae* of Joachim of Fiore," 177, citing Grundmann, "Die Papstprophetien." See Holder-Egger, "Italienische Prophetieen," 98–105; Bignami-Odier, "Deux manuscrits," 219–235; and Reeves, *Influence of Prophecy*, 534–535 for contents of Vat. lat. 3822.

tures, are on two sides of these two sheets, folios 5ᵛ–6ʳ; they begin on 6ʳ and continue on folio 5ᵛ,³ copied at the bottom of the page, after a short sibylline text. Only the texts for prophecies one through eight are recorded in this manuscript; in the adjacent space are either directions to the painter of the miniatures (never executed) or brief descriptions of the miniatures in the exemplar. Although the spaces left for the drawings or miniatures are quite small, it still seems likely that they were intended for the miniatures; otherwise the prophecy written on folio 5ᵛ might well have been squeezed into the remaining space on folio 6ʳ.

The text of the eight prophecies recorded in this manuscript is a "pristine" one (although one with a number of internal corrections); in only three instances does the reading of this manuscript stand alone against the others, and the pattern of variations suggests it is close to the archetype. The prophecies have the short version of the captions, that is, the one-word captions, except for the first prophecy which has the rubric, "Principium malorum secundum Merlinum. Incipit prime."⁴

As has been noted, the version of the prophecies represented by this Vatican manuscript and particularly by the descriptions of the pictures shows many correspondences with the text and pictures referred to in the cardinal or Orsini commentary. The descriptions show no singular affinity with the corresponding pictures in the Leo Oracles, although there is an affinity in two instances with the pictures found in the Douce and Corpus Christi manuscripts.

There are six descriptions or sets of instructions: there are no instructions for the pictures which should accompany texts one and four. The omission of instructions for picture number one is the more surprising one, since it is the first in the series. To be sure, the first picture in the Leo Oracles series, at least according to Lambecius, corresponds in part to the second picture in the *Genus nequam* series. The important consequence is that it is unclear with whom the series is to begin or even if the series is to begin with a pope.

---

³ The foliation is inconsistent; I have followed the foliation indicated by arabic numerals in the manuscript, following Holder-Egger et al. The manuscript begins with two folios marked in roman numerals one and two, then is followed by the folio marked arabic numeral one. There is one readily identifiable hand, first appearing on folio one (arabic numeral one), which continues through folio 4ᵛ and picks up again on folio 7ʳ. Not only is the hand distinct, but the page layout and decoration are distinctive as well. There are large five-line "built-up" initials, with the letter indicating the initial still remaining in the margin. The initials on the next folio are small, only two-line initials, but there are the same letters in the margin. The hands on folio 5ʳ–6ᵛ, except for that in column one of 6ᵛ, are very similar, but none is the hand of folios 1ʳ–4ᵛ.

⁴ Lerner (personal communication) reads for "Incipit prime," "Rᵃ prima."

Only one of the descriptions or instructions refers unequivocally to a pope, that for picture number six: "Fiat figure summi pontificis et una vacca." The instructions for picture number two refer to the central figure as a "diaconus," and in instruction three, an "imago similis priori cum corona sancti et cruces in manum," including references to the "aquila," "puer," and "unicornis," elements found in the corresponding image in the other copies of the *Genus nequam* prophecies. A "diaconus" is of course an ecclesiastic; the figure is described as wearing a "bitortu" in two[5] and a crown in number three.[6] The Leo Oracles show no human figure in the first three pictures; all the other manuscripts under consideration show a pope.

The instructions for picture number five, a picture which came to be identified with Celestine V, describe a "juvenis" holding a sickle in one hand, a rose in the other. Most of the other fourteenth-century copies of the prophecies show a monk, or, as in the case of the Lunel manuscript, a monk in priestly garb, also with sickle and rose. The Douce and Corpus Christi manuscripts show similar figures, a man (of uncertain age) holding a sickle in one hand and an angel in the other. In neither instance is a tonsure visible; both figures are, however, barefoot and are dressed in a very simple belted robe, brown and not quite ankle-length in Douce. The Douce and Corpus Christi manuscripts combine the texts of four and five and conflate the pictures of four and five, so what Vat. lat. 3822 and these two manuscripts really have in common is that there is no connection in either between this image and Celestine V. There is one additional correspondence: for picture number seven, Vat. lat. 3822 calls for a king, as is found in the Leo Oracles, and as is found in the Douce and Corpus Christi manuscripts.

What conclusions can be drawn from these observations? It would seem that the texts, at least for the first eight prophecies, are presented here in their stable form, but that the referents for these texts were unclear. The whole, that is, the eight texts, the one-word captions, and the descriptions for six pictures, did not refer to a series of popes; in fact only one does so directly.

The dating of this version, then, remains open. Lerner suggests shortly after 1294, because a prophecy on folio 5[v] "appears to center around a prophecy *ex eventu* for 1294,"[7] and, in fact, the date 1294 is written in at the

---

[5] Grundmann, "Die Papstprophetien," 77–140, here 103, n. 1, reads *birotro*(?) and suggests the word should be *birotum* or *birotrum*.

[6] Rehberg, " 'Kardinalsorakel'," 67–68; see also "Relation of MSS" for further discussion.

[7] Lerner, "On the Origins," 635. Lerner also notes the barefoot friars in the drawing on folio 5[r], suggesting that their presence supports Holder-Egger's theory of Franciscan origins; he sees these friars as fairly clearly preaching against the terrible dragon.

bottom of the page, although probably in a later hand. Examination of folios 5ʳ–6ᵛ provides a few clues about the sequence in which the texts were copied. The hands on folios 5ʳ–6ᵛ, except for that in column one of 6ᵛ, are very similar. The arrangement of the eight texts and the sets of directions on the two pages suggests that folio 6ʳ must have been blank, for the *Genus nequam* prophecies occupy the entire page. Folio 6ᵛ must have had the text in column one, otherwise the norm would have been to continue the text on folio 6ᵛ rather than on the previous page, folio 5ᵛ. Thus there is nothing in the physical evidence to question a date of shortly after 1294. The attribution of the series to Merlin is less puzzling, for as others have noted, Merlin was a favored prophetic figure in Italy, and he was often identified particularly with lists of rulers and prophecies containing animal symbolism.[8]

Instructions for Miniatures

1. missing

   fol. 6ʳ

2. Hic fiat ymago unius diaconi cum cruce in manu, cum bitorto in capite. In alio latere serpens cum ii corvis qui eruunt serpenti oculos.

3. Hic fiat ymago similis priori cum corona sancti et cruces in manum et supra ymaginem una aquila sit cum corona et ab uno latere unus puer et ab altero unicornis.

4. missing

5. Hic fiat juvenis cum falce in dextra et rosa in sinistra.

6. Fiat figure summi pontificis et una vacca.

7. Hic fiat una civitas.(crossed out and repeated below) Fiat ursa cum iiii catulis et cum ymagine Regis.

   fol. 5ᵛ

8. Hic fiat una civitas.

---

[8] Bernard McGinn, *Visions of the End*, 181. McGinn cites in particular the work of Paul Zumthor, *Merlin le Prophète* (Lausanne, 1943). See also Caroline Eckhardt, ed., *The "Prophetia Merlini" of Geoffrey of Monmouth: A Fifteenth-Century English Commentary*, Medieval Academy of America Speculum Anniversary Monographs 8 (Cambridge, Mass., 1982), for the identification with Merlin of prophecies "with a penchant for animal symbolism," as well as prophecies of rulers, i.e., "Six Last Kings," 6–7, 32, also 3–8 *passim*.

C. CAMBRIDGE, CORPUS CHRISTI COLLEGE, MS 404, FOLS. 88ᴿ–95ᴿ

Description: Montague Rhodes James, *A Descriptive Catalogue of the Manuscripts in the Library of Corpus Christi College, Cambridge* (Cambridge, 1912), 2: 269–177, no. 404; Neil Ker, *Medieval Libraries of Great Britain*, 2nd ed. (London, 1964), 17; Richard H. Rouse, "Bostonus Buriensis and the Author of the *Catalogus Scriptorum Ecclesiae*," *Speculum* 41 (1966): 471–499; B. Degenhart and A. Schmitt, *Corpus der italienischen Zeichnungen 1300–1450* (Berlin, 1968), Pt. 1,1: 216–227, and Pt. 1,3: pls. 167–170; Reeves, *Influence of Prophecy*, 93–95, 193–195, 403–405, 539; eadem, "Some Popular Prophecies," 107–134; Lucy F. Sandler, *Gothic Manuscripts 1285–1385* (Oxford, 1986), 2: 102–103, no. 95; Robert Lerner, "On the Origins," 633–634.

This manuscript is on vellum and measures 213 x 142 millimeters; it consists of three flyleaves plus 107 folios in twelve quires and is written in several hands of the fourteenth century. Folios 88ʳ–95ʳ constitute the 10th quire and contain the *Genus nequam* prophecies; folio 41ʳ records a fragment of the sequence beginning *Ascende calve*.

An anthology of prophecies, this manuscript was compiled by Henry of Kirkestede in the fourteenth century at Bury St. Edmunds and catalogued by him with the pressmark *P 163* for *Prophetia 163*. Richard Rouse, who has provided the most detailed study of Henry's accomplishments as bibliographer and librarian, notes that Henry claims to have copied much of this manuscript himself.[9] On flyleaf iiiᵛ above the table of contents is recorded in Henry's hand at the top in red, "Quaternus monachorum S. Edmundi quem scripsit pro maiori parte ffrater Henricus de Kirkestede in quo subscripta continentur videlicit," and on folio 1 again in Henry's hand at the top in red, "Liber S. Edmundi," and the pressmark "P 163" in black. Although Henry was at Bury St. Edmunds by 1346, he probably began working on this anthology sometime before 1352 and added notes to it as late as 1378.[10] The first date is based on the evidence of the prophecies recorded on folio 41ʳ; these prophecies, in Henry's hand, were copied apparently sometime before Clement VI's death in 1352.[11] Rouse identifies the "last datable note" in Henry's hand as one on a passage giving the date of

---

[9] Rouse, "Bostonus Buriensis," 493.

[10] Rouse, "Bostonus Buriensis," 494; Lerner suggests possibly as late as 1381 (*Powers of Prophecy*, 93–94, n. 19).

[11] Rouse, "Bostonus Buriensis," 481–486, 493–494; see also Reeves, "Some Popular Prophecies," 119–120, and Lerner, *Powers of Prophecy*, 96–97, n. 28; 90, n. 20.

Pope Gregory XI's death in 1378.[12] There is, in addition, the headline on folio 95^r, "Urbanus VI" (1378–1389).

According to the evidence of his notes both in the various Bury manuscripts and in his great *Catalogus,* Henry was concerned with identifying copies of Bury texts held elsewhere, and, in general, with supplying information which would make the texts contained in these manuscripts more accessible and more reliable for the user.[13]

In addition to the table of contents on flyleaf iii^v and the inscription noted above, Henry made a number of notes on individual texts in this Corpus Christi manuscript, particularly on those concerning the Antichrist. As elsewhere, here too he noted texts which were incomplete and took considerable pains to point out similarities among texts, referring to holdings in libraries other than Bury. It apparently was also his custom to leave space in the manuscript for additional material to complete texts he had identified as incomplete.[14]

The table of contents provides some clues to Henry's methods.[15] The order of the items in the table of contents suggests that they were arranged roughly by subject, with space left between groups to accommodate further additions. And, in at least one instance, a section of a text was singled out for identification by subject. Arrangement within each group is chronological by folio with the exception of items six and seven in group one, perhaps simply because he could identify item number six more specifically than he could number seven.

The reference to folio numbers on the contents page, the foliation numbers within the manuscript, and the relation between quiring and text in combination provide evidence as to the sequence in which the manuscript was put together. With the possible exception of item number six, i.e., the reference to the *Genus nequam* prophecies ("Prophecie Joachim abbatis de papis"), the first eight entries on the contents page show the distinctive earlier form of the arabic numerals four, five, and seven, contrasting with what is now the more familiar form of these numerals in all other entries on the contents page. The last folio reference in the old style on the contents page is to folio 42, a prophecy on the mendicant orders, within the longer text, "De seminibus literarum." The reference to the "De seminibus"

---

[12] Rouse, "Bostonus Buriensis," 494; see Lerner, *Powers of Prophecy,* above n. 11.

[13] Rouse, "Bostonus Buriensis," 491–493.

[14] Rouse, "Bostonus Buriensis," 494.

[15] Although I have relied heavily on Rouse's work, the analysis of the table of contents and the resulting conclusions are dependent upon my own examination of the table of contents.

prophecy is the first item in the next group of three items on the contents page and the reference number, 44, is in the modern style.

The evidence of foliation and quiring suggests that Henry probably catalogued the contents of this manuscript in at least two stages.[16] The first stage or group would include the miscellaneous prophecies contained in quire one, the prophecies of Hildegard in quires two, three, and four (for which Henry supplied additional division markers at the top of each folio), the fragment of the *Ascende calve* sequence in quire five, and the text "De seminibus literarum" in quires six and seven. Since on the contents page he identified the text contained in quire five as "alia prophecia de papis," it is safe to assume that at the time he grouped these items on the contents page he had in hand quire ten containing the *Genus nequam* prophecies. Whether he added the folio reference, "88," at this time or later is subject to question, for the "8"s have distinctive flourishes which do not correspond to the "8"s elsewhere in the manuscript.

The *Genus nequam* prophecies recorded on folios 88^r–95^r are not in Henry's hand but in an earlier, regular Gothic hand.[17] They could have been either copied in Bury St. Edmunds or acquired elsewhere and bound in by Henry. Item six on the contents page describes these as "Prophecie Joachim abbatis de papis." The text of each prophecy with its caption occupies the upper third of each page; on the lower two-thirds are clear line drawings. Henry has added headlines above the captions identifying the popes from Nicholas III onwards as well as footnotes below the drawings, beginning with number eight (corresponding to number nine in the usual ordering) through the final picture, giving the dates of the popes.

An important characteristic that the Corpus Christi manuscript shares with Douce 88 (see below) is a combination of texts that occurs twice, and a conflation of pictures four and five. In the first case the last paragraph of what in the other manuscripts forms the second paragraph of prophecy

---

[16] Within the manuscript, the form of foliation numbers changes at 45^r, with the second page of the text "De seminibus literarum." Folio 44^r is marked in the old style, folio 45 and all subsequent folios in the new. This text, folios 44^r–66^v, constitutes quires 6 and 7. The quiring shows quire 1 as a unit, quires 2, 3, and 4 as a textual unit, quire 5 as a short unit of only 4 folios containing the fragment of the *Ascende calve* series of prophecies, quires 6 and 7 as a unit, 8 and 9 as a unit, 10 as a unit, and 11 and 12 as a unit. Relying again on the changes in form of arabic numerals on the contents page and the change noted above between folios 44^r and 45^r, Henry must have numbered the first folio of quire 6 at one time and the rest of the folios at another.

[17] See Lerner, "On the Origins," 633–634, citing Lucy Sandler, who assigns an East Anglian origin to this quire and suggests a date of ca. 1320, and Nigel Morgan who "posits 'c.1330 or 1340 at the very latest.'"

number one is run together with the text of number two. A possible explanation for this anomaly is that, since the picture for the second text shows a serpent, the copyist chose to begin this text with the first allusion to a serpent, which occurs in the last paragraph of text one.[18] The next combination of texts constitutes a more important aberration: the fourth prophecy is run together with the fifth, separated only by a space equivalent to three or four letters, and the short caption for prophecy number five.[19] In this instance pictures four and five are conflated rather than combined. Generally these two texts and pictures are held to represent Nicholas IV and Celestine V respectively. Henry's headline reads "Prophecia de papa Nicholas iiii de ordine minorum." Clearly Henry was not familiar with the tradition of identifying the figure with a sickle and rose, or in this case angel, as Celestine V, and thus the headline for the next picture, number six (five here), identifies Celestine V. From this point onwards, the identifications do not correspond to the usual ones, and the sequence totals only fourteen popes, ending with Gregory XI (fol. 94ᵛ). This "mistake" too can be explained by the appearance of a rose and sickle in both texts, but it distorts the meaning of the prophecies, since the identification of Celestine with this figure prefiguring the "angelic pope" to come seems to have been a crucial interpretation in the other versions.

Lerner and others see the missing fifteenth pope as represented in this manuscript by a unique drawing on folio 95ʳ.[20] At the top is the headline "Urbanus VI" and in the lower left-hand section is a drawing of an animal by someone other than the artist of the earlier pictures. The animal appears to be a beaver: its characteristics correspond to Albert the Great's descrip-

---

[18] The commentary on the cardinal prophecies contains no glossing of this last paragraph; perhaps, although Rehberg does not refer to this paragraph in his discussion of the Douce manuscript, this paragraph was not part of the prophecy being glossed and its addition to prophecy one came when the "anonymous author" went back to the Leo Oracles to expand the sequence of six or eight prophecies into fifteen. With the exception of the last sentence, and part of the previous sentence, the first paragraph of prophecy one is not drawn from the corresponding Leo oracle; the final paragraph, however, is based on the Leo oracle. On the other hand, the "long form" of the prophecy is given in the Vatican 3822 copy, another early witness.

[19] See below for version of the caption in the Douce manuscript. Note also that in referring to the prophecies by number, the common enumeration, as in all the manuscripts save Corpus Christi and Douce, is used. Thus what appears in Corpus Christi as number four is described as a combination of four and five.

[20] Unique, that is, among fourteenth-century manuscripts. Vatican Library, MS Vat. lat. 3816, fol. 32ʳ (1448) shows a similar but not identical beaver as the final picture of the series. See Lerner, "Papstprophetien" in Lerner and Moynihan, *Weissagungen*; although I consulted a copy of this two-volume work, my reference is to p. 28 of the typescript that Robert Lerner very kindly sent me.

tion of a beaver in *De Animalibus* as an animal "with webbed hind feet like a goose . . . and forefeet like a dog."[21]

In a fragment of the *Ascende calve* sequence recorded in Henry's hand on folio 41[r] and identified on the contents page simply as "alia prophecia de papis," the last named pope is Clement VI (1342–1352) and the later headlines refer to the series of popes culminating in a final pope identified with the terrible beast of the Apocalypse.

Henry of Kirkestede's main interest in the prophecies appears to have been the approach of the Last Things. He shows no awareness of the angelic pope theme or "renovatio mundi." Indeed, his identification of the image of pope and cow or ox rather than the figure holding a sickle and rose with Celestine V masks the angelic theme by misplacing Celestine V, the prototype of the angelic pope. Henry's concern is rather to enumerate the succession of popes approaching the final drama. The death dates of popes and the length of their pontificates have been added to the last five prophecies in a hand which is recognizably more irregular and shaky. They could have been added after the death of Gregory XI, as also the heading "Urbanus VI" above the beaver. In his interpretation of the *Ascende calve* sequence, the fourth pope after Clement VI, he believes, will be identified with the terrible apocalyptic beast. This pope, is of course, Urban VI. Did Henry at the close of his life really believe that Urban VI was the precursor of Antichrist? Perhaps, but the beaver, rather than any one of the conventional ways of representing the forms of the Antichrist in the Apocalypse, remains a puzzle.[22] It could be that Henry added the headline to a blank page because Urban was pope at the time and that the beaver is just a beaver and not a symbol of the Antichrist.

---

[21] *Albert the Great: Man and the Beasts, De Animalibus (Books 22–26)*, trans. James J. Scanlon, Medieval & Renaissance Texts & Studies vol. 47 (Binghamton, 1987), 90; see also Debra Hassig, *Medieval Bestiaries: Text, Image, Ideology* (Cambridge, 1995), 84–92 and figures 78–91.

[22] On Henry's interest in the Last Things, particularly in CCC 404, see Rouse, "Bostonus Buriensis," 493. The illustrated Apocalypse was a genre very popular in England (and elsewhere but not, significantly, in Italy) during the thirteenth and fourteenth centuries; as a result there were a number of familiar and conventional ways to represent the Antichrist. If the artist had been directed to draw an apocalyptic beast, he would have had at least four models to choose from; on this point but with respect to the *Ascende calve* prophecies, see R. Freyhan, "Joachism and the English Apocalypse," *Journal of the Warburg and Courtauld Institutes* 18 (1955): 211–244, here 242–244. For discussions of illustrated Apocalypses and the representation of the Antichrist in medieval art see Bernard McGinn, "Portraying Antichrist in the Middle Ages," in *The Use and Abuse of Eschatology in the Middle Ages*, ed. W. Verbeke et al. (Leuven, 1988), 1–48; Richard K. Emmerson, *Antichrist in the Middle Ages: A Study of Medieval Apocalypticism, Art, and Literature* (Seattle, 1981); Peter H. Brieger, "The Trinity College Apocalypse: An Introduction and Description," in *Trinity College Apocalypse*, ed. Peter H. Brieger, translation of Anglo-Norman Commentary by M. Dulong. 1 vol. in 2 parts (London, 1967), 1: 1–15; Jessie Poesch, "Antichrist Imagery in Anglo-French Apocalypse Manuscripts" (Ph.D. diss., University of Pennsylvania, 1966); see also n. 44 below.

The text recorded in this manuscript is a most reliable one, containing very few unique readings, in spite of the aberrations in order. It certainly represents an early version of the *Genus nequam* prophecies. The pictures as well represent an early recension; not all the figures are popes, as in the later manuscripts; the details of picture eleven, that is, the figure seated on a sarcophagus rather than a rock, and the form of picture twelve all make it clear that this is an early version, or at least one with clear affinities to the Leo Oracles. It also seems clear that this version was read differently, certainly by Henry, than were the versions represented by the Riccardiana, Yale, Lunel, Monreale, and Vat. lat. 3819 manuscripts. For the first six units, the text and pictures show clear affinities with the version of the prophecies referred to in the cardinal or Orsini commentary.

Description of the Pictures

The pictures are numbered as they appear in the manuscript. Picture number five corresponds to picture number six and so on in all the manuscripts except this one and the Douce manuscript.

1.   (fol. 88^r) Picture number one shows a pope, standing on a small pedestal, wearing a chasuble and the papal tiara, one hand holding a large staff with cross, the other upraised as if in blessing. To the left of this figure is a bear with four nursing young. The papal tiara is tall and pointed, here as elsewhere, in the old style.

2.   (fol. 88^v) Picture two shows a pope standing on a pedestal, wearing chasuble and tiara, one hand holding a staff surmounted by a cross, the other upraised in blessing. At the immediate left of this figure is a long staff with a banner. To the right of the figure is a snake-like serpent with a dog's head, being attacked by two large birds.

3.   (fol. 89^r) Picture three shows a pope in chasuble and tiara. An eagle with nimbus is just above the pope's tiara. At the left is a smaller figure in a short unbelted gown. To the right is a unicorn with upraised paws, facing the pope.

4.   (fol. 89^v) Picture four shows at the bottom left two medallions: within each is the bust of a king wearing a crown. A large, lightly bearded figure, but with no visible tonsure, is to the right: this figure is barefoot, wears a long simple belted gown and holds a sickle in his right hand, the figure of a winged angel in his left. Above the main figure is a large head, with hair and beard arranged like rays, resting on the serrated edge of a sickle.

5. (fol. 90ʳ) Picture five shows a pope standing on a pedestal wearing a chasuble and tiara, holding a staff with cross in his right hand, with left hand upraised in blessing. A cow or ox with horns is to the figure's right, with its face directed towards the pope.

6. (fol. 90ᵛ) Picture six shows a king at the right, holding his robes to his body. To the king's right is a bear with open mouth, and five suckling cubs.

7. (fol. 91ʳ) Picture seven shows a building, perhaps a church, with three towers, but no cross, windows but no doors. In the middle directly below this building is a head, either hooded or contained within some sort of vessel, blowing upwards.

8. (fol. 91ᵛ) Picture eight shows on the far right a pope, wearing chasuble and tiara, holding a staff with cross in one hand and a scroll (?) in the other. In the middle at the bottom is an animal, looking like a cross between a dog and a bear, mouth open, facing away from the pope. To the left of the animal are two outstretched hands. Above the animal and taking up considerable space are three long crossed staffs with banners.

9. (fol. 92ʳ) Picture nine shows a large empty chair or throne. Below it and to the left is an outstretched hand.

10. (fol. 92ᵛ) Picture ten shows a man dressed only in a long cloth from waist to knee. The man has no visible tonsure, is bearded, barefoot, and seated on a rectangular sarcophagus (?). To the figure's immediate right is a rectangle, twice as long as it is wide, with a double-barred cross inside. Above the man and rectangle is a six-pointed star in black. To the main figure's left is a small figure in a long loose robe, arms crossed, one foot resting on the sarcophagus.

11. (fol. 93ʳ) Picture eleven shows an angel holding a tiara in one hand and a scroll (?) in the other, more or less seated on the torso of a beast with no legs but with a bear's head at each end. Two dogs are just below and in front, back to back, dogs being distinguished from bears by the the shape and position of their ears. The dog is identical to the animal in picture eight.

12. (fol. 93ᵛ) Picture twelve shows on the left a pope, wearing chasuble and tiara, one hand holding a staff with cross, the other upraised in blessing. To the pope's left and of equal size is an angel with a nimbus, one hand on the pope's tiara, the other holding a standard or sceptre ending in a modified *fleur de lis*.

13. (fol. 94ʳ) Picture thirteen shows a pope with nimbus, wearing a chasuble and tiara, seated on a bench, with one hand upraised, the other holding a book. Behind him is a decorated arras, held by an angel (of equal size with the pope) on either side.

14. (fol. 94ᵛ) Picture fourteen shows a pope, wearing a chasuble and mitre, holding a tall tiara in one hand and a book in the other.

15. (fol. 95ʳ) Picture fifteen, if it in fact does belong to the series, apparently is drawn by a second artist. It shows an animal, a beaver, with webbed hind feet and a flat tail. The animal is not centered on the page, rather it is in the lower left of the page, facing the inner margin, with either whiskers or rays coming from its muzzle.

D. Oxford, Bodleian Library, MS Douce 88, fols. 140ᴿ–146ᵛ

Descriptions: *A Catalogue of Printed Books . . . Bequeathed by Francis Douce, Esq. to the Bodleian Library* (Oxford, 1840), vol. 2, 10–12 for a table of contents; *A Summary Catalogue of Western Manuscripts in the Bodleian Library* (Oxford, 1897), vol. 4, 516–517; O. Pächt and J.J.G. Alexander, *Illuminated Manuscripts in the Bodleian Library* (Oxford, 1973), vol. 3, 45, no. 487; Lerner, "On the Origins," 633. *Provenance*: Montague Rhodes James, *The Ancient Libraries of Canterbury and Dover* (Cambridge, 1903), 290, no. 70.

The *Genus nequam* prophecies occupy a very small part, seven folios, of a large miscellany, 215 x 165 millimeters, written on paper in a number of thirteenth- and late thirteenth–early fourteenth-century hands. The calendar which opens the volume, and which must have been part of another volume at one time, is dated 1336, but much of the rest of the volume seems more likely to be later thirteenth or early fourteenth century. The catalogue divides this manuscript into five uneven parts, beginning with the calendar, but, apart from a few mutilated pages, missing pages, and interpolations, and apart from the preliminaries, the book has the look of a whole.[23]

Parts B, C, and D may once have been a part of the same volume; the

---

[23] Except for the decoration on folios 50–51, the decorated initials and flourishes are very similar in style. See below, n. 25. The decorated initials in the second bestiary and elsewhere are similar to those in the *Genus nequam* prophecies section. The pictures in the first bestiary are more accomplished than those in the second, and there are, as well, differences in the flourishes of the decorated initials; on English and French styles of pen flourishing, see Sonia Scott-Fleming, *The Analysis of Pen Flourishing in Thirteenth-Century Manuscripts* (Leiden, 1989), 25 and elsewhere.

testimony of the Catalogue of the Abbey of St. Augustine gives evidence that the section of the manuscript containing the *Genus nequam* prophecies (E) was a part of that library shortly before 1497. The table of contents in the Abbey catalogue corresponds to items nine through twenty-nine in the Douce catalogue, that is, folios 68–154.[24] Thus the manuscript can be divided into two parts, one of which we know was a unit before 1497. There are, as well, some connections between the two parts. The decorated initials are in a number of instances very similar, although it is very clear that the artist of the bestiary in part one is considerably more accomplished than the illustrator of the bestiary in part two.[25]

The prophecies themselves begin on folio 140[r], with no preliminaries. The heading is the caption for the first prophecy: "Ypocrisis habundabit. Incipit principium malorum." The two-and-one-half line initials for the opening word of each prophecy are alternating blue and red, and are lightly decorated with flourishes, with touches of blue and red wash. Within each prophecy, division signs (paragraph signs) are alternately blue and red or are filled in with pale washes of of color. There are remnants of marginal rulings on the sides of pages, as well as some line rulings, and the upper edge of the manuscript shows some signs of trimming. The figures are outlined in ink and filled in with pale washes of red, blue, green, and light brown. The illustrations themselves show no particular finesse: the main figures stand on small pedestals or on lightly defined ground lines, and the integration of the parts in each image is awkwardly managed.[26] In all, the illustrations show little evidence of the professional miniaturist, and they may well in fact have been drawn by the scribe.

The manuscript is undoubtedly of English origin; determining a date within the *termini*, 1277–1320, suggested by Lerner, is more difficult.[27] In a recent bibliography, "Manuscripts of Western Medieval Bestiary Versions," the bestiary in the first part of this manuscript is identified as belonging to the Second Family version (principally thirteenth-century manuscripts), and the bestiary in the second part of Douce 88 to the Third

---

[24] I was able to check the description in James, *Ancient Libraries*, giving the notations in the "Catalogue of the Abbey of St. Augustine," against the Bodleian Library's copy of this catalogue.

[25] For Part 2, compare the decorated initial *I* on folio 81[r] with that beginning unit four of the *Genus nequam* prophecies; also the animal on folio 73[r] with that in picture six.

[26] The illustrations for the bestiary on folios 70[v]–115[r] are also crudely done.

[27] Lerner, "On the Origins," 633; see Rehberg, " 'Kardinalsorakel'," 61–70, 97–104. Rehberg follows Lerner's dating of the Douce MS and assumes therefore that the addition of popes to the prophecies happened earlier in England than in Italy (102). See Rehberg, " 'Kardinalsorakel'," 65–67, for correspondences between the pictures associated with the cardinal prophecies and the first six pictures in the Douce MS.

Family version (all manuscripts are thirteenth and fourteenth century).[28] Perhaps a detailed analysis of the five manuscripts in this group might narrow the dates for the Douce version.

The version of the *Genus nequam* prophecies, text and image, in this manuscript is almost identical with that in the Corpus Christi manuscript. On the basis of textual and iconographic evidence, neither is a copy of the other, but both must be based on a very similar exemplar. There are two important features that distinguish this version from that of C: 1) the presentation of unit one, including the form of the caption, a detail of the iconography, and the addition of a short verse above the image, is unique to D; and 2) D gives the long form of the captions (as opposed to the short form in C).

The picture for unit one shows five suckling cubs in D, four in C, making the Douce version, at least in this instance, closer to the version referred to in the commentary on the cardinal prophecies. Above the image, the Douce scribe also adds a brief verse on the pastoral staff, *inc. In baculi forma*, which, according to Lerner, is known solely from another English MS,[29] and the pope is identified as Nicholas III. For unit one the arrangement of the long and short forms of the motto in D is also unique to it: what usually constitutes the amplification, "Ypocrisis habundabit," is centered above the text and set off by pointing. What is apparently the original short form, "Incipit principium malorum," heavily abbreviated, is squeezed into the remaining space between "habundabit" and the right margin.

At this point, at least, only the form of the captions gives clues to the dating of this version. The long form of the captions was in circulation before 1317, for Pipini makes reference to them. The short form of the caption must be the earlier version: the Leo Oracles have only one-word captions; the commentary on the cardinal prophecies refers to the short form only, the *Visio fratris Johannis* makes no reference to the captions, short or long; the *Liber de Flore* (ca. 1304/1305) refers to two of the short forms. The form of the captions then would suggest a date no earlier than 1304–1305 for the version recorded in D, unless the longer forms were added later.

---

[28] Willene B. Clark and Meradith T. McMunn, eds., *Birds and Beasts of the Middle Ages: The Bestiary and its Legacy* (Philadelphia, 1989), 197–200, the list of manuscripts based in part on Florence McCulloch, *Medieval Latin and French Bestiaries* (Chapel Hill, 1962); see also Clark and McMunn, "Bibliography of Bestiary Studies Since 1962," *Birds and Beasts*, 205–214; see also Hassig, *Medieval Bestiaries*; and see above, n. 23 for similarities between decorated initials in the second bestiary with those in the *Genus nequam* section.

[29] Lerner, "On the Origins," 633.

For the most part the Douce scribe seems to distinguish the two parts of the captions, either by leaving a space or by a period. The other manuscripts which have the long form of the caption generally do not make this distinction, but treat the caption as a single sentence. There is no firm evidence to assume that these captions were added later, even though the longer form of the caption on occasion has a tacked-on look, particularly in units one and eight. For unit eight, the short and long forms, while centered in the space above the text, are not quite on the same line. The long form is omitted entirely for unit two, and the single word "Sanguis" is centered in the space above the text. On the other hand, the form of the caption for unit five would suggest the scribe had access to the long form all along, for although the texts of units four and five are run together, the scribe has no trouble accommodating the seven-word caption. Furthermore, in this instance, the one-word caption has been expanded from "Elatio" to "Elatio paupertatis" followed by pointing, the rest of the caption,[30] and rubrication marking the beginning of the text of unit five.

The question remains: were the longer forms added on later or were they a part of the version the D scribe records from the beginning? The evidence is inconclusive, but the physical evidence, the pattern of centering the captions above the main text, apart from the instances of units one and eight, points to the latter conclusion. The caption for unit five is important here, for, as noted above, the scribe has no problem accommodating the long form of the caption, and the rubrication marking the main text is indented fourteen spaces from the margin. If the scribe had simply left space between the two run-on texts, and then had filled in that space with the captions, one would have expected the rubrication for the main text to have begun a line or to have been indented less deeply.

Lerner has argued that the Douce scribe must have worked from two exemplars, i.e., one with short captions and one with the long form. Although the evidence is not adequate to settle the question with certainty, the form of the caption in unit five, an important textual variant in unit eleven (the reading of "virtus" for "unctus"), and the differences between the two series of images (they are not simply additions), all suggest a single exemplar. It does seem clear, however, that the Douce scribe did not understand the significance of the longer captions, particularly that of caption five. The longer form of this caption is usually read as pointing to Celestine V; yet the iconography of the conflated images of units four and

---

[30] One detail of caption five links D with L: both read "gule" for "castrimargie"; DuCange gives "gulae concupiscentia" for "castrimargia."

five (in both C and D) certainly gives no indication that the copyist knew of the connection between the text and image and Celestine V.

The D scribe's exemplar must, however, have looked very much like the version in C. Except for two readings, one in prophecy one and one in prophecy eleven,[31] all the other textual differences are minor, and, like Corpus Christi 404, Douce presents a "pristine" version of the text, one with very few unique readings. Douce also shares with Corpus Christi 404 the peculiarities of arrangement, both of text and picture, noted in the description of Corpus Christi 404.

Apart from the difference noted in unit one, the images in the Corpus Christi and Douce manuscripts are very similar. Several minor differences in the content of the pictures, however, deserve notice: 1) the eagle atop the tiara in picture three has a cross next to it (the eagle in the Corpus Christi copy has a nimbus, but no cross); 2) in picture twelve the angel sits on a cloud, holding the tiara, and above the tiara is an eagle in flight (there is no cloud or eagle in the Corpus Christi copy, and the angel holds a tiara and a scroll). Both the cross in picture three (with a small variation) and the eagle in picture twelve are elements found in the corresponding pictures of the Leo Oracles, placing the Douce version, then, marginally closer to the Leo Oracles than is the Corpus Christi version.

The other differences between the two sets of pictures are mostly matters of style. Although the pictures in Douce are crudely drawn, there is on occasion more decoration than in the corresponding pictures in Corpus Christi 404, i.e., the pedestals, as well as the sarcophagus in picture ten, are decorated in Douce, plain in Corpus Christi 404.

In sum, then, there is little indication of how the scribe or the anthologizer read these prophecies. There is no particular order to the manuscript nor is there any apparent principle of arrangement, and there is nothing in the manuscript as a whole or in the presentation of the prophecies in particular to tell us why the scribe copied them out or how he read them.[32]

---

[31] For prophecy one, see above p. 22. Douce adds "sicut adulatores" to the sentence "Sicut autem bene manens canes nutris novas et habeas istos in medio tempestatum." In prophecy eleven, Douce reads, "Et revelabitur *virtus*" where Corpus Christi 404 reads "Et revelabitur *unctus*."

[32] Could it be that he was simply attracted to the animals represented in the pictures, as a curiosity similar to the marvels of the world, represented elsewhere in the manuscript? On recent interest in medieval miscellanies, particularly discussions on order and coherence, see Barbara A. Shailor, "A Cataloger's View," in *The Whole Book*, ed. Stephen G. Nichols and Siegfried Wenzel, 153–167.

Description of the Pictures

See description of Corpus Christi 404: differences in content are noted below.

picture one: five suckling bears in Douce, four in CC 404.
picture three: a cross to the right of the eagle in Douce and no nimbus.
picture nine: the pope holds what may be a large seal in Douce, a scroll in CC 404; two hands, palms extended, are at the pope's left in Douce (extended toward the inner margin) and to the pope's right in CC 404 (extended towards the animal).
picture twelve: the angel sits on a cloud in Douce and there is an eagle (?) in flight in the upper left of the picture where there is no bird in CC 404.

The effect of three other images is slightly different in the Douce copy from that in the Corpus Christi copy, although this difference may be simply a result of style or the artist's competence:

picture four/five: the severed head in the Douce copy has hair similar to that of the other figure in the image; the head in CC 404 has hair like flames.
picture six: the cow in the Douce copy is positioned differently, and the effect could be seen as more threatening; in the CC 404 copy, all four feet are on the ground line.
picture seven: the position of the king's head and right hand are different in Douce, inclining towards the bear and young.

And, of course, there is no beaver on an additional leaf, as there is in Corpus Christi 404. (Numbering is that of the units as they are generally represented, rather than the numbering unique to this group.)

F. FLORENCE, BIBLIOTECA RICCARDIANA, MS 1222B, FOLS. 1ᴿ–8ᵛ

Description: S. Morpurgo, *Indici e Cataloghi* 15, *Biblioteca Riccardiana* (Rome, 1893), Vol. 1, fasc. 4, 293; Maria Luisa Scuricini Greco, *Miniature riccardiane* (Florence, 1958), 213–214; Gosbert Schüssler, "Reform und Eschatologie in einer Vaticinienhandschrift des frühen Trecento: MS. 1222B der Biblioteca Riccardiana in Florenz," in Ernst Ullmann, *Von der Macht der Bilder* (Leipzig, 1983), 39–53.

This manuscript of eight pages measures 210 x 145 millimeters and has a damaged first page. Of Italian origin, it bears no title on its first page, although "profezie dell'Abate Giochimo" has been added in a modern hand. With the exception of page one, the text occupies the top third of each page; on the lower two-thirds is a roughly drawn picture. There are no captions or headings.

Riccardiana is the only fourteenth-century manuscript under consideration to include identifications of the popes and/or descriptions of the illustrations appended to the text and apparently in the same hand as that of the main text. There are secondary identifications of popes in a much later cursive hand. The last pope identified by this later hand is Innocent VI (1352–1362). It seems fair to assume that the popes were identified by the earlier hand through Benedict XI and perhaps Clement V (1305–1314), depending on how one interprets the abbreviation above picture eight, and that some of these identifications were erased partially or fully as the second glossator sought to bring them up to date, omitting some popes in the historical sequence in order to end with Innocent VI.

The hand is a regular one of the early part of the century, although some of the identifications are not as smooth in execution as is the main part of the text. The pictures show no evidence of being done by a professional illuminator; if it were not for the lack of correspondence between some of the descriptions of the pictures added at the end of some of the texts and the pictures as they actually appear, one would be tempted to say the pictures were executed by the scribe. They are awkwardly drawn and lightly colored in with greens and pale reds predominating. The initials are built-up two-line initials with no decoration. The built-up initial is followed by a letter at least a line and a half high, and then the letters assume a regular size. The identifications and any description of the pictures immediately follow the text. The secondary, later, identifications are written in next to the illustrations in whatever space was available.

The chief characteristic of this scribe is his attempt to interpret or gloss what he was copying. On occasion, he inserts a *vel* followed by a paraphrase or explanatory clause. In text number five, for example, the first sentence reads "Vide iterum alienum modum existentis falcem magnam et rosam manu *qui est manna. vel hoc interpretatur idest quid est hoc erit miraculum magnum* quam fert." The italicized words are this scribe's addition. In this same sentence all the other early witnesses read "existentis modum"; Riccardiana alone transposes these words. In the remainder of text five, except for reading "Tres tres annos" for "tres autem annos" and "vives" for "vivens" in the last sentence, none of Riccardiana's other readings is unique. Thus, although Riccardiana, along with Yale, Marston 225, has statistically the greatest number of variant readings, the statistical summary does not accurately reflect the ways in which Riccardiana's readings differ from the others. In the last example cited above, the Riccardiana scribe makes two sentences from the sentence that is elsewhere a single sentence by changing "vivens" to "vives." The "Tres tres annos" for "Tres autem tres annos," given the rest of the textual evidence, might or might not be an error. The transposition of "existentis modum" probably is an error in copying.

The textual evidence here is complex, for, as in the above instance, the unique reading of "vives" (unique, that is, of the nine copies) agrees with the reading of "vives" in the fifth unit of the commentary on the cardinal prophecies (V:116). On the other hand, the commentary quotes "Tres autem annos vives" rather than "Tres tres annos vives." A number of other readings, some more significant than others, connect the Riccardiana copy to the text quoted in the commentary. The most striking example is the reading of "collateralis" in the opening line of unit four (cf. IV:82), as noted earlier.[33] Iconographic evidence, as well, connects this copy to the commentary, particularly for images one, two, and three.[34]

The Riccardiana scribe apparently identified the popes through Benedict XI (1303–1304) and perhaps through Clement V (1305–1314), although the identifications for both Boniface VIII and Benedict XI have been partially erased. Above picture number eight, that of a besieged city, is an abbreviation: .ꟽ.ᘜ..[35] There are no further identifications until picture number eleven, which reads "papa nudus," perhaps simply a description.[36] For picture number twelve, the identification or description reads "papa cum ovibus ante et cum metria in manu,"[37] a description which does not correspond to the image below it. Above picture number thirteen is "papa coronatus ab angelo," which does correspond to the picture represented below. Text and picture correspond in number fourteen, as the description

---

[33] See above, "Relation of MSS," pp. 28–29.

[34] See Rehberg, " 'Kardinalsorakel'," 68–69, on this point.

[35] Here I am grateful for the opinion of John Monfasani, and to him as well for double-checking my notes on the erasures in the manuscript when he was in Florence. The first letter or symbol in this group is very similar (although slightly more angular) to the uppercase "M" in unit two (fol. 1ᵛ), the "M" in "Miserabiliter"; it lacks only the distinctive decoration of vertical lines within the space of the letter. Cf. the second letter with the "V" in the identification of "Celestine V," unit five (fol. 3ʳ).

[36] Hugh of Novocastro also identifies this figure as "papa nudus" (*Tractatus*, Lib. II, cap. 28); see above, "The Prophecies," n. 6.

[37] *ante* or *autem*? The word is abbreviated and thus there is the possibility of confusion between the abbreviations for *ante* and *autem*, but in this case the abbreviation is consistent with the abbreviations for *autem* elsewhere in the manuscript, thus requiring editorial emendation here.

reads "papa cum duobus angelis." The description in number fifteen reads "papa cum libro in manu et cum metria," although the pope in the picture holds, instead of a book, a staff terminating in the episcopal cross.[38] There is no mention of the curious animal with human face and peculiar headdress at the bottom left of the page.

The discrepancies between image and description in prophecies twelve and fifteen constitute a puzzle. The description in number twelve notes a pope with sheep; the image shows an angel, holding a papal tiara, above a sarcophagus surmounted by an arrangement of two arcs with four animal heads emitting flames or rays. Unless the animal heads are those of sheep, it is difficult to avoid the conclusion that the Riccardiana scribe either knew of or was looking at a different picture than the one drawn below this text. And if such were the case, it was a picture represented by none of the other fourteenth-century witnesses. Other fourteenth-century versions of this picture do show a pope holding a tiara over the heads of animals, in two instances over four rabbits, but usually over a combination of bears and dogs. Fifteenth-century versions routinely show sheep. The image as drawn in Riccardiana has strong connections to that in both the Corpus Christi and Douce manuscripts as well as to the image in the Lambecius version of the Leo Oracles.

All evidence then points to the execution of this manuscript in the early part of the fourteenth century, no later than 1314, if the abbreviation above picture eight refers to Clement V, and as early as 1304–1305, if it does not. The scribe's descriptions of pictures twelve and fifteen suggest one exemplar, and, at least for some of the pictures, another. An additional possibility is that the hand of the descriptions is a somewhat later one, or even the same scribe writing at a later date[39] and "correcting" the image which follows. If such is the case, however, why not "correct" as well the image in picture four?

As far as the pictures are concerned, this manuscript provides a bridge between the version of the *Genus nequam* prophecies witnessed by the Corpus Christi and Douce manuscripts and almost all the others. It has one of the distinctive features of English manuscripts in its version of picture

---

[38] Millet and Rigaux ("Aux origines," 140) suggest that the painter deliberately made this substitution because the sceptre is a more visible sign of power.

[39] Again, John Monfasani agrees with me that the main hand and the hand of the descriptions seem to be one and the same. The description for number twelve, "papa cum ovibus ante et cum metria in manu," is in a slightly smaller script than that of the text before it, suggesting, perhaps, that the scribe fit it in the space available after the picture was drawn. The placement of the description above picture fourteen, "papa cum duobus angelis," also suggests it might have been added in the space available after the picture was executed.

twelve; yet the description of picture twelve, apart from the sheep, corresponds to that in the other manuscripts. For picture eleven, the Riccardiana
manuscript, unlike the two English ones, shows a nude figure emerging
from a cave, which is identified as the "papa nudus." This change, along
with the identification of the figure in picture number five as Celestine V,
points to an interpretation of pictures and texts different from that of the
two English manuscripts. Here there is a Franciscan resonance, and an
emphasis on the angelic pope missing in the other two.[40] There is, as well,
the addition of the curious beast in picture fifteen, with the word "antichrist" on its torso. The form this beast takes, as noted elsewhere, is
unusual, and is not drawn from the considerable repertoire of representations of Antichrist in the illustrated Apocalypses of the period; rather it is
an inverse image of the Lamb of God.[41]

If this manuscript is as early as 1304–1305, then it is the first to present
features of a Franciscan iconography (in picture eleven) and to represent the
apocalyptic beast, which was to become a regular feature, in picture fifteen.
The evidence of the Lunel manuscript provides a slightly different version
of the evolution of the beast in picture fifteen and would suggest a later
date for the Riccardiana version, a date closer to 1314.[42]

Description of the Pictures

1. (fol. 1ʳ) Picture one occupies the lower right-hand corner of the
    damaged first page. The parts of the drawing are separate rather than
    integrated. The partial figure of the pope wears the papal tiara (old
    style, here as elsewhere); one arm is outstretched, the other holds a
    book. To the right is a bear with young.

2. (fol. 1ᵛ) Picture two shows a pope in chasuble and tiara, holding a
    book. To the right is a snake-like serpent with knots in its middle,
    two birds attacking its head and eyes.

---

[40] See above, "Relation of Manuscripts," n. 23: this resonance is enhanced by the
identification of the figure in picture five with Celestine V and by the identification of the figure
in picture eleven with "papa nudus." See also Schüssler, "Reform und Eschatologie," 44–45.

[41] See below, "Picture Tradition," 111–114.

[42] Lerner, "On the Origins," 628, 634, prefers the earlier date, 1304–1305; Rehberg's recent
work on the cardinal prophecies supports the earlier date as well; Schüssler ("Reform und Eschatologie," 42) follows Grundmann in dating this copy to sometime after the pontificate of Benedict XI (1303–1304) and before that of Clement V (1305–1314). There is no background decoration in the Florentine manuscript's miniatures, so the beast could have been a later addition
to the image, added perhaps at the same time the first set of "corrected" identifications were
made. No erasure would have been required.

3.   (fol. 2ʳ) Picture three shows a pope in the center, wearing chasuble and tiara with an eagle perched on top of the tiara. To the pope's right is a figure of equal size in secular dress, hands outstretched and touching the pope. To the pope's right is a unicorn, with horn touching the pope's eye.

4.   (fol. 2ᵛ) Picture four shows a large decorated goblet-shaped object with a large curved piece extending three-quarters of the way over it. Below this curved piece and within the vessel is the bust of a tonsured and bearded figure.

5.   (fol. 3ʳ) Picture five shows a tonsured and bearded figure, dressed in a robe with a V-necked tunic, holding a sickle in one hand and a cluster of five roses (described by the scribe as *manna*) in the other. An angel with nimbus is at the figure's shoulder.

6.   (fol. 3ᵛ) Picture six shows a pope wearing chasuble and tiara. To the pope's right and constituting two-thirds of the image is a large marked-off rectangular space. In the lower portion of this space is a cow or ox with horns and perhaps a human face turned towards the viewer. At the top and above the upper line of the rectangle are busts of two figures, each wearing a mitre.

7.   (fol. 4ʳ) Picture seven shows a large figure of a pope wearing chasuble and tiara. To the left is the smaller figure of a bear and its suckling cub.

8.   (fol. 4ᵛ) Picture eight shows a besieged fortress or city, with a figure in a tower dropping rocks from it. At the bottom right is a head with "breath" or rays directed at the fortress-city, again very crudely drawn. Above the image are two symbols or abbreviations: **.ꝟ. .6.**

9.   (fol. 5ʳ) Picture nine shows a pope wearing chasuble and tiara, holding a key in one hand and a book or a scroll in the other. To the side is a fox, standing on its hind legs, with a key balanced on its head and holding a banner with a large rectangular cross on it.

10. (fol. 5ᵛ) Picture ten shows another crudely drawn fortress or city similar in overall shape to the one in picture eight but against what may be a background of hills. To one side and in the upper corner of the image is a shield pierced by three outstretched arms directed toward the fortress-city.

11. (fol. 6ʳ) Picture eleven shows a naked man emerging from a roughly drawn cave of rocks, arms awkwardly turned about himself. The man

is bearded but with no visible tonsure. To the side is a figure wearing a short belted robe; it is clear this figure has no tonsure. Above the second figure is a six-pointed star.

12. (fol. 6^v) Picture twelve shows a rectangular sarcophagus, surmounted by two large curved pieces (or arcs) ending in animal heads with well-defined muzzles or faces. Their mouths are open and apparently emit flames. In the middle of the curve is an angel with nimbus, holding a papal tiara in one hand; the other hand is extended in blessing or a pointing gesture.

13. (fol. 7^r) Picture thirteen shows, to one side, a pope wearing a chasuble and tiara, kneeling, hands extended in prayer. The pope is being crowned by a large angel in a robe and with nimbus.

14. (fol. 7^v) Picture fourteen shows a pope wearing chasuble and tiara, apparently kneeling, facing the viewer, hands together. The pope is being crowned by two angels, both with nimbus, both in simple robes, one bearing a large simple cross against one shoulder. Above the tiara is the symbol or abbreviation ⁊ℏ. The same symbol occurs at the end of the text.

15. (fol. 8^r) Picture fifteen shows a pope wearing chasuble and tiara, arms extended, taking up the width of the page. He holds a tiara in one hand and a cross with three crossbars in the other. To the bottom left is an animal with human face, with a headdress or crown of ten horns (?) with "anti-christ" lettered on its torso. Above the pope's tiara is the symbol or abbreviation ⟂ (similar to one of the symbols above picture eight, noted above).

L. LUNEL, BIBLIOTHÈQUE DE LOUIS MÉDARD À LA BIBLIOTHÈQUE MUNICIPALE, MS 7, FOLS. 4^R–19^R, 22^V

Description: Catalogue Général des Manuscrits des Bibliothèques Publiques de France (Paris, 1886—), vol. 31, 168. François Avril, "Les manuscrits enluminés de la collection Médard à la bibliothèque de Lunel," in *La Bibliothèque de Louis Médard à Lunel* (Montpellier, 1987), 163–168. *Provenance:* Southern France, perhaps Avignon, 1315–1320 (Avril); Library of Louis Médard; given to the Bibliothèque Municipale, Lunel, by Jean-Louis Médard in 1834.

This manuscript is in two parts: the first part contains the *Genus nequam* prophecies, followed by a series of thirteenth-century texts, including the pseudo-Hildegard "Insurgent gentes," and a text attributed to Joachim of Fiore, *inc.* "In die illa elevabitur draco repletus furore," and the second, in a different hand, a group of prophecies also attributed to Joachim of Fiore. The title page (folio 1ᵛ) is sixteenth century or later. The manuscript has been described briefly by François Avril ("Manuscrits enluminés"), who dates it to the period 1315–1320. The first section is written on vellum, the second section (beginning fol. 23ʳ) on paper, which suggests that the two parts, although perhaps contemporary, were executed separately and later bound together.[43]

The set of *Genus nequam* prophecies begins on folio 3ᵛ, "Incipit liber prophetiarum papalium," followed by the caption "Ypocrisia habundabit," then "Liber primus," and the text of prophecy number one. On folio 4ʳ is a full-page image of a pope and three bears, identified within the image as Nicholas III. Some notes in Latin and in a later hand have been added to the bottom and side of the page. At the bottom of picture fifteen (folio 19ʳ) is the line, in red, "Explicit liber ymaginum papalium." On folio 19ᵛ begins the series of texts including the pseudo-Hildegard and Joachite prophecies. The "In die illa elevabitur draco repletus" text is followed by what in the Monreale and Vatican (3819) manuscripts is the sixteenth picture of the *Genus nequam* sequence, an animal with a human face, wearing a crown, usually identified as the Antichrist.

With the exception of prophecy and picture number one, each of which takes up a full page, all the prophecies are arranged in the same way on the page: caption in red, decorated initial, text, and picture below the text. Five of the pictures have substantial borders with images of grotesques, as does the text of prophecy one. The border of picture one, for instance, shows two headless winged beasts facing one another; in the center is a large crowned head with three faces, one face to each side and one frontal. This same head is repeated in the border of picture eleven, the first of the "angelic" popes.[44]

---

[43] Avril, "Manuscrits enluminés," 164. (I am grateful to Robert Lerner for calling this article to my attention.) This second group, perhaps in several hands, includes a number of Joachite prophecies, including copies of three short prophecies found on fols. 19ᵛ–20ᵛ in the first part as well as a crude copy of the animal with crown and human face. It also has a number of blank pages. The foliation doubles 19, but as the second fol. 19 is blank and the next text is on the folio numbered 20, this enumeration is followed.

[44] There is some uncertainty as to the significance of the various elements in the border decorations. Robert Calkins thinks that they are purely decorative; for a contrasting view of border decoration in general, see Michael Camille, *Image on the Edge: The Margins of Medieval Art* (Cambridge, Mass., 1992), 9 and elsewhere. The same artist undoubtedly did miniature, border and decorated initial, and perhaps the rubrication (the caption above the text). The border is integrated into the miniature, separated only by narrow bands. The pattern of decoration makes

The hand is a clear one and easy to read. There are several *lacunae* in the text, but on the whole, although it is a text with a fair number of unique readings, these tend to be omissions and/or erroneous readings. Although the manuscript is related iconographically to the Monreale (P) and Vatican (V=3819) witnesses, the Lunel version does not share additions to the texts found in P and V, nor the omissions characteristic of the Monreale and Paris (N) manuscripts. For a number of prophecies there are two sets of captions, one at the head of the text executed by the scribe, and a second, contained within the picture and presumably executed by the artist.[45] Both captions are with one exception the long form, rather than the short, but they are not always identical. In several instances the captions above the texts share unusual readings with the Oxford manuscript (D),[46] while the caption within the picture gives the version found in the Monreale, Paris, and Vatican (3819) manuscripts (NPV). In two instances (the captions for units nine and ten), the short portion of the captions shares important similarities with the captions in the Monreale and Paris copies.[47] The only distinctive features of the text are the additions, "liber secundus," "liber tercius," etc., to the captions, the two versions of the captions, and the *explicit*

---

the first twenty-two folios a unit, even though the end of the *Genus nequam* sequence is marked by an *explicit* on folio 19[r]. Mary Alberi suggested to me a connection between this three-headed image and the magician Hermes Trismegistus. Michael Camille, *Gothic Idol*, 271–277, notes the association of a similar image with the Templars, and accusations of idolatry brought against them. See also Freyhan, "Joachism and the English Apocalypse" (214), who comments on the significance of two-headed figures in the Alexander Apocalypse ("denoting the apocalyptic and the historical meaning"), as well as on the tradition of a type of Antichrist with three heads, "a regular feature in the *Bible Moralisée*" (224, n. 4); for more on the three-headed Antichrist figure, see Rosemary Muir Wright, *Art and Antichrist in Medieval Europe* (Manchester and New York, 1995): the "three-headed Antichrist may have derived its formula from pagan images of Janus and guardian gods, but it expressed above all, the all-seeing and overtly human aspect of the Devil sent to operate in historical time, just as his precursors had operated in biblical times" (109). Wright and others note as well the visual tradition "which portrayed the Godhead as having three heads stemming from the same neck, as a symbol of the three persons of the Trinity" (99–100); finally, see Ruth Mellinkoff, *Outcasts: Signs of Otherness in Northern European Art of the Late Middle Ages* (Berkeley, 1993), 1:93: here a three-faced head wearing a crown, identified as a member of the Norwich Jewish community (see fig. III.125, Caricature of Norwich Jews. Head of a roll of the Issues of the Exchequer of 1233. London. Public Record Office); see Wright, *Art and Antichrist*, 108, for further commentary on this image and its connection to the story of Abimelech.

[45] The hand is similar to that of the main scribe. Captions appear within pictures 7–13, and 15. See below, "Description of the Pictures," for these captions.

[46] See specially the caption for unit five, the picture usually identified with Celestine V.

[47] See Millet and Rigaux, "Aux origines," 137–138. They argue that the way in which Arnaud Novgarède (in his testimony after Bernard Délicieux's arrest in 1317) "remembers" the captions for units nine and ten as well as certain details in the tenth picture (the position of the hands) suggests that the copy of the "papalarius" owned by Délicieux was in "close proximity" to the Lunel and Monreale copies, particularly the Lunel copy.

on folio 19^v. The arrangement of texts following prophecy fifteen and the relation of the image of the beast to the sequence of prophecies are unique to the Lunel manuscript. The popes are identified within the pictures from Nicholas III through Clement V.

The pictures are painted with backgrounds of strong tones of alternating red and blue, with the main figures executed in shades of grey, blue, and red. François Avril notes that the style of pictures is more characteristic of the late thirteenth century than of the fourteenth, even though he suggests the manuscript must have been executed after 1314, since Clement V is the last pope named. Avril suggests that the pictures were executed in southern France, perhaps Avignon, for he notes clear affinities with at least two other manuscripts produced in southern France at much the same time.[48] The iconography of the pictures is closely related to that found in the Monreale and Vatican (3819) manuscripts (PV), particularly in picture four which shows a "dolphin," and picture sixteen, the beast with the human face.[49] The *explicit* after picture fifteen noted above makes it clear, however, that the scribe of the Lunel manuscript considered this picture an addition to, rather than a part of, the *Genus nequam* sequence. The Lunel and Vatican (3819) manuscripts also have common features in picture twelve: in each a seated pope (rather than a standing angel) holds the papal tiara over four rabbits (rather than bears or lambs).

Avril dates this manuscript to 1315–1320, on the basis of similarities to the Avignon manuscripts noted above, and, of course, because Clement V (June 1305–April 1314) is the last pope identified in the pictures. Textual evidence links this copy with the Paris, Monreale, and Vatican 3819 copies, and, in several striking instances, in particular with the Monreale copy. Millet and Rigaux's connection of the version of the *Genus nequam* prophe-

---

[48] Avril, "Manuscrits enluminés," 165, 167, n. 9. The affinities he notes between this manuscript and a commentary of Henry de Carreto (see Bibl. Nat., MS lat. 503 and Bibl. Nat., MS lat. 12018) are especially interesting, for, as he points out, Henry de Carreto "defended the cause of the Franciscan Spirituals before Pope John XXII." For borders similar to those in the Lunel MS, compare a Bible from southern France dated to the last quarter of the thirteenth century illustrated in Lilian M. C. Randall, *Medieval and Renaissance Manuscripts in the Walters Art Gallery*, vol. 2: *France, 875–1420* (Baltimore, 1989), no. 43 (Walters MS 123), 103–105 and figures 89, 90. See also the frontispiece to Maurice Fauçon, *La librairie des papes d'Avignon, sa formation, sa composition, ses catalogues (1316–1420)*, vol. 1 (Paris, 1886). This miniature from Bibl. Nat., MS lat. 365, from Avignon, has a decorated initial very similar to those in the Lunel manuscript. (The miniature shows the Dominican, Grenier, offering his commentary on Genesis to Pope John XXII.) The "Catalogue of the Bibliothèque de Peniscola" lists in number 134 (Fauçon, *Librairie*, 2:51–52) "Item prophetia Joachim de papis," in a compilation that includes texts by Joachim as well as Joachite texts.

[49] Although the Vatican MS has features in pictures two and twelve unique to it.

cies as represented by the Lunel and Monreale copies (and particularly the Lunel copy) to that copy of the "papalarius" in the possession of Bernard Délicieux argues for a date before 1317.[50]

There are a number of curious features of this manuscript. The first is a physical one: beginning with the second text and miniature (folio 4^v), each miniature faces a blank page, as if the artist were trying to protect the paint. Certainly these blank folios may have been added at a later date, but the quiring and traces of paint on these pages suggests otherwise. This same pattern of blank folios continues through the first part of the manuscript to folio 23^r, even when, after 19^v, it serves no purpose.

The second feature is of course the way in which the beast with the human face is appended to the sequence. The fifteenth text and picture is on folio 19^r, followed by a clear *Explicit*. Then beginning on folio 19^v, in the same hand, is a series of five prophecies, the longest of which are the pseudo-Hildegard and Joachite texts[51] noted above. The pseudo-Hildegard prophecy was often quoted in anti-mendicant propaganda and its presence here is a little puzzling.[52] Whether the Lunel scribe saw this prophecy "in the particular," that is, as anti-mendicant propaganda, or "in the general," as one of the signs of the Last Things, is impossible to determine with certainty. Its presence in this particular sequence of texts makes the latter reading likely.

---

[50] Millet and Rigaux, "Aux origines," 137–138. I would argue for a date prior to the Council of Vienne. Elsewhere I hope to explore further both the content of the borders and the way in which the border decoration "brackets" prophecies five and eleven, and to show how both are related to issues in the foreground of the Council of Vienne. See above, "Relation of MSS," n. 22, also above, n. 44.

[51] Folio 22^{r-v}. For this text, "In die elevabitur draco repletus furore," see Leone Tondelli, "Profezia Gioachimita del sec. XIII delle regioni venete," *Studi e Documenti*, 4 (Modena, 1940), 3–9, text on 5–6. The version in Lunel is incomplete, and ends with the sentence "Egredietur in die illa agnus de Verona et adiungetur urse virgiliane et occuret leone de Tuscia venienti et eo devicto spoliis leonis gaudebit et continuo ex ea filios," omitting the usual last word of the sentence "procreabit" and omitting, as well, the verses that usually follow giving the date for the coming of the Antichrist (1250, later changed to 1360). On this prophecy see also Reeves, *Influence of Prophecy*, 51 and notes 1–3. It is, perhaps, the presence of this text, with its reference to a lion, immediately preceding the picture of the beast, which causes Avril to identify the beast as a lion ("Manuscrits enluminés," 164), even though the tail of the beast is much shorter than the typical lion's tail.

[52] For the most recent discussion of this prophecy, see Kathryn Kerby-Fulton, "Hildegard of Bingen and Anti-Mendicant Propaganda," *Traditio* 43 (1987): 386–399; also eadem, *Reformist Apocalypticism and "Piers Plowman"* (Cambridge, 1990), 156–158 and Chapter 4 *passim*. The version of the text I have consulted is in Johann Albert Fabricius, *Bibliotheca Latina mediae et infimae aetatis*, vol. 3–4 (Florence, 1858), 243–244, to which, with minor variations, the version in Lunel corresponds. For other transcriptions see Kerby-Fulton, "Hildegard," 396, n. 40. Kerby-Fulton argues convincingly that the prophecy is a product of the "propagandist works of the William of St. Amour School" ("Hildegard," 393–397).

The miniature of the beast on folio 22ʳ is clearly executed by the artist of the *Genus nequam* sequence, and it seems likely it is meant to be a rendering of the Antichrist.[53] It is, as well, identical with the beasts represented in the sixteenth pictures of the Monreale and Vatican 3919 manuscripts. What makes the Lunel manuscript of special significance in the transmission of the *Genus nequam* prophecies is that it provides evidence of how the beast may have become incorporated into the sequence.

Description of the Pictures

1. (fol. 4ʳ) Picture one shows a pope identified as Nicholas III wearing the papal tiara (old style, here as elsewhere), seated on a bench, one hand upraised, a book in the other. There are three bears, one to either side, and one "attacking" the papal tiara. Below is a substantial border, equal to more than one-quarter of the image, containing two headless winged beasts facing each other; in the center is a crowned head with three faces, a face to either side and one frontal. There is a similar border at the bottom of the first text page (fol. 3ᵛ). Here, as elsewhere, the background is painted in alternating blocks of red and blue, with the main figures executed in strong shades of grey, blue, red, and, on occasion, green.

2. (fol. 4ᵛ) Picture two shows a standing pope, identified as Martin IV, wearing the papal tiara, holding a book in one hand and a staff in the other. To one side is a salamander or lizard-like serpent, green with white spots, and with six short legs. Atop the pope's tiara is a bird looking down at the serpent. Below is a double border of grotesques, a beast attacking a detached animal head with human face, a head swallowing a fish, and a curious crowned head in the center of the lower border.

3. (fol. 6ʳ) Picture three shows a standing pope, identified as Honorius IV, wearing the papal tiara, one hand outstretched in a gesture of supplication, the other holding a book. A large bird is resting on the papal tiara. To one side is a unicorn, paws upraised, long horn extending to the top of the image. To the other side is a smaller figure, hands together in supplication.

4. (fol. 6ᵛ) Picture number four, labelled Nicholas IV, shows two columns with a short vessel-like column between them. The center vessel

---

[53] See below, "Picture Tradition," for suggestions as to the derivation of the beast image.

holds the head of a cleric. A hand extending from the right-hand column holds the tail of a "dolphin," which extends over the head of the cleric to "attack" the crowned head on the left-hand column. All three columns are highly decorated in red and blue, white and brown. Below is a substantial border of tendrils and leaves; in the lower center is an animal head, upside down, with human features.

5. (fol. 8ʳ) Picture five, identified as Celestine V, shows a tonsured figure, garbed in liturgical vestments, holding a sickle in one hand and a rose in the other. Over one arm is hung the maniple, worn during the celebration of the mass. The torso of an angel is in the right corner, hands extended to hold the rose. Below is a border with two stylized fish, one with human features; in the center are two heads.

6. (fol. 8ᵛ) Picture six shows a standing pope, identified as Boniface VIII, wearing a mitre rather than the tiara shown in pictures one through three, and holding a book. To the upper left are two crowned heads, facing away from the pope. To the mid and lower left is an ox or cow, hooves upraised.

7. (fol. 10ʳ) Picture seven shows a standing pope, identified as Benedict XI, wearing the papal tiara and gesturing toward a bear with two nursing cubs to one side. This picture also contains a caption, "Occisio filii balas sociabuntur."

8. (fol. 10ᵛ) Picture eight is labelled Clement V and shows a highly decorated cityscape/fortress. On either side, within the towers, are heads of soldiers. An additional head shows in a window. The picture contains a caption, "Sanguis cenobia ad locum pristinum redibunt."

9. (fol. 12ʳ) Picture nine shows a standing pope, wearing the papal tiara and gesturing towards a small fox with a bushy tail at his side. Above and behind the fox are three standards, two each with a cross and a banner, also with a small red cross, the third with a *fleur de lis* at the end and an inscription along it reading "Vulpinam amicitiam similastis [sic]." The picture also contains a caption, "Occasio symonia cessabit." (*Vulpinam figurasti amicitiam* are the opening words of this prophecy.)

10. (fol. 12ᵛ) Picture ten shows a cityscape/fortress with many towers. To the left are two pairs of clasped hands, extended toward the city. A third pair, also clasped in a gesture of supplication, extends from one of the towers. The picture contains the caption "Bona gracia."

11. (fol. 14ʳ) Picture eleven shows a figure, tonsured, clad in a long loin-

cloth, seated on a rock. His hands are held in an *orans* gesture. To his right is a figure of the same size, dressed in a simple robe, half blue, half red, hands awkwardly clasped in supplication. The two figures are looking at one another. The picture contains the caption "Bona oratio thesaurus pauperibus erogabitur." Below the picture is a border of scrolled tendrils and leaves. In the center is a crowned head with three faces similar to the head in the border of picture one.

12. (fol. 14ᵛ) Picture twelve shows a seated pope, tonsured, holding the papal tiara over four rabbits. The pope is gesturing toward the rabbits with his other hand. (The hand, here as elsewhere, has characteristically long thin fingers.) The bench-like throne is highly decorated in red and blue with a gold-brown cushion. Incorporated into the decoration of the throne are pillars or tower-like structures as well as what appears to be a pair of open doors or gates. The picture contains the caption "Bona intentio karitas habundabit."

13. (fol. 17ʳ) (no folio number 15) Picture thirteen shows a standing pope being crowned with the papal tiara by an angel. Angel and pope are the same size. The angel, barefoot, wears clerical garments of red. The pope holds a book in one hand, the other hand extended in a gesture of supplication. The picture contains the caption, "Prehonoratio concordia erit."

14. (fol. 17ᵛ) Picture fourteen shows a pope, seated on an elaborately decorated bench, being ministered to by two angels in liturgical attire. The pope wears the papal tiara; the angel's hands are touching his shoulders and arms. The angels stand behind the bench. The decoration of the bench/throne incorporates motifs similar to those on the bench/throne in picture twelve.

15. (fol. 19ʳ) Picture fifteen shows a standing pope, tonsured, holding a book in one hand and the papal tiara in the other. The picture contains the caption "Reverencie devotio augmentabitur." Below the picture, in red, are the words "Explicit liber ymaginum papalium."

16. (fol. 22ᵛ) Picture sixteen shows a crowned animal with a human face, identified by Avril as a lion ("Manuscrits enluminés," 164). Above it is a text describing the tribulations of the Last Things which mentions the Lamb of God, a lion and a bear and their progeny.

M. Yale, University Library, T. E. Marston MS 225,
fols. 15ᴿ–22ᴿ

Description: Barbara A. Shailor, *Catalogue of Medieval and Renaissance Manuscripts in the Beinecke Rare Book and Manuscript Library, Yale University*, vol. 3: *Marston Manuscripts*, Medieval & Renaissance Texts & Studies vol. 100 (Binghamton, 1992), 424–431. See also Martha H. Fleming, "Sibylla: De Imperatore" (Ph.D. diss., Boston University, 1975).

This manuscript of forty-five vellum folios measures 179 x 121 millimeters. It is bound in worn limp vellum, account book style, and has inscribed on the front cover the words "De Imperatore." An anthology of prophecies, this collection is unusual among fourteenth-century Joachite anthologies in that it is organized around the themes of savior-emperor and holy reforming popes. The manuscript is divided into three sections: the first, with a heading ".De imperatore." in red, contains a version of the Tiburtine Oracle with special reference to the history of Sicily (fols. 2^r–14^v); the second, with no heading or attribution, contains the fifteen *Genus nequam* prophecies, texts and pictures (fols. 15^r–22^r); the third, also with no heading or attribution, contains a group of twenty-six prophecies (fols. 23^r–43^r). Appended to the manuscript is the so-called 1347 revision of the Tripoli prophecy (fols. 43^v–44^v).[54]

Of particular interest is the first prophecy in the third section of the manuscript. It is a Latin translation of what Lambecius called the "Anonymous Paraphrase of the Leo Oracles," and a text to which Paul Alexander has given the less misleading name of "Cento of the True Emperor."[55] The Greek text of the "Cento" appears in the Lambecius edition of the Leo

---

[54] Lerner, *Powers of Prophecy* for the history of the Tripoli prophecy; for the "redated version for 1347," see Lerner, *Powers of Prophecy*, 226–227.

[55] Alexander, *Byzantine Apocalyptic Tradition*, 130–136. Lambecius based his edition of the "Cento" on a sixteenth-century manuscript and it is he who gave it the title "The Anonymous Paraphrase of the Oracles of Leo." Alexander maintained that the text was not a summary or paraphrase of the Leo Oracles, although it clearly drew on them, and thus the title "Cento of the True Emperor" was a less misleading title. The "Cento" was designed, Alexander suggested, "for readers expecting the coming of a Messianic ruler yet aware of the Gospels' warning against 'false Christs' (Matt. 24:23ff.) and therefore anxious to obtain guidance as to how to distinguish the genuine Emperor from pretenders" (*Byzantine Apocalyptic Tradition*, 135). Alexander did not know of the version of the "Cento" in this Yale manuscript. The only other instance that I know in which a copy of the "Cento" immediately follows the *Genus nequam* prophecies is in London, British Library, MS Add. 39660, which gives the expanded version of thirty prophecies, followed by the "Cento."

Oracles and elsewhere, but the Latin version in this Yale manuscript is, to my knowledge, the earliest version in Latin and predates any surviving version in Greek. This prophecy, *inc.* "De laudato paupere et electo imperatore" (fols. 23^r–28^r), makes it clear that the expected ruler is a secular one; in somewhat later versions of this prophecy, "imperator" becomes "pastor." Jean de Roquetaillade cites this prophecy in his *Liber Ostensor* (MS Vat. Ross. 753, fols. 53^v, 78^v), giving only a few lines, and referring to the "pauper" as "imperator." The prophecy is found also in several fifteenth-century collections of prophecies, including MS Vat. lat. 3816, fols. 64^r–67^v. The ordering of the sentences in the Vatican manuscript is quite different, although the wording is very similar. Significantly, the Vatican manuscript reads "pastor" for "imperator."

The body of the manuscript is in a single hand; the Tripoli prophecy appended to the manuscript is in a different, somewhat later hand. Certain portions of the text are annotated in the margins. For the Tiburtine prophecy in part one, the annotator supplies identifications for the initials in the text. Of particular interest are the references to a Sicilian ruler both in the text and by the glossator and to a "dux de Bavaria" . . . "et tunc incipiet initium doloris." The *Genus nequam* prophecies contain a number of blank spaces in the text and in all instances the missing words have been supplied in the margin by the annotator. The only other text to be annotated in some detail is that of the "Cento"; for the remaining prophecies, with the exception of a single gloss, the glossator simply supplies missing words and makes corrections.

It is worth noting the likelihood of two glossators, for the hand of the glossator of the Tiburtine sibyl text is regular and tidy and cannot be distinguished from the hand of the text itself. Beginning with the gloss on folio 21 of the Tiburtine oracle text, there is a clear shift in style. The form and content of the gloss changes; the letters are larger and less regular, there are definite differences in the formation of letters, for instance capital *M* and lower-case *g*. As well, missing words and corrections are supplied in addition to identifications. It is this second glossator who continues the glosses in the rest of the manuscript, including the *Genus nequam* section, here supplying missing words, but making no identifications or commentary. There are a number of erasures in these texts, for the most part corresponding to places in the text glossed in the margins. In summary, then, there appear to be two glossators: the first through folio 10^v is the same as the hand in the text; the second beginning on folio 11^r and continuing to the end of the manuscript in a hand different from but contemporary with the hand of the main text. The main scribe, wherever he was writing, might well have been southern French or even Italian, for he uses some character-istically Italian forms, i.e., "ç" for medial "z."

The dating and provenance of this manuscript are elusive,[56] but an examination of textual and iconographic evidence points to a date after 1322 and certainly before 1349, most likely between 1327–1328 and 1334, that is, during the pontificate of John XXII.

The physical contents and arrangement of prophecies within the manu-script provide one set of clues. The first section, a version of the Tiburtine Oracle, is distinguished from other versions by its references to Sicilian his-tory, ending with one to Conradin (d. 1268) and also by a reference to the "dux" from Bavaria. This prophecy bears the heading ".De imperatore." and, like the Pseudo-Methodian "program", emphasizes a savior-ruler initi-ating a period of *renovatio* before the advent of the Antichrist.

The prophecies in part three supply additional clues for dating this manu-script. A prophecy on fol. 40ᵛ, known to be circulating in this form no earlier than 1322, provides a *terminus post quem*.[57] Clearly the scribe knew the date was no longer appropriate, for a blank space, not an erasure, is left in the text after "MCCC." In the margin the glossator has written "1349." An-other prophecy, on folio 40ʳ, gives the date 1327 within the text.[58]

It would be an exaggeration to claim that the prophecies in part three constitute a clear sequence of events. The first is the longest one, the prophecy of a great pauper king (the Latin version of the "Cento"). The last few sentences of this prophecy are an addition and repeat a line found in unit eleven of the *Genus nequam* sequence (and the last line of number ten of the Leo Oracles). This addition would seem to connect the savior-emperor prophecy with the prophecy in the *Genus nequam* series that marks the "angelic" sequence.[59] The fifth prophecy in this last section can be identified with Celestine V and the sixth with Boniface VIII. The next group refers to a "middle period" corresponding perhaps to pictures eight, nine, and ten, in the papal series, although it is difficult to tell how many

---

[56] Lerner suggests no earlier than the mid 1320s and no later than 1349: "On the Origins," 635.

[57] Lerner, "On the Origins," 635 and idem, *Powers of Prophecy*, 227–231.

[58] The 1327 date appears a second time in a prophecy on fol. 42ʳ; this one is followed by a short prophecy of a "great eagle" in the "imperial court," perhaps a reference to Louis of Bavar-ia, making this a *post eventum* prophecy. If these two are not *post eventum* prophecies, one would expect either the dates to be revised (as is the case for the prophecy on fol. 40ᵛ) or to be able to date the text earlier than 1327.

[59] Bernard McGinn, " 'Pastor Angelicus'," 246–247, for a somewhat different emphasis: "In the Yale collection we find the papal and the imperial myths not so much intermingled as juxtaposed" (247).

popes are included, perhaps only one. Tribulations will increase, and after a long period of suffering, prefiguring the suffering under the final Antichrist, "an outstanding shepherd will sit on the throne, watched over by angels." The next paragraph begins with "a few more things until the end of the era . . .", and three additional shepherds are described as holding the papal office. Echoing the program and language of the *Liber de Flore,* they are described as the first, second, and third pastors following the first "outstanding shepherd."[60] This last shepherd will yield his soul to angels on Mount Zion.

The next group of prophecies backtrack in time as they appear to refer to historical popes. Number nineteen, with its first line a repetition of pope prophecy fourteen, marks the transition to future popes. The remainder of the prophecies describes a period of tribulation, marked by a reforming secular ruler, after whose reign will come the time of Antichrist.

The prophecies in this last section appear at first glance to have little order, but on closer scrutiny show themselves to run more or less parallel to the *Genus nequam* sequence and can be viewed as both a summary and elaboration or amplification of these prophecies. The first prophecy in this last section seems a deliberate link between the last world emperor prophecy of part one and the *Genus nequam* prophecies themselves as well as the summary and amplification which follows. What sets these prophecies apart from the *Liber de Flore* and the much later *Libellus* of Telesphorus, which recapitulates and amplifies these, is the emphasis on a reforming ruler noted in both the first and last sections, and the connection between this ruler and the series of "outstanding shepherds."[61]

There are a number of distinctive features in the miniatures of this manuscript. In number five, for instance, the Celestine V figure is shown as a cowled monk standing in profile, one of the clearest statements in the *Genus nequam* copies. Perhaps the most problematic feature of the iconography

---

[60] For a recent discussion of the *Liber de Flore,* see McGinn, " 'Pastor Angelicus'," 239–242 and notes 51–52. The manuscript version I have used is Nuremberg, Stadtbibl. Cent. IV. 32, fols. 46^r–70^v.

[61] For a partial edition of the *Libellus,* see Emil Donckel, "Studien über die Prophezeiung des Fr. Telesforus von Cosenza, O.F.M. (1365–1386)," *AFH* 26 (1933): 29–104, 284–312. See also Roberto Rusconi, *L'Attesa della Fine. Crisi della società, profezia ed Apocalisse in Italia al tempo del grande scisma d'Occidente (1378–1417)* (Rome, 1979), 171–182. The earliest version extant is represented by copies in two manuscripts: Paris, Bibl. Nat., MS lat. 3184 (1396), and MS Syracuse University Von Ranke 90 (1391). On this last manuscript see R. Spence, "MS Syracuse Von Ranke 90 and the *Libellus* of Telesphorus of Cosenza," *Scriptorium* 33 (1979): 271–274 and Pl. 27. (I thank Robert Lerner for calling the Syracuse MS and this article to my attention.) A third copy, Vat. Lib., MS Reg. 580, has been dated as early as 1387 and as late as the early fifteenth century.

in this manuscript is the substitution of dogs for bears in several pictures, particularly in number one, where bears, natural symbols of the Orsini pope Nicholas III, are the norm. The possible significance of this change is discussed below.[62]

Analysis of variants in the text shows an unusual number of variations in the Yale manuscript, particularly in prophecy number one. It is difficult to determine a pattern in these variations, but it is clear that many are not errors but deliberate changes. In the last sentence, for example, "dux" is substituted for "dominus," not an unusual substitution in itself. In a sentence or two from the end, the Yale manuscript reads, ". . . et manus expandis ut servos Domini pervertas sed autem eos abiciens turpiter," the others ". . . et manus expandis quamvis pedes [with minor variations] pervertas sicut abiciens te ipsum extra res [or *rex*]."

The arrangement and emphasis of the prophecies in the manuscript as a whole, the textual and iconographic evidence within the *Genus nequam* sequence itself, then, point to the same conclusion, that the manuscript was put together during the pontificate of Pope John XXII and particularly during or shortly after the renewal of the controversy over poverty and the Rule.

One would like to narrow the time and place a bit. Robert Lerner has summarized the arguments for southern German provenance, drawing on Cahn and Marrow's testimony that the miniatures show an affinity with those of chronicles later in the century, and the fact that the manuscript can be placed in southern Germany in the sixteenth century.[63] In spite of the emphasis in both the first and last sections on a savior-emperor, the negative reference to a leader from Bavaria in the Tiburtine sibyl section, the vaguely anti-German tone of some of the prophecies in part three, and, as well, the number of prophecies in part three dealing with the program of holy popes make a south German origin less likely than a location at Avignon or its environs.

A number of noble patrons might be posited, for the Spiritual Franciscans both individually and collectively gained considerable support from such figures as Philip of Majorca and Robert of Naples, brother of the canonized Louis of Toulouse, both of whom (Philip and Robert) were unsympathetic to the aspirations of Louis of Bavaria.[64] It seems a reasonable

---

[62] For the substitution of dogs for bears, see below, "Picture Tradition."

[63] Lerner, "On the Origins," 635.

[64] On the noble supporters of the Spirituals, see Oakley, "John XXII," 102, 112, and notes 227–228. For the relation between Louis of Bavaria and the Franciscans, see Gordon Leff, *Heresy in the Later Middle Ages: The Relation of Heterodoxy to Dissent c. 1250–c. 1450* (Manchester, 1967),

hypothesis, then, that this anthology was put together by a Franciscan or Franciscan sympathizer, who was attracted to this combination of texts by a constellation of events: the renewal of the controversy over poverty and in particular the connections between the bulls of Nicholas III and John XXII; the subsequent alliance between some orthodox Franciscans and Louis of Bavaria,[65] whose claims to the crown of the Holy Roman Empire came to a fruition of sorts during John's pontificate; and, finally, the heightened debate over papal and imperial claims for supremacy. This scribe must have had access to texts not easily available, particularly the "Cento," and at least portions of a letter from Arnold of Villanova to a certain Lady Bartolomea, as Robert Lerner has noted.[66] Given the elegance of the miniatures, we can assume a wealthy patron. All these arguments would suggest Avignon or its environs. In or around Avignon seems the most likely location on other grounds as well: it is clear that the compiler of this manuscript drew on a variety of sources such as the *Liber de Flore* and the *Horoscopus,* and that Roquetaillade, writing in the mid-fourteenth century, drew on these same sources, and in particular on the "Cento." Unlike those of the compiler of the Marston manuscript, Roquetaillade's anti-German and pro-French biases are very clear, and although the affinities between the prophecies in the third part of the Marston manuscript and the writings of Roquetaillade have been often pointed out, there are, as well, significant differences in tone and emphasis.[67]

The emphasis on the two roles, those of emperor and pope, suggests, for the main text, a date close to 1328–1329.[68] Paul Alexander wrote of the "Cento of the True Emperor" that it might have been written to provide guidance for those expecting the coming of a Messianic ruler in order that they might distinguish the genuine Emperor from pretenders.[69] The constellation of prophecies in this Marston manuscript might well have served a similar function.

---

vol. 1, 230–255. See also Marc Dykmans, *Robert d'Anjou: la vision bienheureuse,* Miscellanea Historiae Pontificiae 30 (Rome, 1970), 9–46, 66–80.

[65] Ockham, Marsiglio, and Michael of Cesena (head of the Franciscan order) went over to Louis of Bavaria's court. They had persecuted the Spirituals bitterly and continued to remain separate even after the break with the pope (Leff, *Heresy,* 1:238–255).

[66] Lerner, "On the Origins," 629–630, n. 44.

[67] For a summary of Roquetaillade's program, see Reeves, *Influence of Prophecy,* 321–325; also Bignami-Odier, *Jean de Roquetaillade,* 142–156, 343–344; Lerner, "Historical Introduction," in Lerner and Morerod-Fattebert, eds., *Rupescissa, Liber secretorum,* 33–36 and 60–63.

[68] But see above, n. 54.

[69] See above, n. 55.

Apart from the miniatures in the *Genus nequam* section, the manuscript has little decoration. Two-line built-up initials beginning each new prophecy are lightly decorated with pen flourishes extending primarily below the letters, in the case of the capital "I" beginning the first text on folio 1ʳ the entire length of the margin.[70] The initials denoting divisions within the text are alternating blue and red.

Description of the Pictures

1. (fol. 15ʳ) Picture one shows a pope, wearing chasuble and mitre, one hand in blessing, the other holding a book. There is a small dog to each side, each sitting on its hind legs, paws upraised. A third small dog is in running position above the pope's mitre. The colors are a pale wash, soft reds, blues, and ochres predominating. Most of the backgrounds are either a pale wash of color or a lightly diapered pattern of three or four small circles. The borders are narrow bands, and just within the border on some of the miniatures is a simple pattern consisting of three circles on a central stem at intervals along the inner edge of the border.

2. (fol. 15ᵛ) Picture two shows a pope wearing a chasuble and mitre. In one hand he holds a staff and in the other a book. To the pope's right is a small figure, kneeling, hands in supplication. To the pope's left is a tree with a serpent coiled about its trunk; at the top of this stylized tree are two birds.

3. (fol. 16ʳ) Picture three shows a seated pope, wearing a cope and a mitre; one hand is upraised, the other holds a book. To the pope's right is a small kneeling figure, arms outstretched in supplication. Atop the pope's mitre is an eagle. To the pope's left is a unicorn, standing on its hind legs, paws on the pope's shoulder.

4. (fol. 16ᵛ) Picture four shows three columns of equal height. The one in the middle has a curved top like that of a vessel or bowl; and it supports the bust of a tonsured, lightly bearded monk. On the column to the right is a hand holding a sickle over the head of the monk. On the column to the left is a bust of a head wearing a mitre.

5. (fol. 17ʳ) Picture five shows a tonsured and cowled monk in profile. His robe is unbelted, and he holds a sickle in one hand and a stylized

---

[70] For pen flourishing typical of French manuscripts, see Scott-Fleming, *Pen Flourishing*, 27.

rose in the other. In the upper right corner and behind the monk is the bust of an angel with nimbus.

6. (fol. 17ᵛ) Picture six shows a pope with mitre, wearing a belted gown and cloak. Below and to one side is a cow or ox, sitting on its hindquarters, hooves upraised. One of the pope's hands seems to be pointing in the opposite direction, while the other is to his side. In the upper left and right corners are busts, both of secular figures.

7. (fol. 18ʳ) Picture seven shows a pope, wearing a cope and mitre, arms extended in a pointing gesture. To the pope's right is a bear with upraised paws and two nursing cubs.

8. (fol. 18ᵛ) Picture eight shows a fortress or cityscape with three towers. A rounded arched double door, closed, is in the center.

9. (fol. 19ʳ) Picture nine shows a pope, wearing mitre and cloak, one hand upraised as if in blessing, the other holding the cloak together. To his right is a small dog, rather than the usual fox, with three crossed banners or standards above its back.

10. (fol. 19ᵛ) Picture ten shows a different fortress or cityscape, again with three towers. To the left are three outstretched hands extended from the margin towards the fortress.

11. (fol. 20ʳ) Picture eleven shows a half-nude figure, one hand to his face, dressed in a longish loincloth, legs crossed. He is seated on a pile of rocks. To his left is a small figure in a simple unbelted robe.

12. (fol. 20ᵛ) Picture twelve shows a figure with a halo, wearing a robe and cloak, holding a mitre over the heads of two dogs. To the other side are two small bears, like the dogs, facing the margin.

13. (fol. 21ʳ) Picture thirteen shows an angel crowning a pope with the mitre. The pope stands, partially turned towards the angel, one hand upraised. He wears a cloak rather than a cope or chasuble.

14. (fol. 21ᵛ) Picture fourteen shows a seated pope, wearing a cloak, with one hand upraised. In this instance he wears a papal tiara, tall and pointed, old style. He is seated on a bench and behind him stand, also on the bench, two angels holding a decorated arras.

15. (fol. 22ʳ) Picture fifteen shows a pope, wearing a chasuble, holding a book in one upraised hand. His other hand, extended downward, holds the mitre. The pope is clearly tonsured and has a large nimbus.

N. Paris, Archives Nationales, MS JJ 28, Fols. 285ᴿ–291ᵛ

Description: Alfred Maury, ed., *Catalogue des Manuscrits conservés aux Archives Nationales* (Paris, 1892), no. 541; Henri François Delaborde, *Layettes du Trésor des Chartes*, vol. 5 (Paris, 1909), 47–48; *Les Archives Nationales état Général des Fonds*, vol. 1 (Paris, 1978), 217.

This copy of the *Genus nequam* prophecies was added at the end of a register for Philip the Fair, prepared for the chancellor, Pierre d'Étampes, and was first brought to my attention by Elizabeth A. R. Brown.[71] The manuscript is parchment and measures 247 x 180 millimeters. Folios 1–131 contain the History of the Albigensians (1206–1218) by Pierre des Vaux-de-Cernay; the catalogue describes the contents of folios 132–292 as "documents divers" from the period 1291–1303 concerning especially the differences between Philip the Fair and Boniface VIII, along with "des formules de lettres." However, as Brown discovered, folios 285ʳ–291ᵛ actually contain a copy of the *Genus nequam* prophecies, in a different hand from that of the register proper.

The sequence consists of text and captions only; space was left for the miniatures but they were never done. The captions are in red, but the opening initials for each prophecy must have been assigned to the miniaturist as well, for although space was left for two-line initials, they were never added.

The pages are ruled in two columns; the caption is at the top, the text is in one column, and space has been left in the second column for the miniature, one unit to a page. There are exceptions for shorter units, where there are two on a page.

Pierre d'Étampes was keeper of the archives from 1307 to 1324. Brown has suggested that the register was done in the last year of Philip the Fair's reign, that is, some time before 29 November 1314.[72] Decoration of ear-

---

[71] Elizabeth A. R. Brown generously supplied me with copies of her photographs of the manuscript and her transcription of the text. A brief description of the first part of the register, the *Hystoria Albigensis* by Pierre des Vaux-de-Cernay, appears in volume 3, xlv–xlvi, of the three-volume edition of the text: *Petri Vallium Sarnaii monachi Hystoria Albigensis*, ed. Pascal Guébin and Ernest Lyon (Paris, 1926–1939). The *Genus nequam* prophecies are in a different hand from the chancery hand of the rest of the register, in what Brown calls a gothic liturgical script. By 1314 most documents in the register had appended to them the name of the official who ordered them written, and often as well the name of the notary or scribe who wrote them. (See Joseph R. Strayer, *The Reign of Philip the Fair* [Princeton, 1980], 21.)

[72] Brown, personal communication June 1988; see also Elizabeth A. R. Brown and Robert E. Lerner, "On the Origins and Import of the Columbinus Prophecy," *Traditio* 95 (1989–1990): 220–256, here 221.

lier sections of JJ 28 might well be later, even after Pierre's death, or begun before his death and never finished.[73]

JJ 28 is one of a pair of registers copied for Pierre d'Étampes; the second, JJ 29, as Elizabeth A. R. Brown and Robert Lerner have shown, contains a copy of the Columbinus prophecy, again in a register recording papal bulls and royal memoranda. Brown and Lerner note that "the Columbinus prophecy appears to have been kept with royal documents of 1306–1307— and with one that was of special importance to Pierre d'Étampes himself" (i.e., "an undated royal letter to the *bailii* of Caux regarding Philip the Fair's presentation of Pierre d'Étampes to the Norman church of Sommery").[74]

One of the most interesting things about the copy of the *Genus nequam* prophecies is its presence in a register of Philip the Fair. Its proximity to the "divers documents" pertaining to the controversy between Boniface VIII and Philip the Fair, even though these documents apparently reflect the period 1291–1303, means that the *Genus nequam* prophecies were in very wide circulation and were taken quite seriously. Did Pierre d'Étampes, if he were not in fact responding to someone else's request, see in these prophecies an anti-Bonifacian document, suitable to be preserved with other documents in the Philip the Fair-Boniface VIII confrontation? By 1307, Boniface VIII was dead; Nogaret was still pursuing his condemnation, and Philip the Fair had embarked on his attack on the Templars. By 1312, or by the outside date of 1314, the Templars had been suppressed; the Council of Vienne was over (16 October 1311–6 May 1312); on 5 May 1313, Celestine V was canonized; Clement V died in April of 1314, and John XXII was not to be elected pope until early August of 1316.[75] Throughout this period, 1307–1314, Philip had to deal with the consequences of the Inquisition in the Languedoc. Joseph Strayer notes that the period of greatest involvement coincided with Philip's "final struggle with Boniface VIII," although the Inquisition was also a topic of discussion at the Council of Vienne.[76]

---

[73] The last decorated initial is on fol. 120 (Guébin and Lyon, *Hystoria Albigensis*, xiv, n. 1).

[74] See Brown and Lerner, "Columbinus Prophecy," 220–222, here 221.

[75] For this period, 1307–1314, see Strayer, *Philip the Fair*, esp. Chap. 4; Elizabeth A. R. Brown, "Royal Salvation and the Needs of State in Late Capetian France," *Order and Innovation in the Middle Ages: Essays in Honor of Joseph R. Strayer*, ed. William C. Jordan et al. (Princeton, 1976), 365–383; T. S. R. Boase, *Boniface VIII* (London, 1933); Malcolm Barber, *The Trial of the Templars* (Cambridge, 1978); Heinrich Finke, *Aus den Tagen Bonifaz VIII.* (Münster, 1902); Pierre Dupuy, *Histoire du differend d'entre le pape Boniface VIII. et Philippes le Bel Roy de France* (Paris, 1655; repr. Tucson, Ariz., 1963); Tilmann Schmidt, *Der Bonifaz-Prozess: Verfahren der Papstanklage in der Zeit Bonifaz' VIII. und Clemens' V.* (Cologne and Vienna, 1989).

[76] Strayer, *Philip the Fair*, 297.

The text itself is close to that in the Monreale manuscript, although neither can be a copy of the other, since the Paris manuscript lacks pictures, and the Monreale manuscript has additions and omissions not common to both manuscripts. This textual similarity supports a date closer to 1314 than an earlier one.

P. MONREALE, BIBLIOTECA COMUNALE, MS XXV. F.17, FOLS. 1R–17R

Description: Carlo Alberto Garufi, *Catalogo illustrato del tabulario di S. Maria Nuova in Monreale* (Palermo, 1902), 223–226; Angela Daneu Lattanzi, "I 'Vaticinia Pontificum' ed un codice monrealese del sec. XIII–XIV," *Atti della Reale Accademia di scienze, lettere e arti di Palermo* ser. 4, v. 3(2) (1943) [first presented 1942]: 757–792, plus plates; eadem, *I manoscritti ed incunaboli miniati della Sicilia*, vol. 2 (Palermo, 1977), 221–223.

This vellum manuscript of twenty folios measures 145 x 101 millimeters. The *Genus Nequam* prophecies, text and pictures, occupy seventeen folios; blank sheets precede and follow the prophecies. Carlo Alberto Garufi in his *Catalogo* describes a note once attached to page two but now lost, which reads, "Est Monasterii Sanctae Mariae Novae Montis Regalis ad usum D. Dominici B. Gravina," and dates this manuscript to the fourteenth century, locating it in the south of Italy.[77] Angela Daneu Lattanzi, who has provided a detailed description of the manuscript as well as a transcription of the text, argues for a date as early as the last decade of the thirteenth century and suggests a location in the north of France. The binding, she notes, is French and is very similar to those made at Blois for Louis XII between the end of the fifteenth and the first two decades of the sixteenth century. Furthermore, inventories of the libraries of Jean, Duc de Berry and Charles d'Orléans that record, in the first instance, a book of pope prophecies, and in the second, a volume of "prophecies of Joachim," provide a suggestive connection to the royal library at Blois. Finally, on the first white sheet in a cursive style of the fourteenth century and in French is a list of expenses. Daneu Lattanzi identifies the recurring abbreviation "s.p." as "solus parisis."[78]

The script is a transitional one, "not yet decidedly Gothic," as Daneu Lattanzi puts it, and, the abbreviations and spelling are in fact not typically

---

[77] Garufi, *Catalogo*, 223.
[78] Daneu Lattanzi, " 'Vaticinia Pontificum'," 758–759.

Italian. The prophecies are written in a single hand (with five lines of text added to text fifteen in a different hand), but one which could easily be contemporary with the hand of the rest of the manuscript. There is no title page, no attribution, and no heading for the first prophecy. The longer form of the captions is incorporated into the right-hand corner of each text, and is set apart from the text by the rubricator. A fifteenth-century hand identifies some of the popes in headlines at the top of the page, beginning with the first prophecy. The first identification is Calixtus III (1455–1458), and the identifications end with Alexander VI (1492–1503) for prophecy and picture number seven. Also above the pictures is a series of curious abbreviations, again perhaps in a later hand, but not much later than the hand of the main text. Some of these abbreviations look like numbers, the early forms of "3," "6," and "7," for instance. Above five are the words "pius papa, G. s."[79]

The text of each prophecy is on one page and on the facing page is the accompanying miniature, measuring 88 x 46 millimeters. The first letter of each text is decorated, as is the left margin and a portion of the lower margin. The initial letters are decorated in gold and ornamented with leaves and stems. The decoration of the initials frequently extends down the length of the margin and ends in a cusped spiral half-way across the bottom margin. The decoration of the initial extends in a similar way at the top of the page. The decoration along the side often contains dragons or dogs. The miniatures are colored light blue, salmon, orange, red, and white, and outlined in black ink. The backgrounds are gold, blue, pink, or tan, with white or pink crosses or patterns of dots. Each miniature has a border of irregularly shaped rectangles with a pattern of x-shaped crosses against a background of dots. The pattern of the borders and the way the back-grounds are filled are curiously irregular and seem clumsily executed. The figures themselves are elongated, the hands large with long fingers unskill-fully drawn, the cheeks frequently marked by a red dot.

This version of the *Genus nequam* prophecies contains sixteen pictures and texts. The text which accompanies picture sixteen, the image of the beast with a human face, occurs only in this Monreale manuscript and in the Paris Archives manuscript, but it is a regular part of the fifteenth prophecy in late fourteenth- and fifteenth-century versions as well as in the Regiselmo edition. This text, a quotation from Dan. 4:13, reads "Cor eius

---

[79] Here again thanks are due John Monfasani for his observations. The other abbreviations read, 1: S, 2: S, 3: .3., 4: .S., 5: *pius pp* (for *papa*) G. s., 6: .Λ., 7: .s., 8: .s., 9:.s., 10: 9., 12: .3., 13: .i., 14: .3. (See also Daneu Lattanzi, " 'Vaticinia Pontificum'," 775–776.)

ab humano commutetur. et cor fere detur ei. et septem tempora mutentur super eum."[80] The caption incorporated into the corner of the text reads "Corona superbie." This caption also appears in the Paris Archives text.

The Monreale manuscript shares with Vat. lat. 3819 but not with the Paris Archives manuscript the addition of five lines to the text of the fifteenth prophecy, although in the case of the Monreale manuscript the lines are added in a different and perhaps somewhat later hand. The quotation is from Nah., 3:1–2, foretelling the destruction of the city of Nineveh: "Ve civitatis sanguinum, universe mendacii dilaceratione plena. Non recedet at te rapine. Vox flagelli et vox impetus rote et equi frementis." These lines are regularly found just before the quotation from Daniel in the late fourteenth- and fifteenth-century versions of the text, as well as in the sixteenth-century printed editions.[81]

There are several distinctive features in the iconography of the pictures in this manuscript. Especially worth noting is the flying fish or dolphin in picture four, a feature it shares with both the Lunel manuscript and Vat. lat. 3819, and the inclusion of a sixteenth picture, a lamb or sheep with a human head, wearing a crown. The sixteenth picture is found widely elsewhere in later manuscripts, either alone or more usually incorporated into picture fifteen. This beast is found in four of the fourteenth-century copies (FLPV), although, as discussed elsewhere, there are significant differences among the four instances.[82]

Several additional iconographical features of this manuscript are worth noting. Picture fourteen has several minor details that are unique to it. There are two animals in the picture, dogs by the length of their ears rather than bears, standing back to back behind the standing pope. Although these dogs could be part of a throne, the sort which is often embellished with animal heads, the position of the animals does show an affinity with the position of the animals in picture twelve in the Corpus Christi, Douce, and Florence manuscripts (CDF), all of which are connected to images of apotheosis.[83] None of the other manuscripts has animals in picture fourteen.

---

[80] See Daneu Lattanzi, " 'Vaticinia Pontificum'," 792, n. 6, where she calls attention to the similarity to the Tiburtine sibyl: " 'Hic (Antichristus) erit filius perditionis et caput superbiae.' " This caption does not appear in the Leo Oracles.

[81] It seems to have been identified with the sixteenth prophecy rather than with the fifteenth, for when the two texts and pictures were combined in fifteenth-century manuscripts and in sixteenth-century printed editions, the Nahum text is run into prophecy fifteen, and the Daniel text is set somewhat apart below.

[82] See below, "Picture Tradition," 111–114.

[83] See below, "Picture Tradition," 109.

Picture five also has features that are unique to the Monreale copy among the nine fourteenth-century manuscripts under discussion. The main figure in the image is the usual one, a tonsured figure holding a sickle in one hand and a rose in the other. At the lower left is what looks like a sideways "B" but may well be shackles,[84] and to the lower right something that looks like a doubled-headed axe minus the handle. In late fourteenth- and fifteenth-century manuscripts, as well as in the Regiselmo edition, these symbolic objects, the second one now a leg, are regularly included in the picture. To my knowledge neither occurs in any version of the corresponding Leo Oracle picture. Thus, the form picture five takes corresponds only to later versions of the *Genus nequam* sequence. There is always the possibility that these features were painted in at a later time, for two of the miniatures show signs of being tampered with: the background shows signs of erasure in the section of the image containing the "leg", and in miniature fourteen, the face of the pope has been erased.[85]

Picture nine also has several features unique to this manuscript: an unusual arrangement of standards and a bird upside down atop the middle one, and a very small shield (?) in the space between the base of the standards and the pope.

In summary, then, the iconographic features, especially in picture five, the presence of picture sixteen with text and caption added to it, and analysis of the individual texts all point to a date for the execution of the manuscript at least a decade later than the 1294 date posited by Daneu Lattanzi.[86] The version of the prophecies represented in the Monreale manuscript unquestionably belongs to the "mainstream" version, for it shares many features with the Lunel, Paris, and Vatican lat. 3819 manuscripts.

The French style of decoration, the absence of typically Italian abbreviations and spellings in the hand, as well as connections to the Paris manu-

---

[84] Possibly a reference to Celestine V's imprisonment by Boniface VIII, see below, "Picture Tradition," n. 27.

[85] Unfortunately this possibility is difficult to verify, owing to the closing of the Biblioteca Comunale (information from Dottore Giuseppe Schirò, retired Librarian). Charlotte Lacaze plans on investigating these pictures in some detail, but is of the opinion that it would be very difficult to determine with certainty whether or not there was some over-painting in picture number five, even though the marks of scraping are clear.

[86] Daneu Lattanzi dates the manuscript to the last decade of the thirteenth century, and Lerner posits a *terminus post quem* of 1294 and leans to an early date ("On the Origins," 634); see also Millet and Rigaux, "Aux origines," 136–138, who connect the version of the prophecies represented by the Lunel and Monreale copies (particularly on the evidence of the captions for units nine and ten) to the "papalarius" owned by Bernard Délicieux, suggesting then a date before 1319 but after the pontificate of Clement V.

script, point to a French scribe and a French miniaturist, possibly in northern France.[87] Although Daneu Lattanzi describes the miniatures as elegant and polished, the borders of irregularly shaped rectangles with a pattern of x-shaped crosses against a background of dots and the background of the miniatures themselves seem haphazardly executed. The combination of textual evidence, additions to the text, and iconographic evidence points to a date close to but somewhat later than that of the Lunel manuscript.[88]

Description of the Pictures

Thirteen of the sixteen miniatures, omitting numbers one, five and fourteen, are beautifully reproduced in color in Angela Daneu Lattanzi, "Simboli e profezie nel medioevo," *Sicilia* 12 (1955): unpaginated.[89]

1. (fol. 2ʳ) Picture one shows a seated pope wearing a chasuble and papal tiara (old style), and holding a book. There is a small bear to either side and one above the tiara. The bear above the tiara has one paw holding the lower edge of the tiara, a detail peculiar to P. This folio shows distinct signs of wear or damage.

2. (fol. 3ʳ) Picture two shows a standing pope, wearing a cope and tiara,

---

[87] There are some similarities to manuscripts from northern France and even Flanders in the cusped form of the spirals and in the pattern of Xs in the background, and to a lesser degree in the borders: see Patrick M. De Winter, *La bibliothèque de Philippe le Hardi* (Paris, 1985), plates 20 and 22; *Souvenir de l'Exposition de Manuscrits Français à Peintures organisée à la Grenville Library (1932)*, ed. Eric Millar (Paris, 1933), 24 and plate 23. See also Randall, *Medieval and Renaissance Manuscripts in the Walters Art Gallery*, in particular items 38, 39, 40, 41 (Walters 38, 39, 47, 97), a group of mostly Books of Hours from northeast France dated to the last quarter of the thirteenth century, for features similar to those in the Monreale miniatures, i.e., patterns of Xs in the background, decoration along the hems of cloaks, red dots on cheeks, lips, cusped form of the spirals in the margin. Randall notes in connection with another MS (item 51) certain characteristics of northern French influence, including "rudimentary figure style," and "drolleries attached to border terminals" (*Walters*, 129). The decoration in the Monreale MS, as is true of all the copies of the *Genus nequam* sequence under discussion, is characteristic of late thirteenth-century decoration rather than of fourteenth-century later gothic decoration. This may be due to the fact that these manuscripts were decorated locally, rather than being sent out to an up-to-date workshop, and may well account for certain features of the miniatures in this MS, namely the elongated figures, and the pattern of dots (similar to punchmarks) along the hem of the drapery.

[88] See n. 86 above. The evidence linking the Lunel, Paris, Monreale and Vatican 3819 manuscripts is complex: the Vatican MS is the latest of the group, yet there are features the Lunel and Vatican alone share (e.g., features of picture twelve, where they show a pope holding a tiara above four rabbits while the Monreale copy shows an angel holding a tiara over four small bears). This feature of the Monreale copy would seem to link it more closely with the versions in the Cambridge and Oxford copies, and particularly to the Florentine copy, none of which shows a pope.

[89] I am indebted to Robert Lerner for calling this issue of *Sicilia* to my attention and especially to Charlotte Lacaze for making her copy of this magazine available to me.

holding a staff with a white banner in one hand. To the right is an elongated snake with a bird attacking its head.

3.   (fol. 4^r) Picture three shows a seated pope, wearing a cope and tiara. To one side is a unicorn with curved horn touching the pope's eye. To the other side is a small figure in a short robe. The pope's hand is touching the figure's head; the pope holds his cope to him with his other hand. Above the pope's tiara is an eagle.

4.   (fol. 5^r) Picture four shows three pillars of equal height. The middle one, which has a curved top, holds the bust of a monk, tonsured and lightly bearded. Atop the right-hand pillar is a hand holding the tail of a flying fish-like object that curves over the head of the monk and extends to the pillar on the left. This fish has a head with ears. Atop the left-hand pillar is a bust of a secular figure.

5.   (fol. 6^r) Picture five shows a monk holding a rose in one hand and a sickle in the other. Above the rose is the bust of an angel, arms extended and hands holding the rose. Below and to one side is a sideways *B* or shackles and to the other is an object which looks something like the head of a double-headed axe, features unique to this manuscript among those under consideration.

6.   (fol. 7^r) Picture six shows a pope wearing a cloak and tiara. One hand is upraised, the other holds his cloak to his body. To one side is a cow or ox, facing the pope, hooves upraised. In the upper left (and above the cow) are two crowned heads, facing away from the pope.

7.   (fol. 8^r) Picture seven shows a pope wearing a cope and tiara. His head is inclined toward a bear and two cubs below; one hand is upraised, the other points to the bear.

8.   (fol. 9^r) Picture eight shows a fortress or stylized cityscape, with three turrets. Above the middle turret is a large staff with a white banner. Behind the roof of the fortress are the busts of four knights, wearing helmets.

9.   (fol. 10^r) Picture nine shows a pope, wearing a cope and tiara, one arm and hand extended downward. To one side and below is a dog or fox. Above the animal, and apparently held in the animal's mouth, are three crossed standards, one bearing a white banner, another a cross or coat of arms, and the middle one an axe or hatchet (or perhaps a portion of a banner). A bird, upside down, tail resting on the end of the standard, is atop the middle standard. There is a very small shield

(dark, with a blue band, the band decorated with a wavy white line and four white dots) in the space between the base of the standards and the pope. The bird and the shield are unique to P.

10. (fol. 11ʳ) Picture ten shows a different fortress or stylized cityscape, with one turret. Two pairs of hands extend toward the fortress from one side. Another hand rises above and behind the fortress.

11. (fol. 12ʳ) Picture eleven shows a figure, naked except for a long loincloth with a decorated belt. He is seated on a rock, arms raised either in astonishment or in an *orans* gesture. To the right is another figure of almost equal size, dressed in a lightly decorated tunic, with arms crossed over his chest. Neither figure is tonsured.

12. (fol. 13ʳ) Picture twelve shows a haloed figure with long hair (apparently an angel), wearing an alb and cloak, and holding the papal tiara in his outstretched hand. Below in the bottom fifth of the page are four small bears, two facing in one direction, two in the other.

13. (fol. 14ʳ) Picture thirteen shows an angel, dressed in long gown and cloak, crowning a pope with the papal tiara. The pope, wearing a chasuble, holds his arms in the *orans* gesture. The figures are of equal size and are contained within an arch.

14. (fol. 15ʳ) Picture fourteen shows a pope wearing a tiara, and an angel to either side. The wing of one angel extends beyond the border of the miniature into the margin. Below and behind the pope are two large dogs, facing in opposite directions (or a throne or *Faltstuhl* embellished with animal heads). The figures are contained within an arch, and the pope's face is blank, its features having been erased.

15. (fol. 16ʳ) Picture fifteen shows a pope wearing a chasuble, holding the papal tiara in one hand, arm extended, and a book in the other. The figure is contained within an arch.

16. (fol. 17ʳ) Picture sixteen shows an animal with a human head. The head, wearing a crown, faces right.

V. Vatican Library, MS Vat. lat. 3819, fols. 147ᴿ–149ᴿ

Description: Herbert Grundmann, "Die Papstprophetien," 104–106; idem, "Über den Apokalypsen-Kommentar des Minoriten Alexander," MGH, Schriften 25, 2 (Hanover, 1977), 58–60; Bernhard Degenhart and A. Schmitt, *Corpus der italienischen Zeichnungen 1300–1450* (Berlin, 1968), Pt. 1,1: 226; for a partial table of contents, Reeves, *Influence of Prophecy*, Appendix C, 537; Rehberg, " 'Kardinalsorakel'," 94–97; Sabine Schmolinsky, *Der Apokalypsenkommentar des Alexander Minorita: zur frühen Rezeption Joachims von Fiore in Deutschland* (Hanover, 1991), 20–21.

This manuscript is an anthology (of 236 folios) of works in a single hand. It contains "De semine scripturarum" (fols. 1ʳ–18ᵛ), "Expositio in Apocalypsim" by Alexander Minorita (fols. 19ʳ–130ᵛ),[90] "Oraculum Cyrilli" (fols. 131ʳ–146ᵛ), the *Genus nequam* prophecies (fols. 147ʳ–149ʳ), Jerome on Matthew and Mark (fols. 151ʳ–222ᵛ), and "De provincialibus presagiis" (fols. 23ʳ–236ʳ).[91] The pages are ruled and the decoration is minimal: in addition to the pictures in the *Genus nequam* section, there are three pictures in the "Expositio in Apocalypsim" section with spaces left for at least seventy-five additional pictures. There is no contents page.

The set of *Genus nequam* prophecies begins on folio 147ʳ, the equivalent of ten lines down from the top of the page. The page is arranged in two columns as is the immediately preceding text of the "Oraculum Cyrilli." At the top of the page in column one are the last nine lines of the "Oraculum Cyrilli" text, ending with the words "Deo gratias amen." There is a space of one line, and the caption for text number one of the *Genus nequam* series follows: "Incipit principium malorum ypocrisia habundabit." The first decorated initial is that of the first word of the text proper. Thus there is no identification of the text nor any attribution. The initials in this section with the exception of a capital "I" are three lines high and are decorated with pen flourishes.

The text of the prophecies is in column one; in column two are the pictures arranged for the most part in a series of connected rectangles more or less opposite the appropriate text. The sixteen miniatures are simply drawn and warmly colored, with a minimum of decoration, and for the

---

[90] The *explicit* for this section reads "Explicit postilla Joachim super apocalipsim" (fol. 131ʳ); the catchwords also refer to this section as "Joachim super Apocalipsim."

[91] Rehberg (" 'Kardinalsorakel'," 94) suggests that this last text was added when the manuscript was bound.

most part the ground line is the bottom of the frame. Following the text of
the prophecies and opposite the sixteenth picture—not set apart from the
sequence in any way—is a short text beginning "Scitote karissimi fratres,
quondam exibunt gentes incluse de petra reclusa. ..." (fols. 149^r–149^v),[92]
a list of popes through John XXII (1316–1334) (fol. 149^v), and the commentary on the cardinal prophecies (fols. 149^v–150^v), recently transcribed
by Rehberg and discussed earlier.

There are several distinctive features of the text recorded in this manuscript. The most important are the addition of five lines to the text of the
fifteenth prophecy and two lines added to the text of the tenth prophecy.
The first is from Nah. 3:1–2: "Ve civitas sanguinum universe mendacii dilaceratione plena, non recedet a te rapine, vox flagelli et vox impetus rote et
equi frementis," as Nahum, the prophet whose name means "comforter,"
foretells the destruction of the city of Nineveh. These lines are not found
in any of the other early versions, although they have been added in a second hand to text fifteen in the Monreale manuscript. They appear regularly
in all later versions of prophecy fifteen.

Two lines, Dan. 8:14, with some modification, are added to the text of
prophecy number ten. The usual Vulgate text of Daniel reads "Usque ad
vesperam et mane, dies duo, millia trecenti; et *miniabitur sacrificium*" (italics
mine: for the italicized words Daniel reads "mundabitur sanctuarium").
These lines come from the section in Daniel recording the angel's interpretation of Daniel's vision of the ram and the he-goat. It is the answer to the
question, "How much time between the beginning of the persecution of
Antiochus (a figure of the Antichrist) until his death?" The addition of these
lines is unique to this Vatican copy among the early manuscripts.

This witness records as well an unusual error in the opening words of
text number one, the reading of "Senus" for "Genus," an error that it
shares with Yale, Marston 225. The "S" is a decorated initial, so the error
could easily be that of the rubricator rather than that of the scribe.

The pictures also have a number of distinctive features. Unique to this
manuscript among the early witnesses are the crow atop a standard, a definite dragon in number two, three arches, each enclosing a figure or figures,
in number eight, and the donkey in number nine. Both this manuscript and
the Lunel manuscript show a pope (rather than an angel) holding the papal

---

[92] See Donckel, "Studien über die Prophezeiung des Fr. Telesforus von Cosenza," 66–67,
308–309, for references to this text as one of the sources drawn upon by Telesphorus in his
Libellus. The appearance in Vat. lat. 3819 is one of the earliest recorded, if not the earliest,
before its appearance in the *Libellus*. There is no attribution either here or in the *Libellus*.

tiara over rabbits rather than the usual bears or sheep. It also shares with the Lunel and Monreale manuscripts the flying fish or dolphin in number four, and with the Monreale manuscript the sixteenth picture of a lamb or sheep with the head of a crowned king.[93] The Monreale manuscript has a text assigned to this picture; this Vatican mansucript does not, assuming that the text in column one opposite the picture ("Scitote karissimi fratres. . . ." noted above) is not related to the picture.

Grundmann dates this manuscript to after 1314, probably before 1334, and surely before 1369.[94] Physical evidence suggests this to be a later copy than any of the other manuscripts under discussion. In the list of popes named and numbered one through nine on folio 149^v, John XXII is the last pope named (1316–1334). The list is in a slightly smaller size script and appears to have been squeezed into the available space at the bottom of column one after the *explicit* of the "Scitote karissimi fratres" prophecy, although there is still room for two additional lines. The commentary on the cardinal prophecies begins at the top of the next column and continues through fol. 150^v, where all but one line of column two is blank. On fol. 151^r begins Jerome's commentary on Matthew and Mark, and this new text is marked by a seven-line decorated initial. Thus it looks as if the list is contemporary with the text, for there was a larger space available on fol. 150^v.

For this manuscript, a date during the pontificate of John XXII seems most likely. There is no way of knowing whether this scribe's exemplar contained the additions to the text in numbers ten and fifteen or the list of popes on fol. 149^v; there is no record of such an exemplar elsewhere. The addition to prophecy fifteen became standard, but the addition to number ten is unique to this manuscript. These two additions bracket the last five prophecies, making it clear that someone dated the reign of the Antichrist to the reign of John XXII, i.e., to the tenth prophecy. Details in the miniature accompanying the ninth prophecy may well refer to Clement V.[95] Neither picture eight nor picture ten shows a pope, although this lack does not prevent a scribe or glossator from assigning a pope to that prophecy in later manuscripts.

---

[93] The Lunel MS also shows this beast, but it is clearly detached from the *Genus nequam* sequence: see above, p. 65.

[94] Grundmann, "Papstprophetien," 104; see also Lerner, "On the Origins," 635.

[95] The image here shows an animal which looks more like a donkey than a fox, surmounted by three standards, two of which are topped by *fleurs de lis*. Clement V's move to Avignon inaugurated the seventy years of the "Babylonian captivity," although he himself expected the move to be temporary. Clement V, although a compromise candidate of the pro-French and anti-French factions, was in fact much controlled by Philip the Fair. See, however, Sophia Menache, *Clement V* (Cambridge, 1998), for a re-evaluation of the pontificate of Clement V.

An examination of marginal glosses elsewhere in the manuscript suggests a date closer to 1334.[96] The only text that is annotated is the "Oraculum Cyrilli," and there are a number of annotations in the margins identifying popes and rulers and glossing particular portions of the prophecy.[97] Several glosses are of especial interest. Two provide a *terminus post quem*: the reference to the expedition of King John of Bohemia to Italy in the period 1331–1333 (fol. 142), and a note on fol. 141 (in addition to the list on fol. 149) suggesting that Pope John XXII (d. 1334) was still alive.[98] In addition, as Rehberg argues in considerable detail, the glosses indicate the political sympathies of the glossator and ultimately the commissioner of the manuscript itself.

The glosses rehearse, in the reference to Celestine V (fol. 141^v), in the negative reference to the anti-pope Nicholas V ("contra Petrum de corvario," fol. 141^r), and particularly in the revival of resentments against the Orsini ("contra ursos et Ursinos," fol. 142^r), the last note of particular significance as it glosses a neutral reference to the Orsini in the text proper,[99] the long-held animosity of the Colonna towards the Orsini going back to the papal conclave of 1287 and "held in memory," as Rehberg puts it, as a part of the Colonna family tradition.[100] Thus Rehberg not only attributes this manuscript to Colonna circles in Avignon ca. 1334 but also names Giovanni Colonna (cardinal from 1327–1348) as the possible commissioner of the manuscript.[101] The conclusion, then, is that there is no internal evidence, reference to events or persons, that would date the manuscript to a period earlier or later than the reign of John XXII, and Rehberg's dating to 1331–1334 seems most convincing. The additions to the text in units ten and fifteen, assuming them to be those of the scribe copying the text ca.

---

[96] The hand of this glossator is the same as that of the main scribe.

[97] See Paul Piur, "Oraculum Angelicum Cyrilli nebst dem Kommentar des Pseudojoachim," in Karl Burdach, *Vom Mittelalter zur Reformation*, vol. 4 (Berlin, 1912), 223–343, here 276–279.

[98] Rehberg, " 'Kardinalsorakel'," 95.

[99] Rehberg, " 'Kardinalsorakel'," 95.

[100] Rehberg, " 'Kardinalsorakel'," 97.

[101] Rehberg, " 'Kardinalsorakel'," 95–97; Degenhart and Schmitt date this manuscript to the mid-fourteenth century and to Venice (*Corpus*, 226). Lerner, "On the Origins," 635, notes that the grounds for this assignation are not clear. MS Vat. lat. 3819, or an intermediary, undoubtedly did serve as the exemplar for a fifteenth-century manuscript now in the Art Institute of Chicago (MS Buckingham 1944. 165), probably of Venetian origin. (I thank Suzanne McCullugh and Bernard McGinn for calling this manuscript to my attention.) Grundmann, "Papstprophetien," 104–106, suggests southern French or Italian origins, noting that this manuscript is listed in the library catalogue (1369) of Pope Urban V (104, n. 4); on the papal library and Giovanni Colonna see Rehberg, " 'Kardinalsorakel'," 96–97 and n. 241. Rehberg (" 'Kardinalsorakel'," 95) argues convincingly for an Italian or southern French provenance.

1334 during the last year of Pope John XXII's reign, features of the pictures unique to this manuscript, and certain textual variants suggest that the version of the *Genus nequam* prophecies recorded in this manuscript is the latest of the group of nine copies under consideration.[102]

Description of the Pictures

1. (fol. 147ʳ) Picture one shows a pope wearing a chasuble and the papal tiara (old style, here as elsewhere), sitting on a bench with a bear to either side, paws upraised and touching the pope's robes, and a third bear above and behind the tiara.

2. (fol. 147ʳ) Picture two shows a standing pope, wearing chasuble and tiara, holding a book in one hand, and in the other, a staff with a large bird in profile surmounted on it. To the right is a dragon-serpent, facing the pope. These last two details are unique to V among the fourteenth-century manuscripts.

3. (fol. 147ᵛ) Picture three shows a seated pope, wearing a chasuble and tiara. Atop the tiara is a large bird in profile perched on the tiara slightly to one side and extending through the border of the picture into the top margin. To the left is a small figure in a short gown. To the right is a unicorn, paws upraised, horn touching the pope's head.

4. (fol. 147ᵛ) Picture four shows a low pedestal with a bowl-like top containing the bust and torso of a naked tonsured figure. To either side is a column. Atop the column on the right is an extended hand, apparently holding a fin of a large flying fish or dolphin. The tail of this open-mouthed dolphin extends from the top of the middle vessel, over the head of the tonsured figure, to the bust of the crowned head atop the column on the left.

5. (fol. 147ᵛ) Picture five shows a tonsured figure wearing a chasuble, holding a sickle in one hand and a rose in the other. At the top right is the bust and torso of an angel, arms extended toward the figure and hands touching the rose.

6. (fol. 148ʳ) Picture six shows a pope wearing chasuble and tiara, one hand raised as in blessing, the other holding a book. To the left is a

---

[102] The reading in sentence one in prophecy eleven is an important one: the two early readings would appear to be "unctus" and "virtus." V reads "vinctus" or "iunctus." This and other readings make it clear that while the version of the prophecies represented in V could be earlier than 1328, it is not among the earliest versions.

cow with front legs upraised. Above the cow are the heads of two men wearing crowns, facing away from the pope.

7.   (fol. 148ʳ) Picture seven shows a pope wearing chasuble and tiara. To the left is a bear with young. The bear has upraised paws, touching the pope's robes.

8.   (fol. 148ʳ) Picture eight shows three arches with crenelations along the top. Within the left and middle arches are two figures, apparently soldiers, with shields and helmets. In the third arch to the right is a single larger figure with a shield and a visor covering his face. This image is unique to V among the fourteenth-century manuscripts.

9.   (fol. 148ʳ) Picture nine shows a pope wearing chasuble and tiara. To the left is a donkey, facing away from the pope. Behind the donkey are three crossed standards, the middle with three crosses at the top, the other two with stylized *fleurs de lis*. The donkey is unique to V.

10. (fol. 148ᵛ) Picture ten shows a fortress or stylized cityscape. At the upper left are two hands, fingers extended toward the fortress. Slightly above the fortress is another hand, fingers extended away from the fortress.

11. (fol. 148ᵛ) Picture eleven shows a figure, tonsured, naked except for a long skirt-like cloth, one hand upraised, one arm extended, seated on a rock. To the right is a figure of equal size, wearing a short gown and hood, one hand upraised, the other extended toward the seated figure.

12. (fol. 148ᵛ) Picture twelve shows a seated tonsured figure, wearing a chasuble, and holding a papal tiara over four rabbits. One finger appears to be pointed at the rabbits. The rabbits are in the lower left, two facing the pope and two facing the border.

13. (fol. 149ʳ) Picture thirteen shows a pope, wearing a chasuble and seated on a bench, being crowned with the papal tiara by an angel. The pope holds a book in one hand; the other hand is upraised. The angel is of the same size as the pope and its wings extend beyond the boundary of the border into the margin.

14. (fol. 149ʳ) Picture fourteen shows a pope seated on a bench, with a book resting in his lap and held by both hands. He wears chasuble and tiara. Two angels, one to the right and one to the left, standing on the bench, are crowning the pope.

15. (fol. 149^r) Picture fifteen shows a pope, tonsured, wearing a cope over chasuble and alb. With arms extended, he holds a book in one hand and the papal tiara in the other.

16. (fol. 149^r) Picture sixteen shows a large animal with a lamb's body and a human head wearing a crown.

The Picture Tradition

This section brings together all the significant variations in the manuscripts, tracing, where relevant, what appears to be the evolution of the picture tradition. It discusses some of the more important iconographical features, but does not aim to give a full iconographical study.

Analysis of the picture tradition reinforces the groupings of manuscripts
noted earlier, that is, A–CD and LNPV, with F and M closely aligned to
the latter group. Analysis of the images underscores as well the many variations within each group and both the ways in which the groups are discrete
and the ways in which they overlap. The Yale manuscript, for instance,
shows characteristics of both early and late features: details of image four
(the columns, the scimitar) link this version most closely to fifteenth-
century and later versions of the image; yet there is is no beast in the final
image of the series, a detail present in some form in LPV as well as in F.
Each witness has some unique feature, e.g., dogs instead of bears in the Yale
manuscript, a slightly different arrangement of elements in the image,
slightly different background detail. Some of the variations clearly have
referents that are for now at least lost to us: both the Lunel and Vatican
3819 witnesses, for instance, show the pope in the angelic series (image
twelve) holding his tiara over four rabbits. In the much later Regiselmo
edition of the pope prophecies, the rabbits have become sheep: whatever
specific referent the rabbits might have called to mind has been lost or is no
longer relevant and the image is now the more generalized one of the papal
shepherd "feeding his sheep."

Analysis of the picture tradition makes it clear as well that individual
variations in the images are not only of interest but also that certain images
in the series emerge as crucial, affecting in particular the cumulative effect
of the images. Images five, eleven, and fifteen are important in this context.
In CD, for instance, there is no explicit reference to Celestine V in image
five, and no beast in image fifteen, even though there is a clear angelic sequence in images eleven through fifteen. The instances in which Celestine
is clearly identified in image five allow for a slightly different reading of
image eleven, the summoning of the angelic pope, a reading with a particu-

lar Franciscan resonance, as has been discussed earlier. Thus even minor changes in image five alter the cumulative effect of the series more substantially than do the greater variations in images four and twelve, for instance.

Certain patterns emerge. In the earlier versions represented by CD, the last five images were probably read as the progress of a single holy pope; in the later versions the single pope has become a series of holy popes. Local references (rabbits, dogs, the substitution of a donkey for a fox in image nine in V) are lost and the image becomes more generalized. One explanation suggests that when memories of a particular historical pope in the series are fresh, local references abound; as the lives of these popes recede into the distant past, the images lose these local references and the images become more stable.

The images in the Lunel manuscript represent a version that with some exceptions can be termed the established version or what will become the established version in much later manuscripts. The serpent that looks like a salamander in image two will become a stylized serpent; the flying fish in image four will become a scimitar, details will be added to the image of Celestine V (image number five), rabbits will become sheep in image twelve, and images fifteen and sixteen will become combined, the only truly substantial change.

PICTURE 1

The picture tradition for the first image is remarkably consistent, showing as it does a pope and bears; and there seems to be little doubt that the series was meant to begin with the Orsini pope, Nicholas III (1277–1280). This unanimity is all the more remarkable since in most of the extant Greek manuscripts of the Leo Oracles (all post-dating the *Genus nequam* prophecies), the first image is that of a serpent.[1] The bear symbol obviously pointed to the Orsini family, suggesting Giovanni Gaetano Orsini (Nicholas III) as the first figure in the series. Dante's characterization of Nicholas as "son of the she-bear" and representative of the simoniacal popes not only testifies to the familiarity of the association but also may indicate that he had seen this picture.[2]

The common version for picture one, represented by LMPV, shows a

---

[1] MS Oxford, Bodleian Library, Barocci 170, a sumptuously decorated sixteenth-century copy, does show a bear with three nursing cubs as the first picture. For the Barocci copy, see Rigo, *Oracula Leonis*, 17–48.

[2] Dante Alighieri, *The Divine Comedy*, trans. Charles S. Singleton (Princeton, 1970), *Inferno*, 19: 69–72. See also Lerner, "Recent Work," 149, n. 18.

pope, surrounded by three animals, bears in LPV and dogs in M. CD show
a pope and to one side a large bear with nursing cubs (figure 1), four in C,
five in D, similar to figure six in the Leo Oracles, which shows a large bear
with three nursing cubs. The F scribe left little space for the picture, which
shows the torso of a pope and to the upper side a bear with young (the
number of the young is uncertain as this portion of the page has been damaged). The picture is not described either in A or by Pipini, although Pipini
notes that the series begins with Nicholas III (Cap. xx, cols. 724–725). As
discussed above, the commentary on the cardinal prophecies notes five cubs
(identified with five cardinals), and although the commentary makes it clear
that the subject of unit one is Giovanni Gaetano Orsini (Nicholas III), it is
not certain that the image included a human figure as well as the figure of
the bear with five cubs.[3] Thus, of the copies under consideration, only the
Vat. lat. 3822 copy leaves in doubt the subject of the unit.

If it were not for the testimony of the commentary on the cardinal prophecies, the variations in the image might seem minor, but given this testimony, it is clear that the five cubs in the early versions had specific referents. It is tempting then to see significance in the heretofore considered
minor difference in detail between the Cambridge and and Oxford copies
(four cubs rather than five).[4] In the later versions, as seen in the Lunel witness, the placement of the bears in the image has changed; Nicholas III is
clearly referred to in his capacity as pope, and the reference to bears is
"generic" rather than specific.[5]

The significance of the substitution of dogs for bears in the Yale manuscript (one executed no earlier than the mid-1320s) is unclear.[6] An obvious

---

[3] As noted elsewhere, Rehberg makes the point that the commentary would have followed
a copy of text and pictures; therefore there was no need for the commentator to describe the
picture in detail.

[4] See also the reference to the death of Nicholas III in unit three of the commentary (66–
69), and the seemingly gratuitous observation that the death left only four cubs. It is clear that
the first three units of the prophecies (as represented by the cardinal oracle) were *ex eventu*, for
the commentator was familiar with events of Honorius IV's pontificate. The fourth cub, Latino
Malabranca, died in 1294, the fifth, Giordano Orsini (according to Rehberg's enumeration), died
earlier in 1287, and the second cub, Matteo Rosso Orsini, died in 1305. Since there is some
debate about the identity of the fifth cub, the missing cub in the Cambridge copy (if not the
result of simple error) points either to Latino Malabranca or to Matteo Rosso Orsini. If this
hypothesis can be sustained, it would date the version represented here to no earlier than 1294
and more likely, in my opinion, to sometime after Matteo Rosso Orsini's death in 1305.

[5] I.e., the reference to the Orsini, to nepotism and simony.

[6] For dating, see "Description of Manuscripts," pp. 74–75. Lerner ("On the Origins," 617
and n. 13) notes that the Monreale, Vat. lat. 3819, and Yale manuscripts "delete the she-bear
and show a pope surrounded by three dogs, conceivably with the intention of toning down the
anti-Orsini bias" (n. 13). The animals in the Monreale and Vatican manuscripts certainly appear
to be bears rather than dogs (size and position of ears, short tail) particularly in the case of the

explanation might be that they referred to the emblem of a particular patron, one for whom the manuscript was produced. On the other hand, if no such connection between emblem and patron can be identified, their presence could point to a larger symbolic meaning. As James Marrow has discussed in his study of Passion iconography, there are many references in this period to dogs as the tormentors of Christ, drawing on the language and images of Ps. 21:17, "Quondam circumdederunt me canes multi; / Concilium malignantium obsedit me."[7] Even more particularly, references to dogs and their "snapping" are found not only in the Franciscan discourse surrounding the promulgation of "Exiit qui seminat," by Nicholas III (1279), but also in the prologue to the bull itself.[8]

When Nicholas III became pope, the Franciscans petitioned him to rule on the issue of poverty and the Rule, and with his ruling, "Exiit qui seminat," began a series of debates both within the Order and between the Order and the Papacy that continued for the better part of four decades, debates which were not resolved until the series of bulls issued by John XXII, and then not to the Spirituals' satisfaction. There was a series of bulls in between, under Martin IV (1283) and Clement V (1312).

Pope John XXII addressed himself to these same issues in 1317 when he ordered the Spirituals to conform to the moderate position, in particular

---

Monreale manuscript, if they are compared with the dogs in the Yale manuscript and with the animal in picture nine in P, which does in fact look like a dog rather than a fox. (See also Daneu Lattanzi, " 'Vaticinia Pontificum'," 777–778.)

[7] James Marrow, *Passion Iconography in Northern European Art of the Late Middle Ages and Early Renaissance* (Kortrijk, Belgium, 1979), 39; see also 33, 36–39. Kerby-Fulton, "Hildegard," 397, notes references to dogs "to signify the ungodly" in Mark 7:28 and 3 Kings 14:11.

[8] " . . . Interdum aemulatores agitatos invidia, iracundia et indiscreta iustitia concitavit mordentes fratres et eorum regulam quasi illicitam, inobservabilem et discriminosam caninis latrantibus lacerantes, non attendentes hanc sanctam regulam, ut praedicitur, praeceptis ac monitis salutaribus institutam, apostolicis observationibus roboratam, per plures romanos pontifices approbatam et etiam per sedem apostolicam confirmatam . . ." from "Exiit qui seminat," quoted in Fidelis Elizondo, "Bulla 'Exiit qui seminat' Nicholas III (14 August 1279)," *Laurentianum* 4 (1963): 59–119, here at 86; idem, Appendix, 189–219, for comparison of "Quo elongati" (Gregory IX), "Ordinem vestram" (Innocent IV), "Exiit qui seminat" (Nicholas III), and "Exivi de paradiso" (Clement V). For the frequency of "dogs" in Franciscan discourse surrounding the promulgation of "Exiit," see David Burr, *Olivi and Franciscan Poverty: The Origins of the "Usus Pauper" Controversy* (Philadelphia, 1989), 153–154 and notes 49–52. Some of the "biting dogs" were "domini canes," and Burr notes that "it is hard to read 'Exiit' without recognizing it as an answer to certain claims advanced by Aquinas, Kilwardby, and other Dominicans at Franciscan expense" (*Olivi and Franciscan Poverty*, 154); Burr reiterates this latter point in a review of Andrea Tabarroni, *Paupertas Christi et apostolorum: L'ideale francescano in discussione (1322–1324)* (Rome, 1990) in *Speculum* 67 (1992): 749, in which he argues that more attention must be paid to "the internecine political and intellectual warfare between Franciscans and Dominicans in the late thirteenth and early fourteenth centuries," that period between the promulgation of "Exiit" in 1279 by Nicholas III and the promulgation of "Quia nonnunquam" by John XXII in 1322.

banning their short habits and calling on them to observe the "moderate use" rule.[9] Later in 1322 and 1323 the Franciscan order under Michael of Cesena was at clear odds with John XXII's teaching on Christ's and the Apostles' ownership of goods. In 1325 a portion of the order separated itself from the rest, and a small group including Michael of Cesena eventually took up residence at the court of Louis IV of Bavaria in 1329. Pope John's bull of 1329 "Quia vir reprobus" articulated once again his position on the right to hold property, based on his interpretation of Scripture that Christ and his Apostles did in fact hold property, a position clearly at odds with the Spirituals' position and as well that of the Michaelists, the latter once the "personification . . . of orthodoxy."[10]

The dogs in the first image then may well provide a connection between the pontificates of Nicholas III and John XXII, for not only did each pope make a major statement on poverty and the Rule, but if "dogs were snapping" at the Franciscans at the time of "Exiit," which Nicholas III implied in the prologue to that bull, then they were clearly gaining in numbers and force by the time of John XXII's bulls. Moreover, Pope John's bull "Quia nonnunquam" (March 1322) declared that as pope he had the authority to alter rulings established in earlier bulls, in this case with specific reference to "Exiit."[11]

Certainly at the distance of John's pontificate, Nicholas's bull was a "friendly" one, but, as well, it also marked the "initium malorum" noted in the usual caption to picture and text number one.

PICTURE 2

Of the key items in picture two, pope (usually identified as Martin IV, 1281–1285), serpent and one or two crows, only the two crows attacking a snake-like serpent appear in the corresponding image of the Leo Oracles.

---

[9] A recent discussion of John XXII and his confrontation with the Franciscan order is that of Oakley, "John XXII." He gives a more sympathetic view of Pope John's motives and thinking than do the standard authorities: Decima Douie, *The Nature and Effect of the Heresy of the Fraticelli* (Manchester, 1932); Malcolm Lambert, *Franciscan Poverty* (London, 1961); Leff, *Heresy*; and John Moorman, *A History of the Franciscan Order* (Oxford, 1968). See also Burr, *Olivi and Franciscan Poverty*; Tabarroni, *Paupertas Christi*; and Roberto Lambertini, *Apologia e crescita dell'identità francescana (1255–1279)* (Rome, 1990), 154–186.

[10] Leff, *Heresy*, 238.

[11] An irony, since, as Thomas Turley points out, the Spiritual Franciscans on the whole supported the notion of papal infallibility and of course John came to be the proponent of such a notion. See Thomas Turley, "The Ecclesiology of Guido Terreni" (Ph.D. diss., Cornell University, 1979). See also Brian Tierney, *Origins of Papal Infallibility 1150–1350*, 2nd ed. (Leiden, 1988, originally published 1972).

Pipini in his description uses the term *anguilla* or "eel" instead of "serpent," and elsewhere in the passage refers to Martin IV's fondness for eels. With the exception of A, which describes a *diaconus*, CDFLMPV show a pope, in some instances holding a pastoral staff (a standard with a cross at the top). CDFP show a snake-like serpent (figure 2) similar to the one in the Leo Oracles, although C's and D's have dog-like heads and D adds forepaws to the snake's body. L, M, and V show distinct variations: L a green spotted salamander-like serpent with six legs; the bird in L is atop the papal tiara and appears to be looking down at the serpent; M shows a serpent entwined about a tree trunk, two birds sitting in leaves at the top of the tree, and a small kneeling figure to the pope's other side (figure 3); V a pope holding a book in one hand, a dragon figure to one side, and a standard with a large bird, beak open, atop it (figure 4).

The testimony of the commentary on the cardinal prophecies makes it clear that in the earliest version the subject of the prophecy was a cardinal, Matteo Rosso Orsini. Rehberg argues, as noted elsewhere, that the *diaconus* referred to in the Vatican 3822 copy is probably a cardinal. The commentary also identifies Matteo Rosso Orsini with the "flying serpent," so it is not altogether certain from the commentary (apart from the evidence of the Vatican 3822 copy of the prophecies) that the earliest version of the image showed a human figure.[12] It is easier to see how the figure became a pope, given Rehberg's dating of the commentary. It is difficult to determine at what point the elements of serpent and crows ceased to retain specific references to the Orsini and anti-Orsini forces; certainly Pipini did not read the image in that way.

PICTURE 3

The key items in picture three include a pope (usually identified as Honorius IV, 1285–1287), a smaller figure, usually supplicating, to one side, an eagle surmounting the papal tiara, and a unicorn, in some instances with its horn touching either the pope's eye or the base of the tiara. This picture corresponds to figure three in the Leo Oracles, which shows, in two different versions, the imperial eagle with a cross hanging from its beak, and a large unicorn with a smaller figure to one side. Pipini describes the animal as a rhinoceros, a not uncommon confusion (Job 39: 9–12).[13] A describes the main figure as *imago similis priori*, that is, another *diaconus*, but includes

---

[12] Rehberg, " 'Kardinalsorakel'," 53.
[13] See Albert the Great, *Man and Beasts*, 47, 160.

the other items, calling the small figure a *puer*. In CD and M, the unicorn is not attacking. All show the eagle, although in V, the bird is in profile and not clearly an eagle. A cross is next to the eagle's head in D; the eagle has a nimbus in C.

In medieval iconography the unicorn has two contrasted meanings. On the one hand, it is associated with the virgin who easily lures it into docile captivity by her purity. This is a common medieval theme, which derives ultimately from the Greek *Physiologus*.[14] On the other hand, fierce unicorns are frequently identified with the persecutors or enemies of Christ, a figure drawn from Ps. 22:23.[15] In the *Genus nequam* prophecies the most common rendering of the unicorn is obviously reminiscent of the virgin and unicorn tradition—as distinct from the Greek tradition of the Leo Oracles, where the unicorn rears itself alone—but its fiercely attacking horn suggests the second interpretation. Perhaps the double image is intentional. What relation, if any, this image has with a prophecy recorded by Bartholomew Cotton (d. ca. 1298), as from Joachim of Fiore, *inc.* "Egredietur unicornis de plaga occidentali cum vexillo leopardorum . . ." is uncertain.[16]

The commentary on the cardinal prophecies mentions explicitly the unicorn and eagle (and apparently refers to the cross); the subject of the text is Jacopo Savelli, a member of the Orsini party that elected Nicholas III, but who as Honorius IV worked to retrieve Sicily for the French. The commentator glosses "unicorn" by noting Jacopo Savelli's role as "defender of the bears." Rehberg connects the text and picture referred to in the commentary to the description in the Vat. lat. 3822 manuscript (a *diaconus* with *corona*) and also to the picture for unit three in the Florentine manuscript.[17]

PICTURE 4

There is considerably wider variation in the picture tradition for unit four. LPV show two columns and between them a vessel with the head of a cleric. A hand extends from right-hand column and holds the tail of a "dolphin" or flying fish which in turn extends over the head of the cleric

---

[14] See Rudiger R. Beer, *Unicorn: Myth and Reality*, trans. Charles M. Stern (New York, 1977); Nikolaus Henkel, *Studien zum Physiologus im Mittelalter* (Tübingen, 1976). I thank David Heffner for these references.

[15] Marrow, *Passion Iconography*, 33–43.

[16] *Historia Anglicana*, ed. Henry Richards Luard, Rolls Series (London, 1859), 239–240; see also Reeves, *Influence of Prophecy*, 75, and Rupert Taylor, *The Political Prophecy in England* (New York, 1911), 87.

[17] Rehberg, " 'Kardinalsorakel'," 68–69, esp. n. 92.

apparently to "attack" the crowned head on the left column. F shows a single vessel similar to the middle vessel (or capital) in LPV, with the head of a cleric and curved handle-like attachment extending over this head (figure 5). M shows three columns, a crowned head on the left-hand one, a cleric's head on the middle column and a hand from the right-hand one holding a scimitar over the head of the cleric. Pipini's description mentions a head of a bird (*avis*), its beak supporting a nest (*rostra sustinens nidum*), which, in turn, holds the head of a cleric.[18] This does not correspond to any one picture: none shows the bird or the nest. *Nidum* can be a "nest-shaped bowl," or "goblet"; L, F. and V show a vessel of this sort. "Rostrum" can be a "beak-like" shape as in the prow of a ship, perhaps similar to the curved "inverted handle" attached to the vessel in F.

Of the manuscript group ACDF, none has columns; A has no description for this picture; F has the vessel noted above with the bust of a tonsured figure. In C and D, pictures and texts for units four and five are presented together on a single page (figure 6). The portion of the combined picture that can be called four shows a head resting on the serrated edge of a sickle.[19] The hair stands out like rays in C.

The commentary on the cardinal prophecies helps to account for the evolution of this fourth image, for the commentary notes a severed head and sickle in the picture, elements found in the Cambridge and Oxford copies and alluded to in the Florentine copy, in the form of the handle-like attachment. The subject of the commentary is Latino Malabranca, particularly in his role as pope-maker and manipulator of papal elections.[20] The relation of this image to those in the corresponding Leo Oracles is complex. The Lambecius version (PG 107:1153) shows the king with sickle and rose appropriated in most *Genus nequam* copies to number five. Jeanne Basquin-Vereecken's work has demonstrated, however, that there is considerable variety among the manuscript witnesses of the Leo Oracles, both in the arrangment of the sequence and in the content of the images. One group of witnesses corresponds to the Lambecius version; a second group shows a head, and yet a third group shows a combination of the head and

---

[18] Pipini's description: "[Pontifex] est enim inclusus Columnae, ita ut nonnisi caput appareat mithratum, & ante se alias duas habet columnas, in quarum una est caput avis, rostro sustinens nidum, in quo est caput senis Clerici." (*Chronicon*, Cap. 23, col. 728.)

[19] The conflated image in CD includes elements of pictures four (head resting on serrated blade), five (figure with sickle and angel), and six (heads of two kings). The head resting on on the serrated blade is unique to CD and to the version adduced from the commentary (in M the instrument is held over the head of the cleric; however, in the fifteenth-century MSS and in the sixteenth-century printed editions, the scimitar is below the head).

[20] Rehberg, " 'Kardinalsorakel'," 56.

a king with sickle and rose.[21] It would seem that, in the case of the manuscript group LPVN, this uncertainty in the source (and change of referent) allowed for the elaboration of columns, retaining the middle column or vessel. This would offer an opportunity for direct political allusion. Thus the columns surely refer to the Colonna family while the clerical head emerging from the vessel points to Nicholas IV (1288–1292) who was dependent on the Colonna family.

The significance of the flying fish or dolphin is more puzzling: the possibilities include reference to the Dauphiné, to the heir to the French throne, or to the dolphin as a symbol of resurrection and salvation. Joseph Strayer traces the history of its identification first of all with the counts of Vienne in the area known as the Dauphiné,[22] and after 1334 as an emblem of the heir to the French throne. By 1349 Philip VI had determined that it should be the eldest son who should rule this territory of Dauphiné.[23] The problem is that no satisfactory connection can be made to the pope usually identified with this picture, Nicholas IV. Philip the Fair was king of France during Nicholas's reign, but Charles V (1364–1380) was the first royal dauphin.

Perhaps M's version of the picture in its later form which, significantly, is closest to most fifteenth-century forms, as well as to the Regiselmo printed edition, gives the best possible key to the transmission from the earlier form of the image to the later. Here, instead of a dolphin, a scimitar is held over the tonsured head (figure 7). Thus the interpretation might be: the columns, the Colonna family; the crowned head, Philip the Fair; the cleric, Nicholas IV; the scimitar, perhaps a reference to the aborted crusades of Philip the Fair and Edward I and/or the fall of Acre in 1291.

PICTURE 5

The pattern of variations in picture number five is linked to that in number four, although all manuscripts contain some combination of the key

---

[21] This information is based on the as yet unpublished edition of the Leo Oracles which has been prepared by Dr. Jeanne Basquin-Vereecken of Ghent; see also Reeves, "The *Vaticinia*," 148–149, n. 13; and above, "The Prophecies," n. 17.

[22] "Dauphin," *Dictionary of the Middle Ages*, 10 vols. (New York, 1984–1989), vol. 4: 107–108. Strayer notes that ". . . originally the name seems to have been only a way to distinguish the counts, most of whom were called Guigues, from other men of the same name. . . . By 1248 *dalphinus* was becoming a title; by the 1280's [sic] it had supplanted that of count" (107).

[23] See William M. Hinkle, *The Fleurs de Lis of the Kings of France 1285–1488* (Carbondale and Edwardsville, 1991), 44–45 and Pl. 16, Secret Seals of Charles V, 1376, which shows two dolphins very similar in design to those in the Lunel, Monreale, and Vatican 3819 MSS.

elements: monk or figure holding a sickle and a rose, and an angel (cf. Apoc. 14:14–16). The corresponding Leo Oracle picture (number five, PG 107:1553) shows an emperor or king, holding a crook or sickle in one hand and a rose in the other, being crowned by an angel.[24] The conflation of pictures four and five (and one element of picture six) in C and D reflect both the multiple versions of unit four in the Leo Oracles, and also the connections between units four and five of the commentary on the cardinal prophecies. Rehberg describes unit five as the "companion" to unit four, here describing or referring to Latino Malabranca's role in the papacy of Celestine V.[25] The commentary refers to the figure holding a rose and a sickle, the rose a symbol of the papacy and the sickle apparently connected to the "cutting of the rose."[26]

The important variations are not so much in the images themselves as in the way(s) the images do or do not point to Celestine V (5 July–13 Dec. 1294). While the description in A makes no mention of an angel, the important difference is that the main figure is described as a "juvenis." C and D show a figure (of uncertain age) holding a sickle in one hand and an angel in the other (omitting the rose). The figure, although simply dressed and barefoot, is not clearly a monk and certainly not a pope. Thus what distinguishes A–CD as a group is the absence of any identification of the main figure with Celestine V.

Pipini, identifying the pope as Celestine V and noting his canonization in 1313, describes the figure as a religious, tonsured, and wearing a hood (concullam), holding a reaper's sickle in his right hand and a rose in his left. M is noteworthy in that it is the only one to show a hooded figure (as described by Pipini), while the main figure is in profile rather than in the usual frontal position (figure 8). P contains the only other significant variation: the addition of a symbol variously interpreted as either a sideways "B" or shackles, and an unidentifiable object on the right, which in the printed edition of 1589 (figure 9) is a leg. Robert Lerner first suggested that the sideways "B" might be a shackle or leg manacle, an allusion to Celestine V's

---

[24] For interpretation of the Leo Oracle, particularly its reference to Andronicus I Comnenus, see Mango, "Legend of Leo the Wise," 64. Not all copies of the Leo Oracles show the angel (Reeves, "The Vaticinia," 148–149).

[25] On references to Celestine V in units four and five, see Rehberg, " 'Kardinalsorakel'," 58–59 and commentary V:111–112, 118–119.

[26] In unit four, the rose points to Latino Malabranca as pope-maker (Rehberg, " 'Kardinals-orakel'," 55, n. 41, references to the rose and sword in papal ceremonies and to Salimbene's Cronicon [p. 572], where Rehberg notes, "Is it a coincidence that before the description of the pontificate of Honorius IV there is a long excursus on the golden rose?" [my translation]).

imprisonment by Boniface VIII.[27] Whether the two additional symbolic objects were part of the original image in P or were added later remains to be determined.[28]

PICTURE 6

The key elements in picture number six include the pope, usually identified as Boniface VIII, and a cow (*vacca*), elements which are common to all the manuscripts (although the enumeration is different in CD), and to Pipini's description. The corresponding Leo picture (number six, PG 107: 1154) shows a cow and two heads. These heads are mitred in F, crowned in FLPV (CD shows them in the combination picture 4–5); M shows two heads with secular headgear, not crowns.

The commentary on the cardinal prophecies refers to a cow and two crowned heads as well as to the "fifth son of the bear," identified by Rehberg as Giordano Orsini.[29] All versions of the *Genus nequam* prophecies show a pope in this image, and the description of the picture in the Vatican 3822 copy is the only one of the descriptions to refer explicitly to a pope. The text of the commentary in what Rehberg considers to be an interpolation (ca. 1297) does refer to Celestine V's death and to Boniface VIII; nonetheless it is impossible to determine with certainty if the original image referred to showed a human figure. The reference to bulls or calves as the tormentors or enemies of Christ might well be based on imagery drawn from Ps. 21:13–14;[30] however if, as the commentary suggests (VI:122–

---

[27] In fifteenth-century manuscripts like that of Vatican Library, MS Ross. 374, the shackle alludes to "Baldassare Cossa's imprisonment by the Council of Constance," and the "leg" a visual representation of the name "Cossa" (Lerner, personal communication, 24 June 1988); see also David Heffner, "*Eyn wunderliche Weyssagung von dem Babstumb*: Medieval Prophecy into Reformation Polemic" (Ph.D. diss., University of Pennsylvania, 1991), 115, n. 61, and 91–96 for evidence that this object, "shackles" or "stocks," is, in later versions of the pope prophecies, a fire-steel. See also two copies of the *Ascende calve* series, one in Vienna, Österreichische Nationalbibliothek, MS 13648 [Suppl. 1071], fol. 4, for a prisoner of Boniface VIII's wearing shackles (here similar to stocks), and another in Saint-Gall, Vadianische Bibliothek, MS 342, fol. 4, where the prisoner is wearing similar shackles. To my knowledge the shackles do not appear in any copy of the *Genus nequam* prophecies before the appearance of the stocks in the St. Gall and Vienna copies of the *Ascende calve* series.

[28] See above, "Description of MSS: P." p. 83 and n. 85.

[29] See commentary VI:120–123 and Rehberg, " 'Kardinalsorakel'," 59–61.

[30] Marrow, *Passion Iconography*, 34, also 261, n. 121, and Fig. 3, "Christ Encompassed by Bulls," reproduced from the 9th-century Stuttgart Psalter, Württembergische Landesbibliothek, MS Biblia, fol. 23; although the Latin text reads "vacca," clearly the Leo picture was read as a bull: see Mango, "Legend of Leo the Wise," 62–64.

123), Giordano Orsini is signified by the figure of the cow and one of his attributes is that he is "a friend of the friends of the church" (III:123), then it is necessary to look elsewhere for the significance of the cow.

PICTURE 7

For picture number seven, in some manuscripts identified with Benedict XI (1303–1304), all show a pope, bear and nursing young, except for ACD, which substitute a king for the pope. The Leo Oracles (number seven, PG 107:1153) show only the bear and three or four cubs. The key element in the picture, apart from the main figure of the pope or king, is the bear and cubs. The cubs vary in number from one to five (there is no longer the testimony of the commentary on the cardinal prophecies):[31] Pipini describes a bear and twin cubs (*gemini*); LMPV show two cubs, CD five, F one; Pipini describes the bear as touching the right side of the pope, but only V shows the bear touching the pope.

It is unclear how or even if the iconography of the bear and cubs relates to Benedict XI. The first bear picture in the Leo Oracles was clearly fitted to the Orsini pope, Nicholas III, but this second one may be used simply because the first line of the relevant Oracle text requires it. In biblical imagery, the she-bear robbed of her cubs is a simile for human anger (2 Sam. 17:8, Isa. 59:11); a bear alone is a simile for a wicked ruler (Prov. 28:15); and in the imagery of the Apocalypse is a component of the composite beast in Apoc. 13:2 and Dan. 7:15. The suckling bear alone or with two cubs is also an image of Rome.

PICTURE 8

Picture number eight shows a cityscape or fortress apparently under siege; only the L illuminator identifies this picture and prophecy with Clement V (1305–1314). F has the symbol $\mathcal{D}$. .6. below the text and above the cityscape (figure 10). The corresponding Leo picture (number eight, PG 107:1154) shows a city and below it a head in a vessel. Rays extend from this head toward the city. Only CD and F show both these features, the head and the rays, although the vessel is missing in F. F's drawing is distinguished by a figure in a tower dropping rocks on those below. V alone shows three arches instead of the cityscape: two each contain two

---

[31] On the number of units in the commentary on the cardinal prophecies, see Rehberg, " 'Kardinalsorakel'," 100–101; see also Lerner, "Recent Work," 154 and n. 29.

soldiers with shields, the third has a single figure with shield, wearing a visor over its face (figure 11). Pipini makes no reference to this image.

PICTURE 9

Although Pipini identifies the pope in picture nine as Clement V, iconographical analysis supports the assumption that in the earliest version no reference to Clement V was intended. The key elements in the image are a pope and an animal, usually a fox, with crossed standards arranged above its back. The corresponding Leo picture (number nine, PG 107: 1155) shows a fox with three crossed standards above its back, each bearing a cross. Pipini describes a pope and a fox with the three standards, more or less as represented in LM. CD show a pope carrying a pastoral staff in one hand, and scroll or large seal (D) in the other. The animal in C looks like a bear and in D rather like a dog; the animal in P looks more like a dog than a fox, in V it is a donkey. CD show as well the two extended hands (signs of threat or supplication) usually found in picture ten. The other details, crossed standards and the pope, are consistent throughout the manuscripts, although P has several details unique to it, a bird, upside down, atop a standard and a small shield (figure 12).[32] There is a *fleur de lis* atop one of the standards in L and atop two in V.[33] F shows a pope holding a large key in one hand and either a scroll or book in the other. To the side is an upright animal, most likely a fox, with a key balanced on its head and holding a single large banner with a large cross on it. F's iconography suggests a threat to the papacy itself, as the fox carries off the symbols of the papacy, the key and the banner so often found in conjunction with representations of the Lamb of God Triumphant.

PICTURE 10

For picture number ten, CD show an empty throne and below it a hand extended towards the throne (figure 13), similar to the corresponding picture in the Leo Oracles (number ten, PG 107:1156).[34] FMLPV show a

---

[32] This shield in the lower third of the image is dark with a blue band decorated with a wavy line and four white dots.

[33] See Hinkle, *Fleurs de Lis*, 112, also 171, n. 1. The Lunel MS also shows a standard bearing the *fleur de lis* but identifies prophecy eight with Clement V. The Douce and Corpus Christi manuscripts show an angel holding a standard bearing the *fleur de lis* in picture thirteen (twelve in CD's numbering).

[34] Although the text of prophecy ten corresponds to Leo Oracles ten and eleven, the image of prophecy ten is drawn only from Leo Oracle number ten. Jeanne Basquin-Vereecken argues

cityscape or fortress with three hands to one side, extended towards the city.[35] In LPV one of these hands emerges from the battlements of the city. The hands in L and P are in pairs, held in a gesture of supplication. In F the city is superimposed against a series of "lumps," perhaps meant to represent the seven hills of Rome.[36]

Although the number and position of the hands might seem minor, this element (along with the evidence of the captions) helps to date the LMNPV group. Millet and Rigaux have argued persuasively that the copy of the "papalarius" owned by Bernard Délicieux was in close proximity to the Lunel and Monreale copies.[37] V, a copy quite certainly later than LP or N, shows the hands in the same position, but does not share features of the captions.

PICTURE 11

For prophecy eleven all pictures show a main figure, nude or clothed only in a loincloth, seated or reclining on a sarcophagus or rock, with a smaller figure to one side. This corresponds to number twelve in the Leo Oracles; the *Genus nequam* sequence omits Leo Oracle eleven, a unicorn. The images vary only in details (figures 14–17). The main figure is clearly tonsured only in LV. His gestures vary somewhat: he has one hand to his head, the other to the side in CDM (as in the Leo picture); one hand extended as if in blessing in F,[38] hands raised in the *orans* gesture in LP, one hand extended, the other part-way to the head in V. The loincloth in P has a decorated band at the waist and the figure in F is naked. The smaller figure wears a simple robe, belted in D, unbelted in C, arms crossed in front. In M the smaller figure is tonsured, arms extended down to side front. In V this figure, the same size as the main figure, has arms extended as if in conversation and wears a short robe and long hood. In F his arms are extended and he wears a short belted robe. The figure in L has hands

---

that units nine and ten were interpolated in the Oracles (personal communication from Marjorie Reeves).

[35] CD alone show two supplicating or threatening hands in picture nine (eight in CD's enumeration).

[36] Lerner, "On the Origins," 621, n. 24, sees in the image of the city in F the "remnants of a throne."

[37] Millet and Rigaux, "Aux origines," 137–138, call attention to the position of the hands in this image (and to the captions), noting the correspondence between the image in the Lunel and Monreale MSS and the copy of the "papalarius" owned by Bernard Délicieux.

[38] See Fleming, "Metaphors," 145, n. 33: in antique art, the hand to the head denotes dreaming, arms wrapped about the body, sleeping. The former gesture is also associated with grief or mourning.

clasped as if in prayer. CDF add a sun or stylized star, following the Leo Oracle feature of a stylized sun and moon. CD add a rectangle containing an ecclesiastical cross with two crossbars, not found in the Leo Oracles. Thus manuscripts of the *Genus nequam* sequence all show the same main image: a figure being called from sleep or great solitude by a herald or this person's awakening being witnessed by another.[39] (The figure has as well all the attributes of "Job on the the Dungheap."[40]) The addition of the ecclesiastical cross in CD, particularly in conjunction with the sun (Mal. 4:2), as well as the F scribe's identification "papa nudus," suggests that from the earliest point this figure was meant to signify a pope.[41]

Brief reference must be made here to the puzzling problem of whether or how the legend of Gregorius, the hermit who becomes pope, relates to this image in the *Genus nequam* prophecies. The main elements in the climax of the story—the miraculous directions from God, the finding of the holy hermit on the rock, the summons to become pope—are similar to the dramatic calling of the hermit-pope in the *Genus nequam* sequence. The Gregorius story goes back at least to the 1180s. Strangely, the Leo Oracles, which are undoubtedly the main source of the *Genus nequam* prophecies, appeared at the same period and with a similar image. Was there an older piece of folklore concerning a holy hermit on a rock miraculously summoned to become emperor/pope? If so, this may have contributed to the evolution of the angelic pope myth as developed later from Joachim's prophetic utterances which do not include this specific image.[42]

---

[39] For some of the many references to the sleeping hero awakened, see Fleming, "Metaphors," 146, n. 39; see also Heffner, "*Eyn wunderliche Weyssagung*," 33–41.

[40] Fleming, "Metaphors," 145, n. 33; Heffner, "*Eyn wunderliche Weyssagung*," 34–35, and 47, n. 4; also most recently Samuel Terrien, *The Iconography of Job Through the Centuries: Artists as Biblical Interpreters* (University Park, Pa., 1996). Characteristic features include the Job figure seated on stones or on a bench, foot on stool, often wearing classical pallium covering left shoulder, right side bare or garment with ends draped over arm, hand on knee, other hand on bench. Over time Job was seen less as righteous king and more often as suffering martyr, a forerunner of the suffering Christ or a type of the suffering Church against heretics, or as prophet of new life, linked to John the Baptist (Terrien, *Iconography of Job*, 90). Hand gestures changed to a flexed arm with head on fist or one hand to head; often one hand on knee, one leg still raised as if supported by a footstool, but no footstool. Job is often shown with Elihu, with Elihu either gesturing in debate or with arms crossed on chest. Many of these features are found in unit eleven of the *Genus nequam* images: the only element consistently missing is Job's sores, to be sure an element not always present in the traditional images of Job.

[41] Hugh of Novocastro, writing as early as 1315, refers to a "libellus of Roman pontiffs" and calls particular attention to the "papa nudus."

[42] On the Gregorius legend, see Heffner, "*Eyn wunderliche Weyssagung*," 39–41.

PICTURE 12

For picture number twelve, CDF's iconography (figure 18) is based on that of Leo Oracle thirteen, which shows a shroud-wrapped figure, sometimes identified as an emperor by the eagle near its head, borne aloft on the backs of four animals (although only three show clearly), while an angel anoints the figure with oil. CDF have these elements with minor variations, except that, instead of the shroud-wrapped figure, an angel holds a papal tiara over the four animals. CF omit the bird, D shows it in flight. F shows a sarcophagus, surmounted by arcs bearing four animal heads (figure 19). The animals in CD are two bears and two dog-like animals. What CDF and the Leo Oracle pictures have in common is an image suggesting both death and ascension, that is, the summoning of a "dead" figure to life. The number and position of the animals, the arc in F, the angel holding a scroll in C, call to mind the iconic language of Ezekiel's vision (Ezek. 1:1–28), the ascension of Elijah (2 Kings 2:11), as well as the language of the Apocalypse.[43]

In another group of manuscripts only residual traces of the dead figure remain in the supporting animals. MP show a haloed figure, apparently an angel, holding a papal tiara (a mitre in M), over the heads of two or four animals, four cubs in P, two bears and two dogs in M. The figure in M holds a book as well. Only LV show a tonsured pope on a throne or bench holding the tiara over the heads of four rabbits, with one hand, and with the other pointing towards the rabbits. The four copies LMPV retain in the number and position of the animals something of the iconographical significance of the more explicit imagery in CDF. Later copies of the *Genus nequam* prophecies show here a pope holding the tiara over the heads of sheep, the sheep in a cluster, mouths touching the flaps or fanons of the tiara, an image of the papal shepherd "feeding his sheep." The variations in treating this image may reflect the fact that the logical order in the source has been disturbed, that is, that the "mummified" figure should precede the man awakening.[44]

---

[43] For a recent discussion of the transmission and transformation of the images of apotheosis and ascension, see Michael Lieb, *The Visionary Mode: Biblical Prophecy, Hermeneutics, and Cultural Change* (Ithaca, N.Y., 1991); for antecedents and analogues see H. P. L'Orange, *Studies on the Iconography of Cosmic Kingship in the Ancient World* (Oslo, 1953), especially p. 36 on medieval symbols of cosmic kingship (sun, moon, stars), Fig. 88, a relief fragment of the ascension of Alexander (Castel S. Angelo, Rome), Fig. 89, ascension of Alexander (ivory casket in Darmstadt) and the connection between apotheosis and throne-ritual.

[44] See above, n. 34.

PICTURE 13

For picture thirteen, there is little variation: all are essentially similar, showing a pope being crowned by an angel. In all but V the pope is standing; in M the pope wears a mitre rather than the papal tiara (characteristic of M, only in picture fourteen does the pope wear a tiara). In LP the pope's gestures are similar to those in picture eleven. In CD the pope holds a pastoral staff, the angel a standard with a stylized *fleur de lis* atop. This picture corresponds to a combination of numbers fourteen and fifteen in the Leo Oracles, showing a king holding a sceptre, and an angel holding a vessel from which oil flows.

PICTURE 14

The key elements in picture fourteen are a pope and two angels. In some versions of the fifteenth Leo Oracle picture, the angel is anointing a kneeling king. Only F and V show the pope being crowned by the two angels; in all the others the two angels stand one at each side holding a tapestry or decorated cloth behind the bench or throne. The image in P has several features unique to it: the pope stands, facing front (his face blotted out), pope and two angels enclosed in a decorated arch. Below and to each side are the torsos of dog-like animals. The number and position of these animals call to mind both the images of apotheosis noted above in picture twelve and as well the so-called "throne of Dagobert," the folding chair, which "after its restoration at Saint-Denis in the twelfth century ... was regularly used for the coronation of the kings of France."[45]

PICTURE 15

The picture tradition for the fifteenth prophecy encompasses three versions and represents a clear departure from the concluding picture in the Leo Oracles, which shows emperor and patriarch together, the priestly figure in some examples anointing the secular figure, with no eschatological overtones. In what is apparently the earliest version, the fifteenth picture shows a pope holding a papal tiara in one hand and a book in the other, as in CDM. A second version, as in LPV, shows the pope holding tiara and

---

[45] Sumner McKnight Crosby, edited and completed by Pamela Z. Blum, *The Royal Abbey of Saint-Denis: From Its Beginnings to the Death of Suger, 475–1151* (New Haven, 1987), 45–46, here 45, also Fig. 19; see also François Bucher, *The Pamplona Bibles* (New Haven, 1970), vol. 1, 127–128, n. 70.

book as the fifteenth picture, and a crowned beast with human face, alone in LV, accompanied by a short prophecy in P, as a sixteenth image. The third version, as in F (figure 20) and characteristic of fifteenth-century manuscripts as well as the printed editions of the sixteenth century (figure 21), shows a pope holding a book in one hand and the papal tiara in the other, held over the head of a crowned and horned animal with human face. C is unique among fourteenth-century copies in showing a beaver as the sixteenth image.[46]

There are, as well, significant differences among the manuscripts showing the beast, FLPV. The Vatican copy shows the beast picture, with no accompanying text, but it adds a text from Nah. 3:12, foretelling the destruction of the city of Nineveh, to the body of the fifteenth prophecy. The Lunel manuscript shows the beast picture separately. The scribe and artist thought of it as an addition, for there is an *explicit* after picture fifteen, and it is preceded by five texts, including the pseudo-Hildegard "Insurgent gentes," and the Joachite text, "In die illa elevabitur draco. . . ."[47] The Monreale copy includes the caption, "Caput superbie," and a text from Dan. 4:13.[48] (The Paris Archives manuscript has the same caption and the text from Daniel, but the picture, here as elsewhere, has not been executed.) The Florentine manuscript shows a beast incorporated into picture fifteen, but one quite different from that in the Monreale, Lunel, and Vatican manuscripts, even allowing for the fact that F's artist was no professional. The beast in F, identified on its torso as Antichrist, has a headdress of ten horns or feathers, rather than a crown.[49]

The sequence of these additions needs some examination. Which came first? The image of the beast, then the Daniel text and caption, or was the text from Nahum added before the Daniel text? It can be said with certainty that the characteristic version of the late fourteenth century, and all subsequent versions, has the beast of picture sixteen incorporated into picture fifteen, and both texts, the Nahum text incorporated as the last sentence of prophecy fifteen, and the Daniel text usually following, but set

---

[46] See above, "Description of Manuscripts: C."

[47] See above, "Description of Manuscripts: L."

[48] See Daneu Lattanzi, "I 'Vaticinia Pontificum'," 792, n. 6; the text from Nahum is added below the Daniel text but in a later hand.

[49] F shows a pope, arms extended, holding a papal cross (with three crossbars) in one hand and the papal tiara in the other. Below the text of the prophecy in the same hand is the line: "papa cum libro in manu et cum metria." There is no book in the picture and the scribe makes no mention of the animal. See also Millet and Rigaux, "Aux origines," 140; Ruth Mellinkoff, *The Devil at Isenheim: Reflections of Popular Belief in Grünewald's Altarpiece* (Berkeley, 1988), 48–49, esp. Fig. 33; also eadem, "Demonic Winged Headgear," *Viator* 16 (1985): 367–381, esp. n. 71.

apart a bit. Since neither the Lunel nor the Florentine copy has the Nahum and the Daniel texts, while Vat. lat. 3819 has only the Nahum, and Paris Archives and Monreale only the Daniel text (with the Nahum text added separately and later in Monreale), the key question seems to be which came first, the addition of the text from Nahum or Daniel or the addition of the image?

Although it is clear that the Lunel, Paris, Monreale, and Vat. lat. 3819 versions belong to the same family, establishing the exact relation among them is more problematic. It is tempting to see the Lunel version as the earliest of the group, for its scribe clearly did not know of the addition of either the Daniel or Nahum text (although the Lunel copy does share with the Vatican copy a "later" version of picture twelve). The Vatican copy was executed later than any of the others and is the only one of the group to contain the Nahum text, so, on the basis of this admittedly limited evidence, it can be assumed that the Nahum text was a later addition than the Daniel text. The key issue, that is, were the texts in the Lunel copy and the Daniel text in the Monreale copy added to make sense of the image of the beast or was the beast an illustration of the texts, cannot, on the basis of the evidence at hand, be resolved. All that can be said with confidence about this middle stage is that, at one point, the beast appeared alone as a sixteenth prophecy, and that, at almost the same point, the text from Daniel (and the caption) were added to "complete" the prophecy.

The Yale and Florentine manuscripts represent slightly different recensions, even though the Yale version has clear affinities with LNPV, and the Florentine manuscript with A–CD. Iconographic features, particularly those in picture four, mark the Yale manuscript as a later version, yet picture fifteen shows only a pope and the prophecy has neither the Nahum nor the Daniel verses. The Florentine manuscript also does not have these verses, but shows a pope holding the papal tiara over a beast labelled "antichrist." It may well be that the beast was not part of the original image, for, as noted elsewhere, there are inconsistencies between the scribal description of the picture in F and the picture represented; the prophecies show signs of having been brought up to date where original identifications have been incompletely erased and new identifications substituted.[50]

Given the evidence of FNP, the beast must be a form of the Antichrist, yet, as a representation of the Antichrist, it is apparently unique to the *Genus nequam* prophecies. It is certainly not characteristic of the representations of the Antichrist found in the illustrated Apocalypses of the

---

[50] See above, "Description of Manuscripts: F."

period.[51] It shows similarities to beasts shown in some secular texts, as in a London manuscript (a Middle English version of *Mandeville's Travels*): Michael Camille describes this beast as a parody of the Muslim sacred cow, which is shown as half ox, half man, crowned and bearded.[52] A second instance, a beast uncrowned and lying on a covered altar, is shown in a Paris manuscript from the Duc de Berry's *Livre des Merveilles du Monde*, under the heading "Child Sacrifice to Muhammad."[53]

The simplest explanation may well be that the beast in the *Genus nequam* prophecies is an anti-type of the Lamb of God, although how common such a representation might be is open to question. Perhaps it is an anti-type in the guise of a secular ruler (i.e., Nebuchadnezzar as he is described in Dan. 4:30). In the Monreale manuscript, as noted above, the picture of the beast is accompanied by a text from Dan. 4:13: "Cor eius ab humano commutetur, et cor fere detur ei, et septem tempora mutentur super eum." This is a reference to King Nebuchadnezzar's dream, to be interpreted by Daniel. In Dan. 4:30 Nebuchadnezzar "was driven away from among men, and did eat grass like an ox, and his body was wet with the dew of heaven: till his hairs grew like the feathers of eagles, and his nails like birds' claws" (Douay-Rheims translation). The king must stay in exile until he realizes that the source of his power comes from God. The lines could be interpreted as meaning Nebuchadnezzar actually would change shape, and, in fact, Nebuchadnezzar is represented as an animal eating grass in an early fourteenth-century French *Bible Historiée* in the illustration for Dan. 4:30.[54]

If the beast is a representation of the Antichrist, then McGinn is correct in interpreting the scene "as the abdication of the pope before the coming of the Antichrist, a parallel to the similar abdication found in the imperial myths,"[55] but not, as noted above, in the final picture and text of the Leo Oracles. This view is supported by the testimony of the *Liber de Flore* and, later, the *Libellus* of Telesphorus, both of which describe the coming of the

---

[51] See above, "Description of Manuscripts," n. 22.

[52] Camille, *Gothic Idol*, 156–159 and Fig. 87, "The most holy idol of the Muslims" (London, British Library, MS. Royal 17.c.XXXVIII, fol. 38ᵛ).

[53] Camille, *Gothic Idol*, 159, Fig. 88 (Paris, Bibl. Nat., MS fr. 2810, fol. 185ʳ); in this instance the animal has the body of a lion.

[54] New York, Public Library, Spencer Collection MS. 22, Bible Historiée; for Nebuchadnezzar as a type of Antichrist, see Emmerson, *Antichrist in the Middle Ages*, 25–26. McGinn, *Visions*, 329 n. 17 notes a passage in a Joachite *Commentary on Jeremiah* ". . . in which Nebuchadnezzar and the Babylonian exile are used as a concordance for the coming imperial persecution of the Church." According to Reeves (*Influence of Prophecy*, 56), this text "was in existence at the latest by 1248 and probably by 1243."

[55] McGinn, " 'Pastor Angelicus'," 239, n. 49; see also Reeves, *Influence of Prophecy*, 403.

Antichrist during the reign of the third successor to the angelic pope.[56]

If it were not for the testimony of the *Liber de Flore* and the *Libellus,* there would be good reason to agree with McGinn's earlier assessment of the image, that it "might signify papal domination over the empire," an interpretation suggested earlier as well by Reeves.[57] This interpretation is not incompatible with viewing the beast as a secular Antichrist, as Reeves also has noted, but it departs somewhat from the particular eschatological emphasis of the *Liber de Flore* and the *Libellus* of Telesphorus. What seems very clear is that the shifting features of the final prophecy, text and image, could and did generate a variety of interpretations.[58]

---

[56] On the *Liber de Flore* and the *Libellus* see above, p. 4 and n. 13, also "Description of MSS," n. 60.

[57] McGinn, *Visions of the End,* 330, n. 56; Reeves, *Influence of Prophecy,* 403, eadem, "Some Popular Prophecies," 114.

[58] Reeves, "Some Popular Prophecies," 123; Heffner, "*Eyn wunderliche Weyssagung,*" 56–57 and 85; see also Lerner, "On the Origins," 623, n. 7 and 628, n. 42, where he suggests that the iconography of CD ". . . and the textual evidence of Hugh de Novocastro . . . show that the last pope is setting down his tiara, the symbol of the papacy's worldly rule, in favor of a mitre, the symbol of spiritual rule." Elsewhere Lerner notes that the originator of the prophecies "surely . . . believed or hoped that after the succession of corrupt pontiffs an eschatological revolution would install one or more humble and just popes who would reign under the aegis of angels and that one such pope would lay down his tiara before the coming of Antichrist" (628).

Vrsus vegni vrsa catulos pariens. et in V roman septus
cruciabit nonā. et in xxxvi. annos miser ambulabit
primus finis fere habentis. v. filios. A. figurie. n. vno
due vt. Siea autē tempus vmbaros vre recipe. Cum antē
ruderis vrsam matre caui. miserabiliter luge. in latitudine
teh in latitudine teh vt a deo confectris. aurihii. multa de
cipis nequissima sub pelle ahena. purtata eo. vr vrsum faci
lem coniti. Sirus abstondis dereptom. inimicos facientem.
Sicut autē bene manes tales. nutris vonos. vt lulvas
ustos in medio tempestatū siunt adulatores. et temp ma
infestabit cogitacones.

In batent forma psul dic her t nouma.
Attrahe ꝑ primū medio rege. pringe ꝑ imu
Cothge sustenta. sumula usa. morbidi lenta.

Figure 1: *Vaticinium I:* pope, bear, and nursing cubs.
Oxford, Bodleian Library, MS Douce 88, fol. 140ʳ.

Serpens qn̄ onis consumpt uelone nū bꝰ quos lactas ⁊ leneris penast̄ ⁊ mor̄ er
prudis ginus peter pinas fue abraes scipm̄ et̄ res · ser dn̄s ypoclim̄ ostret quo
enī mali faues · o tu liens faue canis ad mirē alieno mortuu quo tu sers bonū ꝙ
misto qui apis os ad pusillos quo cructab̄ ubū intet · ⳨ et̄o a⸱ filis alia serā uo
ras ⳨ prns ad mdia tue ingro ⁊ mḡ tot̄ pūal liue atonis mamfestas se͛
ssigurīs uisilibꝰ qui succedit pino suu cristes serpēs miser restructor urse · o
quo es esca nisor cornor criste · eni genus ablhinabile cor ⁊ ab onēr mirabilis
turlans te ipm̄ simil ⁊ auutaue genū tuū cab̄ stępt tueti.

Figure 2: *Vaticinium II*: pope, serpent, and birds.
Cambridge, Corpus Christi College, MS 404, fol. 88ᵛ.

Figure 3: *Vaticinium II:* pope, tree with birds and serpent, kneeling figure.
Yale, University Library, T. E. Marston MS 225, fol. 15ᵛ.

Figure 4: *Vaticinium II:* (lower register) pope, bird on standard, dragon.
Vatican Library, MS Vat. lat. 3819, fol. 147ʳ.

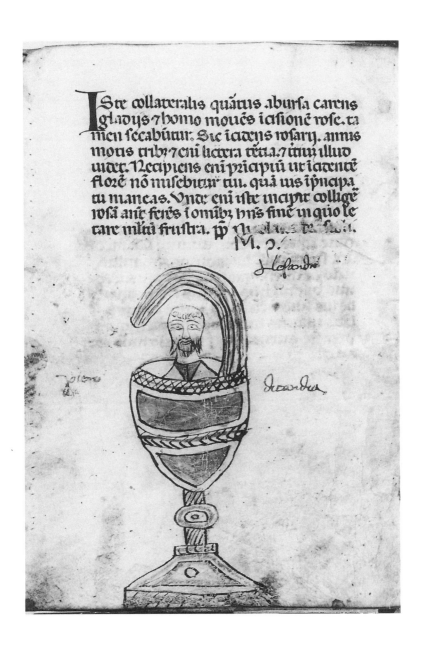

Figure 5: *Vaticinium IV*: vessel or font and head.
Florence, Biblioteca Riccardiana, MS 1222B, fol. 2ᵛ.

Figure 6: *Vaticinia IV–V:* sickle-bearer.
Cambridge, Corpus Christi College, MS 404, fol. 89v.

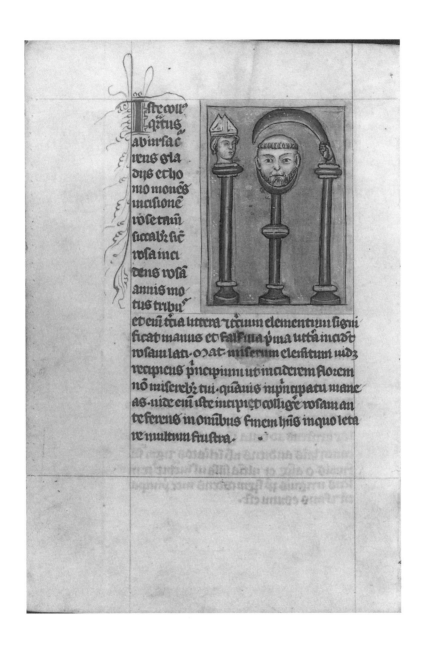

Iste collo=
quitur
ad uniuerfa=
cetens ola
dus et ho=
mo monet
incisione
role tantu
fucabit fic
rosa inca
dens rofam
annis mo=
tus tribu=
et enim tria littera ї tertium elementium figni=
ficat manus et falſma pma utta incabs
rosam lati ozat miferum cleriſtrum uidz
recipiens principium ut incaderim florem
no mifereb tui quamus inprincipatu mane=
as nide enim iſte incipirp colligie rosam an=
te ferens in onubus finem hus inquo leta
re multum fruſtra

Figure 7: *Vaticinium IV*: columns, heads, scimitar.
Yale, University Library, T. E. Marston MS 225, fol. 16ᵛ.

Figure 8: *Vaticinium V*: sickle-bearer (monk with cowl, small figure).
Yale, University Library, T. E. Marston MS 225, fol. 17[r].

ª Elatio ᵇ paupertatis, obedientia, caſtitas, Caſtrimargiæ,
& Hypocritarum deſtructio.
ª al. legitur folummodo vox Elatio pro titulo, & nil aliud.
a al. paupertas.

VATICINIVM XX.

VATICINIO XX.

ª *Elatione* ᵇ *della pouertà, obedientia, caſtità, deſtruttione della cupidigia sfrenata di mangiare, & de gl'Hipocriti.*
a al. ſi legge in alcuni libri ſolamente la uoce Elatione, per titolo, & nien
te altro. *b* al. pouerta.

Figure 9: *Vaticinium V*: sickle-bearer (pope).
Pasquilino Regiselmo, *Vaticinia sive Prophetiae Abbatis Joachimi
et Anselmi Episcopi Marsicani* (Venice, 1589), unpaged, *Vaticinium XX*.

Heu. heu miſeria ſuſtinene colores ꝑpaſſiones. Ciuitas eni miſerabile ut appareat luiii mos tenebit arcaiia paruur tꝑs. occeus cui ire ꝫeffuſio ſanguinu. Jn cenaiiu incipiente no cōfidct i quique principatus. Jno narchia tua draconem ꝯſtringet que occidit libm. fruſtra lauabut membra no ceſſa. ꝫadpuꝑgna iteſtina exacata inumerabile multitudinem oc ōc gladio amiliaria ſex ſeptē numeratas. Et omnis multiplicabitur formicatioiii. Et occet maculatus adulter raptor ꝫiuuſtus ſoꝯmita uidebit ulamu luiii aiic oculos.

.M. .6.

Figure 10: *Vaticinium VIII*: cityscape or fortress under siege.
Florence, Biblioteca Riccardiana, MS 1222B, fol. 4ᵛ.

item conulcta falafer quatuor in e̅
cum te ſcribo prīncipatus aut omī
quem oſumpſeri gladio trīpla
ypolonum poſt paululum reſuſcita
to tres aut annos in mundo uniⁱ
ſener uato in inſulim dieabi tribi
ſombt in medio ſmaſio yparatus
in abhomīnacione erit·

☩laca antem quartum qꝫ fi
 lius urſe paſcentis figura
manifeſtat locam amoꝰ
bice adiuncꝰ ſolus manifeſta
bit micḣ armais ·prīnas enim
lus urtutum alioꝛ plus adviſpe
ct arra armos pꝫn inueniſti fine
dulaſſimū ſolus columabis a g̅
a et morturis reliquies potentaſ
ſime potenaas fic cum viibiem
bere nuentes potenaas· Deo fi
in balahe ſectabuntur·

☩ha urſa piſceus catulus
ſe m onimbꝫ illa prīma
in umbra trū ſcapta ua·
tempoꝛ natuitas aboꝛtiua in ul
tima ei ſcabit ultime cſoclaueꝛ ꝫ
aut uraaſqꝫ coronas manifeſtat
oniuocuem totus potꝛue· po
teſtas ceuobra ad locū pꝛimum
en inuⁱſa tui woibunt
rtineus paſſiones autea
muſabit ut appat inue
moꝛ tenebit arra prūm tempuꝰ
ceoruꝰ e̅ ut te effuſio ſaṅguinū·
unrẽ nam incipicutres nō retia
eut et quinqꝫ prīnapatus amo
nintha tua diadonii contingẽt
quedadit libin fruſtratim laii
abiut membra ultuꝰ nō cella a
ad pugnā inteſtina ceritata a n̅
naturabile multitudinem ceⁱſ
gladio ad onliariam ſer ſeptrin
inniata quomo impliet forti
catōue·e cete magalatus adulf
raptor muiſtus ſodomita urde
bunt urtmū lumen au̅ ocluſ·
Dona gꝛū ſȳmoia ceſſabit·

☩bpinam figuraſti anni
caam pacem ſenſu urſ
nium ſicut mulai ſener
attuiato ḣus ſenſum uemeus

Figure 12: *Vaticinium IX:* pope, crossed standards or banners, fox. Monreale, Biblioteca Comunale, MS XXV.F.17, fol. 10ʳ.

ᵖᵗᵉſᵗₐₛ.

Figure 13: *Vaticinium* X: empty throne.
Cambridge, Corpus Christi College, MS 404, fol. 92ʳ.

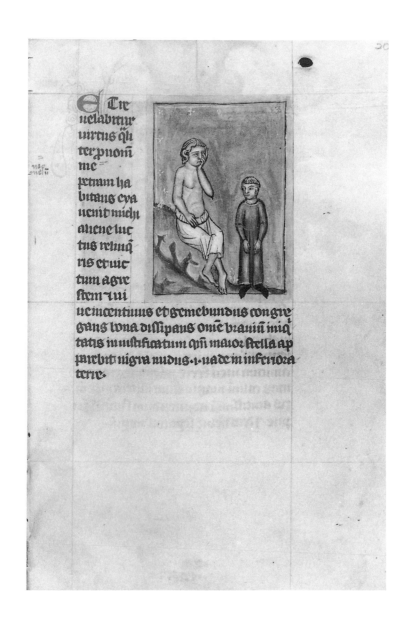

uc incentiuus et gemebundus congregans bona dissipans omne brauium iniq
tatis in iustificatum cpm maior stella ap
parebit nigra nudus .i. uade in inferiora
terie.

Figure 14: *Vaticinium XI*: figure on rock (hermit summoned forth).
Yale, University Library, T. E. Marston MS 225, fol. 20ʳ.

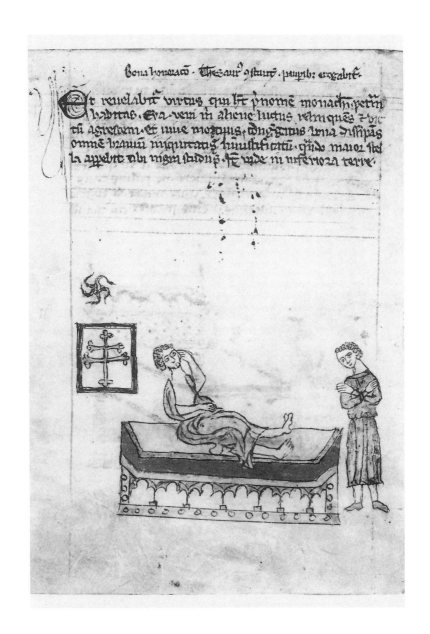

Figure 15: *Vaticinium XI:* figure on sarcophagus (hermit summoned forth).
Oxford, Bodleian Library, MS Douce 88, fol. 144ᵛ.

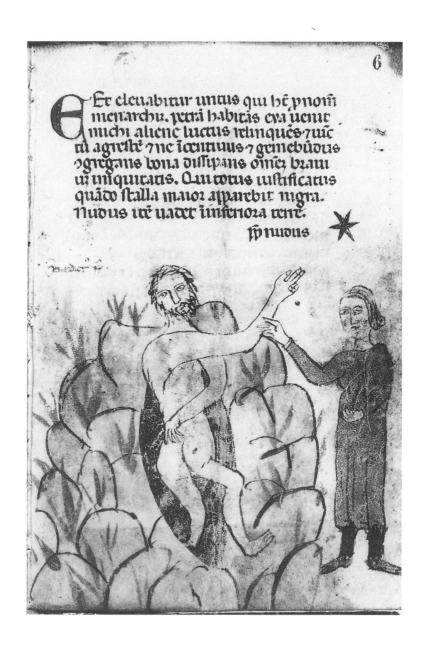

Er eleuabitur untus qui bē pnoīn
menarchu. petra habitas eva uenit
michi aliene luctus relinques 7 uīc
tū agrestē 7 nic īcontinuus 7 gemebundus
egregans bona dissipans omeq braui
uz iniquitatis. Qui totus iustificatus
quōto stalla maior apparebit nigra.
Nudus ite uadet inferiora tenē.
sp nudus

Figure 16: *Vaticinium XI:* naked figure emerging from rock
(hermit summoned forth).
Florence, Biblioteca Riccardiana, MS 1222B, fol. 6ʳ.

Figure 17: *Vaticinium XI:* seated figure (hermit summoned forth).
Monreale, Biblioteca Comunale, MS XXV.F.17, fol. 12ʳ.

Mortuus nñe + obltᵉ alþᵃⁱˢ noiūñc mula q̄ūuˢ nullus ꝯtū iuicat. Sⁱᵉ
ab ebiͤctate meᵃuiſᵉⁿᵘˢ ex in ſtᵃⁱˢ ſtᵉpᵉ tūbʳᵉ iſtⁱ ꝼpꝯ ʒ al° enⁱ mⁱᵃⁱⁿ
ꝼceⁱ iͤlo cõtea ꝓ iuiabⁱl e damabⁱ maxⁱñe · itͤ ꝵ ſetⁱⁿacoͤ aᵈ
ocucᵉtᵉ ſtᶜpⁱcoll ꝼuetueⁱ uⁱᵃ ꞇꝵtoʳᵉ aⁱua meⁱ ſeʳe iſⁱ iⁱᵉgⁱaˢ tᵒ
mos coluⁱ mⁱᵃⁿſueⁱ meꞇᵉ alꞇᵉ uↄeus aↄcutⁱſ̄ſumᵃ aᵈ uⁱᵈeᵈᵘ ſiꞇunⁱ papꞇe
et itͤ ſ̄obⁱe ſtᶜpⁱcollꞁⁱs muꝯⁱā

Iſtͤ ꝼuⁱt mᵍᵒ mↄᶜꝵ ⁊ a bediͤ ꞇ papacⁱᵃ tᵉꞇᵉ aⁿⁱᵒ
⁊ obiⁱt aⁿ ſin ſⁱⁱ ⱥⁿↄyͤ a° dⁿⁱ · ⁀ⁱ · ꞇꞇⁱ · ꞁoⁱ°   iↄ ꝺcetʳ

Figure 18: *Vaticinium XII*: angel holding papal tiara born aloft by animals.
Cambridge, Corpus Christi College, MS 404, fol. 93ʳ.

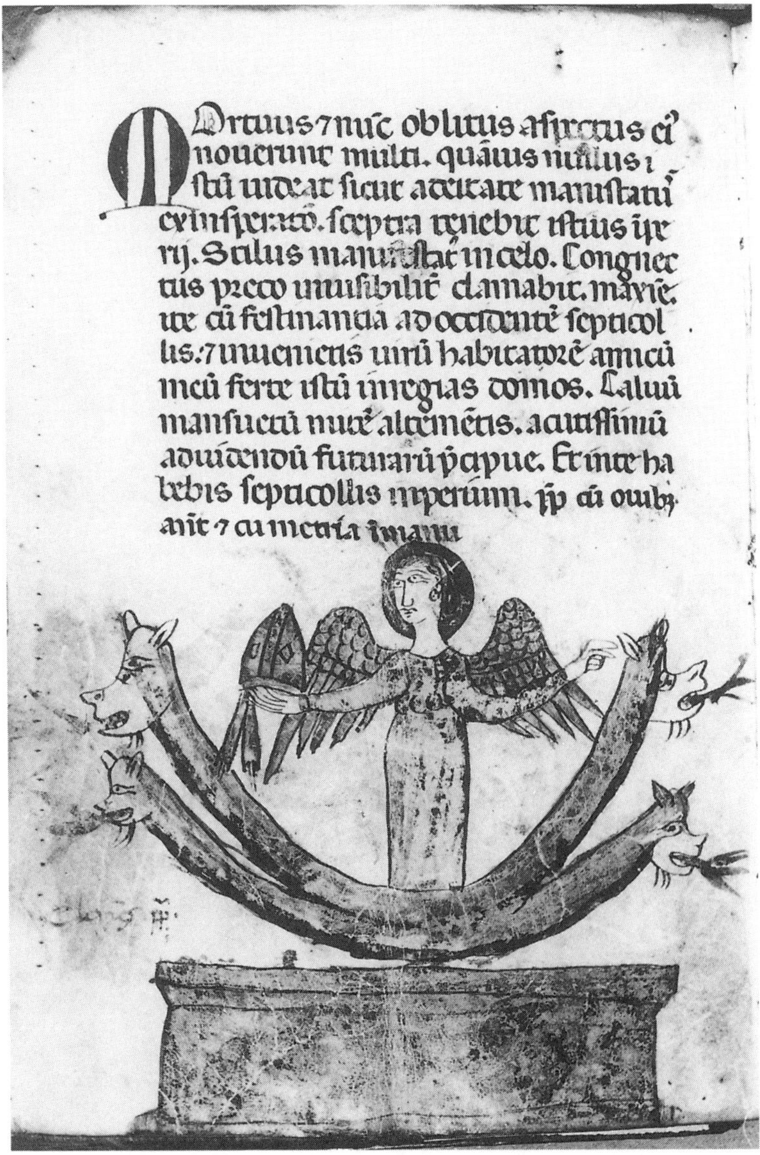

Ortuus 7 nuc oblitus aspectus est
nouerunt multi. quauis nullus i
stu uideat sicut aoctate manifestatu
et inspectato. sceptra tenebit istius ir
rij. Salus manifestat in celo. Congruec
tus preco inuisibilit clamabit. marie.
tur cu festinancia ad occidente septicol
lis. 7 inueniens uiru habitatore amicu
meu ferre istu inuegras domos. Caluu
mansuetu nudu alce metis. acutissimu
aduidendu futurarum papue. Et inter ha
bebis septicollis imperium. sp cu omib3
anit 7 cu metria in manu

Figure 19: *Vaticinium XII:* angel holding papal tiara, sarcophagus,
arcs with animal heads.
Florence, Biblioteca Riccardiana, MS 1222B, fol. 6ᵛ.

Bona uita muenusti ab ingeneratioe.
a uirtute aut acepisti plusq fortuna.
ß nequaq uirtuosa luctaberis gsam
Inuidia eni ptingnens iudicia tibi no
centia. No priuaberis aforte desup deo
gratias amen. C ꝑ cu libro in manu
꩜ cu metria.

Figure 20: *Vaticinium XV*: pope, beast with human face.
Florence, Biblioteca Riccardiana, MS 1222B, fol. 8ʳ.

Figure 21: *Vaticinium XV*: pope, beast with human face.
Pasquilino Regiselmo, *Vaticinia sive Prophetiae Abbatis Joachimi et Anselmi Episcopi Marsicani* (Venice, 1589), unpaged, *Vaticinium XXX*.

Bibliography: Works Cited

MANUSCRIPTS

Austria
Vienna. Österreichische Nationalbibliothek, MS 13648 [Suppl. 1071].

France
Arras. Bibliothèque Municipale, MS 138.
Carpentras. Bibliothèqeue Inguimbertine, MS 340.
Lunel. Bibliothèque de Louis Médard à la Bibliothèque Municipale, MS 7.
Paris. Archives Nationales, MS JJ 28.
———. Bibliothèque Nationale, MS]at. 503.
———. Bibliothèque Nationale, MS lat. 3184.
———. Bibliothèque Nationale, MS lat. 12018.

Germany
Nuremberg. Stadtbibliothek, MS Cent. IV.32.

Great Britain
Cambridge. Corpus Christi College, MS 404.
London. British Library, MS Add. 39660.
Oxford. Bodleian Library, MS Douce 88.
———. Bodleian Library, MS Barocci 170.

Italy
Florence. Biblioteca Riccardiana, MS 1222B.
Monreale. Biblioteca Comunale, MS XXV.F.17.
Vaticano, Città del. Biblioteca Apostolica Vaticana, MS Vat. lat. 3816.
———. Biblioteca Apostolica Vaticana, MS Vat. lat. 3819.
———. Biblioteca Apostolica Vaticana, MS Vat. lat. 3822.
———. Biblioteca Apostolica Vaticana, MS Reg. 580.
———. Biblioteca Apostolica Vaticana, MS Ross. lat. 374.
———. Biblioteca Apostolica Vaticana, MS Ross. lat. 753.

Switzerland
Sankt Gallen. Vadianische Bibliothek, MS 342.

United States
New York. Public Library, Spencer Collection MS 22.
Syracuse, New York. MS Syracuse University Von Ranke 90.
New Haven, Conn. Yale, University Library, T. E. Marston MS 225.

PRINTED SOURCES AND SECONDARY WORKS

Albert the Great: Man and Beasts, De Animalibus (Books 22–26). Translated by James J. Scanlon. Medieval & Renaissance Texts & Studies vol. 47. Binghamton, 1987.

Alexander, Paul J. "Byzantium and the Migration of Literary Works and Motifs: The Legend of the Last Roman Emperor." *Mediaevalia et Humanistica* (1971), n.s. 2: 47–82.

———. *The Byzantine Apocalyptic Tradition*. Edited by Dorothy deF. Abrahamse. Berkeley, 1985.

Avril, François. "Les manuscrits enluminés de la collection Médard à la bibliothèque de Lunel." *La Bibliothèque de Louis Médard à Lunel*, 163–168. Montpellier, 1987.

Baethgen, Friedrich. *Der Engelpapst: Idee und Erscheinung*. Leipzig, 1943.

Barber, Malcolm. *The Trial of the Templars*. Cambridge, 1978.

Beer, Rudiger R. *Unicorn: Myth and Reality*. Translated by Charles M. Stern. New York, 1977.

La Bible Moralisée conservé à Oxford, Paris et Londres. Reproduction intégrale du manuscrit du XIIIe siècle, 5 vols. Études sur la Bible Moralisée illustrée, edited by A. de Laborde. Paris, 1911–1927.

Bignami-Odier, Jeanne. "Notes sur deux manuscrits de la Bibliothèque du Vatican." *Mélanges d'archéologie et d'histoire de l'École française de Rome* 54 (1937): 211–241.

———. *Études sur Jean de Roquetaillade*. Paris, 1952.

Boase, T. S. R. *Boniface VIII*. London, 1933.

Brown, Elizabeth A. R. "Royal Salvation and the Needs of State in Late Capetian France." In *Order and Innovation in the Middle Ages: Essays in Honor of Joseph R. Strayer*, edited by William C. Jordan, Bruce McNab, and Teofilio Ruiz, 365–383. Princeton, 1976

———, and Lerner, Robert E. "On the Origins and Import of the Columbinus Prohecy." *Traditio* 95 (1989–1990): 220–256.

Burr, David. *The Persecution of Peter Olivi*. Transactions of the American Philosophical Society, vol. 66, part 5. Philadelphia, 1976.

―――. *Olivi and Franciscan Poverty: The Origins of the "Usus Pauper" Controversy.* Philadelphia, 1989.

―――. Review of *Paupertas Christi et apostolorum: L'ideale francescano in discussione (1322–1324)* (Rome, 1990). *Speculum* 67 (1992): 748–750.

Calkins, Robert G. *Illuminated Books of the Middle Ages.* Ithaca, New York, 1983.

Camille, Michael. *The Gothic Idol: Ideology and Image-Making in Medieval Art.* Cambridge, 1989.

―――. *Image on the Edge: The Margins of Medieval Art.* Cambridge, Mass., 1992.

A Catalogue of Printed Books . . . Bequeathed by Francis Douce, Esq. to the Bodleian Library. Oxford, 1840.

Clark, Willene B., and McMunn, Meradith T. eds. *Birds and Beasts of the Middle Ages: The Bestiary and its Legacy.* Philadephia, 1989.

Crosby, Sumner McKnight. *The Royal Abbey of Saint-Denis: From Its Beginnings to the Death of Suger, 475–1151.* Edited and completed by Pamela Z. Blum. New Haven, 1987.

Daneu Lattanzi, Angela. "I 'Vaticinia Pontificum' ed un codice monrealese del sec. XIII–XIV." *Atti della Reale Accademia di scienze, lettere e arti di Palermo* ser. 4, vol. 3 (2) (1943): 757–792.

―――. *I manoscritti ed incunabli miniati della Sicilia,* vol. 2. Palermo, 1977.

―――. "Simboli e profezie medioevo." *Sicilia* 12 (Dec. 1955), unpaginated.

Daniel, E. Randolph. *The Franciscan Concept of Mission in the High Middle Ages.* Lexington, 1975.

Dante Alighieri. *The Divine Comedy.* Edited and translated by Charles Singleton. 3 vols. Bollingen Series 80. Princeton, 1970.

de Dmitrewski, Michel. "Fr. Bernard Délicieux, O.F.M., sa lutte contra l'Inquisition de Carcassonne et d'Albi, son procès, 1297–1319." *AFH* 17 (1924): 183–218, 313–337, 457–488; 18 (1925): 3–22.

Degenhart, Bernard, and Schmitt, Annegrit. *Corpus der italienischen Zeichnungen 1300–1450.* 5 vols. (vol. 1, Parts 1–4). Berlin, 1968.

Delaborde, Henri François. *Layettes du Trésor des Chartes.* vol. 5. Paris, 1909.

De Winter, Patrick M. *La bibliothèque de Philippe le Hardi.* Paris, 1985.

Donckel, Emil. "Studien über die Prophezeiung des Fr. Telesforus von Cosenza, O.F.M. (1365–1386)." *AFH* 26 (1933): 29–104, 284–312.

Douie, Decima L. *The Nature and Effect of the Heresy of the Fraticelli.* Manchester, 1932.

Dugan, Joseph J. "Editing Medieval Texts: How to Do It." *University Publishing* 9 (Summer, 1980): 12, 17.

Dupuy, Pierre. *Histoire du differend d'entre le pape Boniface VIII. et Philippes le*

Bel Roy de France. Paris, 1655. Reprint. Tucson, Ariz., 1963.

Dykmans, Marc. *Robert d'Anjou: la vision bienheureuse.* Miscellanea Historiae Pontificiae 30. Rome, 1970.

Eckhardt, Caroline, ed. *The "Prophetia Merlini" of Geoffrey of Monmouth: A Fifteenth-Century English Commmentary.* Medieval Academy of America Anniversary Monographs 8. Cambridge, Mass., 1982.

Elizondo, Fidelis. "Bulla 'Exiit qui seminat' Nicholas III (14 August 1279)." *Laurentianum* 4 (1963): 59–119.

Emmerson, Richard K. *Antichrist in the Middle Ages: A Study of Medieval Apocalypticism, Art, and Literature.* Seattle, Wash., 1981.

Fabricius, Johann Albert. *Bibliotheca Latina mediae et infimae aetatis,* vol. 3–4. Florence, 1858.

Fauçon, Maurice. *La librairie des papes d'Avignon, sa formation, sa composition, ses catalogues (1316–1420).* Paris, 1886.

Finke, Heinrich. *Aus den Tagen Bonifaz VIII.* Vorreformationsgeschichtliche Forschungen, vol. 2. Münster, 1902.

Fleming, Martha. "Sibylla: De Imperatore." Ph.D. dissertation, Boston University, 1975.

———. "Metaphors of Apocalypse and Revolution in Some Fourteenth-Century Popular Prophecies." *The High Middle Ages,* edited by Penelope Mayo. ACTA 8 (Binghamton, 1980): 131–146.

Foulet, Alfred, and Speer, Mary Blakely. *On Editing Old French Texts.* Lawrence, Kans., 1979.

Freyhan, R. "Joachism and the English Apocalypse." *Journal of the Warburg and Courtauld Institutes* 18 (1955): 211–244.

Friedlander, Alan. "Jean XXII et les Spirituels: le cas de Bernard Délicieux." *La papauté d'Avignon et le Languedoc 1316–1342.* Cahiers de Fanjeaux 26 (Toulouse, 1991): 221–236.

Garufi, Carlo Alberto. *Catalogo illustrato del tabulario di S. Maria Nuova in Monreale.* Palermo, 1902.

Greco, Maria Luisa Scuricini. *Miniature riccardiane.* Florence, 1958.

Grundmann, Herbert. "*Liber de Flore*: Eine Schrift der Franziskaner-Spiritualen aus dem Anfang des 14. Jahrhunderts." *HJ* 49 (1929): 33–91.

———. "Die Papstprophetien des Mittelalters." *Archiv für Kulturgeschichte* 19 (1929): 77–138. Reprinted in *Ausgewählte Aufsätze. 2: Joachim von Fiore.* MGH Schriften 25, 2. Hanover, 1977.

———. "Über den Apokalypsen-Kommentar des Minoriten Alexander." MGH, Scriften 25, 2. Hanover, 1977: 58–69.

Guébin, Pascal, and Lyon, Ernest, eds. *Petri Vallium Sarnaii monachi Hystoria Albigensis.* Paris, 1926–1939.

Hall, J. B. "The Editing and Emendation of Medieval Latin Texts: Two Case Histories." *Studi Medievali* 3rd ser. 19.1 (1978): 443–466.

Hassig, Debra. *Medieval Bestiaries: Text, Image, Ideology.* Cambridge, 1995.

Heffner, David. *"Eyn wunderliche Weyssagung vom dem Babstumb:* Medieval Prophecy into Reformation Polemic." Ph.D. dissertation, University of Pennsylvania, 1991.

Herde, Peter. *Cölestin V (1294): der Engelpapst.* Stuttgart, 1981.

Henkel, Nikolaus. *Studien zum Physiologus im Mittelalter.* Tübingen, 1976.

Hinkle, William M. *The Fleurs de Lis of the Kings of France 1285–1488.* Carbondale and Edwardsville, 1991.

Historia Anglicana. Edited by Henry Richards Luard. Rolls Series. London, 1859.

Holder-Egger, O. "Italienische Prophetieen des 13. Jahrhunderts III," *NA* 33 (1908): 97–187.

Hugh de Novocastro. *Tractatus de victoria Christi contra Antichristum.* Nurenberg, 1471.

Hult, David. F. "Reading It Right: The Ideology of Text Editing." *The New Medievalism.* Edited by Marina Brownlee, Kevin Brownlee, and Steven G. Nichols, 113–130. Baltimore, 1991.

Imperator Leonis Cognomine Sapientis Oracula cum Figuris et Antigua Graeca Paraphrasi [Leo Oracles], ed. Petrus Lambecius. In *Patrologus Cursus Completus: Series Graeca,* ed. J. P. Migne, 107: 1121–1168. Paris, 1857–1876.

James, Montague Rhodes. *The Ancient Libraries of Canterbury and Dover.* Cambridge, 1903.

———. *A Descriptive Catalogue of the Manuscripts in the Library of Corpus Christi College, Cambridge.* Cambridge, 1912.

Joachim, Harold, and McCullugh, Suzanne. *Italian Drawings from the Art Institute of Chicago.* Chicago, 1979.

Johannes de Rupescissa. *Liber secretorum eventuum.* Edited and translated by Christine Morerod-Fattebert, Historical Introduction by Robert E. Lerner. Freiburg, Switzerland, 1994.

Kelly, Samantha. "The *Visio Fratris Johannis:* Prophecy and Politics in Late-Thirteenth-Century Italy." *Florensia: Bollettino del Centro Internazionale di Studi Gioachimiti* 8–9 (1994–1995): 7–42.

Ker, Neil. *Medieval Libraries of Great Britain.* 2nd ed. London, 1964.

Kerby-Fulton, Kathryn. "Hildegard of Bingen and Anti-Mendicant Propaganda," *Traditio* 43 (1987): 386–399.

———. *Reformist Apocalypticism and "Piers Plowman."* Cambridge, 1990.

Kermode, Frank. *An Appetite for Poetry.* Cambridge, Mass., 1989.

————. *Poetry, Narrative, History.* Cambridge, Mass., 1990.

Lambert. Malcolm D. *Franciscan Poverty.* London, 1961.

Lambertini, Roberto. *Apologia e crescita dell'identità francescana (1255–1279).* Rome, 1990.

Leff, Gordon. *Heresy in the Later Middle Ages: The Relation of Heterodoxy to Dissent c. 1250–c. 1450.* 2 vols. Manchester, 1967

Lerner, Robert E. *The Powers of Prophecy: The Cedar of Lebanon Vision from the Mongol Onslaught to the Dawn of the Enlightenment.* Berkeley and Los Angeles, 1983.

————, and Moynihan, Robert. *Weissagungen über die Päpste: Vat: Ross 374 (Einführungsband zur Faksimile ausgabe de Cod. Vat. Ross. 374).* Stuttgart, 1985.

————. "On the Origins of the Earliest Latin Pope Prophecies: A Reconsideration," *Fälschungen im Mittelalter,* MGH Schriften 33, 5 (Hanover, 1988): 611–635.

————. "Recent Work on the Origins of the *Genus nequam* Prophecies." *Florensia: Bollettino del Centro Internazionale di Studi Gioachimiti* 7 (1993): 141–157.

Lieb, Michael. *The Visionary Mode: Biblical Prophecy, Hermeneutics, and Cultural Change.* Ithaca, N.Y., 1991.

L'Orange. H. P. *Studies on the Iconography of Cosmic Kingship in the Ancient World.* Oslo, 1953.

Mango, Cyril. "The Legend of Leo the Wise." *ZRVI* 6 (1960): 59–93.

Mann, Horace K. and Johannes Hollnsteiner. *The Lives of the Popes,* vol. 16. London, 1932.

Marrow, James. *Passion Iconography in Northern European Art of the Late Middle Ages and Early Renaissance.* Kortrijk, Belgium, 1979.

McCulloch, Florence. *Medieval Latin and French Bestiaries.* Chapel Hill, 1962.

McCann, Jerome J. *A Critique of Modern Textual Criticism.* Chicago, 1983.

McGinn, Bernard. "Angel Pope and Papal Antichrist." *Church History* 47 (1978): 155–173.

————. *Visions of the End: Apocalyptic Traditions in the Middle Ages.* New York, 1979.

————. "Portraying Antichrist in the Middle Ages." *The Use and Abuse of Eschatology in the Middle Ages,* edited by Werner Verbeke, Daniel Verhelst, and Andries Welkenhuysen, 1–48. Leuven, 1988.

————. " 'Pastor Angelicus': Apocalyptic Myth and Political Hope in the Fourteenth Century," *Santi e santità nel secolo XIV,* 221–251. Perugia, 1989.

————. *Antichrist: Two Thousand Years of the Human Fascination with Evil.* San Francisco, 1994,

Mellinkoff, Ruth. *Outcasts: Signs of Otherness in Northern European Art of the Late Middle Ages.* Berkeley and Los Angeles, 1993.

———. *The Devil at Isenheim: Reflections of Popular Belief in Grünewald's Altarpiece.* Berkeley and Los Angeles, 1988.

———. "Demonic Winged Headgear." *Viator* 16 (1985): 367–381.

Menache, Sophia. *Clement V.* Cambridge Studies in Medieval Thought and Life, Fourth Series. Cambridge, 1998.

Millet, Hélène, and Rigaux, Dominique. *"Ascende calve:* Quand l'historien joue au prophetè." *Studi Medievali* 33 (1992): 695–720.

———. "Un puzzle prophétique dans le manuscrit 6213 de la Biblioteca Nacional de Madrid." *Revue Mabillon* n.s. (=64) (1992): 139–177.

———. "Aux origines du succès des *Vaticinia de summis pontificibus.*" *Fin du monde et signes des temps: visionnaires et prophètes en France méridionale (fin XIIIᵉ–début XVᵉ siècle).* Cahiers de Fanjeaux 27 (Toulouse, 1992): 129–156.

Mitchell, W. J. T. *Picture Theory: Essays on Verbal and Visual Representation.* Chicago and London, 1994.

Mollat, Guillaume. *The Popes at Avignon 1305–1378.* London and New York, 1963.

Moorman, John. *A History of the Franciscan Order: From its Origins to the Year 1517.* Oxford, 1968.

Nichols, Stephen G., and Wenzel, Siegfried, eds. *The Whole Book: Cultural Perspectives on the Medieval Miscellany.* Ann Arbor, Mich., 1996.

Oakley, John Patrick. "John XXII, the Franciscans, and the Natural Right to Property." Ph.D. dissertation, Cornell University, 1987.

Ong, Walter J. *Orality and Literacy: The Technologizing of the Word.* London, 1982.

Pächt, Otto, and Alexander, J. J. G. *Illuminated Manuscripts in the Bodleian Library.* 3 vols. Oxford, 1973.

The Pamplona Bibles. Edited by François Bucher. 2 vols. New Haven, 1970.

Patterson, Lee. "The Logic of Textual Criticism and the Way of Genius." *Negotiating the Past: The Historical Understanding of Medieval Literature.* Madison. Wisc., 1987, 77–113.

Pickens, Rupert. *The Songs of Jaufré Rudel.* Toronto, 1978.

Pipini, Francesco. *Chronicon.* In *Rerum Italicarum Scriptores,* edited by L. Muratori. OS 9: cols. 724–751. Milan, 1721.

Piur, Paul. "Oraculum Angelicum Cyrilli nebst dem Kommentar des Pseudojoachim." In *Vom Millelalter zur Reformation,* edited by Karl Burdach, vol. 4, 223–343. Berlin, 1912.

Poesch, Jessie. "Antichrist Imagery in Anglo-French Apocalypse Manuscripts." Ph.D. dissertation, University of Pennsylvania, 1966.

Randall, Lilian M. C. *Medieval and Renaissance Manuscripts in the Walters Art Gallery*, vol. 2: *France, 875–1420*. Baltimore, 1989.

Reeves, Marjorie. *The Influence of Prophecy in the Later Middle Ages: A Study in Joachimism*. Oxford, 1969.

———. "Some Popular Prophecies from the Fourteenth to the Seventeenth Centuries." In *Popular Belief and Practice*, edited by G. J. Cuming and Derek Baker. *Studies in Church History* 8 (1972): 107–134.

———. "The *Vaticinia de Summis Pontificibus*: A Question of Authority" [for "Authorship"]. In *Intellectual Life in the Middle Ages: Essays Presented to Margaret Gibson*, edited by Lesley Smith and Benedicta Ward, 145–156. London, 1992.

———, and Hirsch-Reich. B. "The *Figurae* of Joachim of Fiore: Genuine and Spurious Collections." *Medieval and Renaisance Studies* 3 (1954): 170–199.

Rehberg, Andreas. "Der 'Kardinalsorakel'-Kommentar in der 'Colonna'-Handschrift Vat. lat. 3819 and die Entstehungsumstände der Papstvatizinien." *Florensia: Bollettino del Centro Internazionale di Studi Gioachimiti* 5 (1991): 45–112.

Regiselmo, Pasqualino. *Vaticinia sive Prophetiae Abbatis Joachimi et Anselmi Episcopi Marsicani*. Venice, 1589; repr. Leipzig, 1972.

Registres de Benoît XI, edited by C. A. Grandjean. Paris, 1885, fasc. 3, #1099, 656–657.

Rigo, Antonio, ed. *Oracula Leonis: Tre manoscritti greco-veneziani degli oracoli attribuiti all' imperatore bizantino Leone il Saggio (Bodl. Baroc. 170, Marc. gr. VII.22, Marc. gr. VII.3)*. Venice, 1988.

Rouse, Richard H. "Bostonus Buriensis and the Author of the *Catalogus Scriptorum Ecclesiae*." *Speculum* 41 (1966): 471–499.

Runciman, Steven, *The Sicilian Vespers: A History of the Mediterranean World in the Later Thirteenth Century*. Cambridge, 1958.

Rusconi, Roberto. *L'Attesa della Fine. Crisi della società, profezia ed Apocalisse in Italia al tempo del grande scisma d'Occidente (1378–1417)*. Rome, 1979.

Russell, Daniel S. *Emblematic Structures in Renaissance French Culture*. Toronto and Buffalo, 1995.

Sandler, Lucy. *Gothic Manuscripts 1285–1385*. Oxford, 1986.

Schein, Sylvia. *Fidelis Crucis: The Papacy, the West, and the Recovery of the Holy Land 1274–1314*. Oxford, 1991.

Schmidt, Tilmann. *Der Bonifaz-Prozess: Verfahren der Papstanklage in der Zeit Bonifaz' VIII. und Clemens' V.* Cologne and Vienna, 1989.

Schmolinsky, Sabine. *Der Apokalypsenkommentar des Alexander Minorita: zur frühen Rezeption Joachims von Fiore in Deutschland*. Hanover, 1991.

Schüssler, Gosbert. "Reform und Eschatologie in einer Vaticinienhandschrift des frühen Trecento: MS. 1222B der Biblioteca Riccardiana in Florenz." in Ernst Ullmann, *Von der Macht der Bilder*, 39–53. Leipzig, 1983.

Schwartz, Orit, and Lerner, Robert E. "Illuminated Propaganda: The Origins of the *Ascende calve* Pope Prophecies." *Journal of Medieval History* 20 (1994): 157–191.

Scott-Fleming, Sonia. *The Analysis of Pen Flourishing in Thirteenth-Century Manuscripts*. Leiden, 1989.

Shailor, Barbara A. *Catalogue of Medieval and Renaissance Manuscripts in the Beinecke Rare Book and Manuscript Library, Yale University*. vol. 3: *Marston Manuscripts*. Medieval & Renaissance Texts & Studies vol. 100. Binghamton, 1992.

Souvenir de l'Exposition de Manuscrits Français à Peintures organisée à la Grenville Library (1932). Edited by Eric Millar. Paris, 1933.

Spence, R. "MS Syracuse Von Ranke 90 and the *Libellus* of Telesphorus of Cozenza." *Scriptorium* 33 (1979): 271–274.

Strayer, Joseph R. *The Reign of Philip the Fair*. Princeton, 1980.

Tabarroni, Andrea. *Paupertas Christi et apostolorum: l'ideale francescano in discussione (1322–1324)*. Rome, 1990.

Tanselle, G. Thomas. *A Rationale of Textual Criticism*. Philadelphia, 1989.

Taylor, Rupert. *The Political Prophecy in England*. New York, 1911.

Terrien, Samuel. *The Iconography of Job Through the Centuries: Artists as Biblical Interpreters*. University Park, Pa., 1996.

Tierney, Brian. *Origins of Papal Infallibility 1150–1350*. 2nd ed. Leiden, 1988.

Tondelli, Leone. "Profezia Gioachimita del sec. XIII delle regioni venete." *Studi e Documenti* 4, 3–9. Modena, 1940.

Trinity College Apocalypse. Edited by Peter Brieger, translation of Anglo-Norman Commentary by M. Dulong. 1 vol. in 2 parts. London, 1967.

Turley, Thomas. "The Ecclesiology of Guido Terrini." Ph.D. dissertation, Cornell University, 1979.

Verbeke, Werner; Verhelst, Daniel; and Welkenhuysen, Andries, eds. *The Use and Abuse of Eschatology in the Middle Ages*. Mediaevalia Lovaniensia 15. Leuven, 1988.

Weitzmann, Kurt. *Illustrations in Roll and Codex: A Study of the Origin and Method of Text Illustration*. Princeton, 1947.

Wright, Rosemary Muir. *Art and Antichrist in Medieval Europe*. Manchester and New York, 1995.

Zumthor, Paul. *Toward a Medieval Poetics*. Translated by Phillip Bennett. Minneapolis, 1992.

———. *Merlin le Prophète*. Lausanne, 1943.

The Late Medieval Pope Prophecies:

The *Genus nequam* Group

Picture I: MS Lunel, fol. 4[r]

om. description A. **pope seated:** pope standing CDFMP, on pedestal CD, pope wears mitre (throughout) LM, old–style papal tiara (throughout) in CDFPV. **upraised hand:** holds staff with cross CD, extended F. **hand holding book:** *om.* book, hand upraised CD. **bears:** dogs M. **bears, position:** bear with four nursing cubs to side C, bear with five nursing cubs to side D, bear and nursing cubs (number unclear) to side F, paws touching pope PV. **bear over crown:** (*om.* CDF), leaping M, in motion PV.

Vaticinium I

Principium malorum.

Ypocrisis habundabit.[a]

Genus nequam, ursa catulos pascens, et in quinque Romam sceptra
conturbat novam, et in xxxvi annos miser ambulabit. Primus finis[b] fere
habentis quinque filios.[c] A figuris enim modus est. Erea autem civitas,
barbaros item recipe. Cum autem videris ursam, matrem canum, miserabiliter luge in latitudine celi[d] ut a deo consequaris auxilium.[e] Multos decipis,
nequissima,[f] sub aliena pelle. Imitata[g] enim es, visum fallacem converti.[h]
Intus abscondis deceptionem inimicos facientem. Sicut autem bene manens
canes nutris novos ut habeas istos[i] sicut adiutores in medio tempestatum.
Sed Christus[j] manifestabit cogitationes.[k]

Serpens autem omnes consumit velociter cum hiis quos lactas. Et letaris penaliter et manus expandis, quamvis pedes pervertas,[l] sicut abiciens te
ipsum extra res. Sed dominus ypocrisim tuam ostendet. Quid enim mali
facies, o tu habens faciem canis admixtus alieno morsui? Quomodo tu
feres bonum? Quid mundo, qui aperis os ad pusillos? Quomodo eructabit
verbum bonum civitati?[m]

5

10

15

1–2. Caption: *om.* FM *throughout. Here as elsewhere line one gives the short form of the caption as
it appears in* AC; *lines one and two together constitute the long form of the caption as it appears
in* DLNPV. Principium . . . habundabit: Ypocrisis habundabit. Incipit [*literally* ⋎]
principium malorum D.

1. Principium malorum: Incipit principium malorum NPV, Incipit liber prophetarum
papalium L.

2. Ypocrisis habundabit: secundum Merlinum incipit prime A, *om.* C, Ypocrisia habundabit LPV, *add.* liber primus L.

3. Genus: Sevus (*or* senus) MV, [G]enus N *here as throughout, blank space left for decorated
letter; before the space is a lower-case letter indicating letter to be supplied* [E.A.R. Brown].
ursa: ursus M, versa N. et in quinque: *om.* L lacuna *sufficient for nine–ten letters.*
Romam: novam C. sceptra: septris D, sceptris M, sceptri FNPV, *om.* L.

4. conturbat: conturbans A, turbat M. novam: non enim M. et in: *om.* M. xxxvi: trigita sex F, 36 NP. annos: annis AMV, annus N. miser: misera FLMV. finis: filius FM. filios: oculos LMNP, *om.* V.

5. enim: *om.* L. modus: medius F. autem: quoque F. civitas? D.

6. item: inte L, inde M, iterum N, ante V. videris: viderit NP. ursam: ursa N. matrem: *om.* N lacuna *of five or six letters* [18mm E.A.R. Brown]. canum: cane C.

6.–7. miserabiliter: *om.* L, *literally* miserabil'e M, in altitudinem miserabiliter NP.

7. luge in latitudine celi: *repeat* in latitudine celi D, in altitudine celi luge L, quam captivabis celi luge M, luge in altitudinem celi FV, luge in altitudine celi NP. a: an L. deo: domino AMP. consequaris: consequeris V. auxilium: *om. sed add. in margine* M. Multos: multa D, cunctos M. decipis: decipies F, *add.* misera LPMV.

8. nequissima: *om.* NM, tibi ne conmissa sint M. sub: *om.* M. aliena pelle: *om.* pelle C, pelle aliena D. Imitata : inmutata FM, *om.* L, mutata NP, imita? V. enim es: es enim D. enim: *om.* FLMV. es: *om.* ALNP, est V. Visum: ursum D, Rursum F, visum enim M. fallacem: facilem CD, falcem NP, in falcem LMV. converti: convertis N.

9. Intus: intra CFLPV, *om.* N. abscondis deceptionem: deceptionem abscondis M. abscondis: a[b]scondis F. inimicos facientem: in multos facientes F, inmutas faciem L, immutas faciem inimicos facientem M, immutas faciem NP (frem' *cancelled* N), mutas faciem inimicos facientem V. Sicut: Dicis N. autem: enin FM. bene manens: bene manes DNP, manens bene F.

10. canes: *om.* C. nutris: *add.* no (*excised*) L. istos: ipsos FL. sicut adiutores: *om.* CD, sicut adultores L. tempestatum: *add.* sicut adulatores D.

11. Sed: set CF. Christus: tempus ACD, alias Christus *in superscript* A, Christus? V. cogitationes: *add.* et t'vum ? C. In C *and* D *texts unit one ends at this point; the paragraph printed here occurs as first part of unit two.*

12. consumit: consumet ACF, consumi D. lactas: lectas M, lateris N, lactans P. Et: *om.* N.

12–13. letaris: lactaris F, *om.* L lacuna *sufficient for five–six letters*, letans NP.

13. expandis: expendis C, espandis P. quamvis pedes: quamvis manus pedes que F, *om.* quamvis L, ut servos Domini M. pervertas: *manuscript damaged but appears to be* perversitas L, vertas P.

13–14. sicut abiciens te ipsum extra res: sed autem eos abiciens turpiter M. sicut: *add.* autem V. te: et N. extra: *om.* N, *add.* alias contra exemplum N. res: eres L, rex NP.

14. Sed: set CL. dominus: dux M. ypocrisim: intercesimum M. tuam: *om.* CDM, tua F. ostendet: *literally* ondet CM.

14.–15. Quid enim mali facies, o tu ... morsui?: *om.* NP. Quid: ann? F. mali facies: malum facies D, maliefacies V. canis: *om.* F. admixtus: ammistam F, amistam L, admixtam AM. morsui: morsu FLMV.

15.–17. Quomodo ... civitati? *om.* L. Quomodo: Quo *for* Quomodo C, Quo F, Quado L, Quando P.

16. feres: fers C, ferens FPV, feceris N. bonum: *om.* M. Quid mundo: qui mundo L, quo modo N. mundo: mondo V. qui: *om.* FNPV, ad M. aperis: quos M. os: hos, L, *om.* MNP. ad pusillos: ad pupillos D, apullos F. eructabit: *literally* eructab' C, eructabis DV, *om.* L.

17. verbum: *om.* LM. bonum: *om.* CDL.

Picture II: MS Lunel, fol. 4ᵛ

pope standing: *unius diaconi cum bitortu in capite* A, on pedestal CD. **hand holding staff:** cross in hand A, *add.* staff with pennant to side CD, holds staff with pennant MP, holds staff with bird atop V. **hand holding book:** *om.* A, *om.* book, hand upraised CD, *om.* book, hand extended downward P, book extended towards serpent V. **serpent:** *serpens* A, snake-like with animal head C, snake-like with two paws and animal head D, snake-like with knots in middle F, snake-like, wound around tree trunk M, snake-like P, dragon V. **bird:** two *corvis* attacking serpent's eyes A, two birds attacking serpent's head CDF, two birds resting atop tree, facing pope M, one bird attacking serpent's head P, *om.* attack, bird on opposite side atop staff, beak open, parallel to pope's head V.

Vaticinium II

Sanguis.

Decime dissipabuntur in effusione sanguinis.[a]

Secundus autem filius, alia fera volans, serpens ad meridiem iunctus[b]
nigro. Et niger[c] totus privatus lumine a corvis[d] manifestans tempus. In[e]
5   figuris litteralibus qui succedet paterno fini existens serpens miser destructor urse. O quomodo es esca miserorum corvorum, existens enim genus
abhominabile eorum ab oriente. Miserabiliter turbabis teipsum simul et
civitatem tuam gemitum dabis in tempore meti.[f]

1.   Sanguis: *om.* C.
2.   Decime dissipabuntur in effusione sanguinis: *om.* D. in effusione sanguinis: *om.* L. *After each caption* L *adds* liber secundus, *etc.*
3.   autem: est MNPV. filius: *om. but add. in margine* M, finis A, *add.* est F. autem filius: filius est L. alia fera: fera aliis M. volans: vorans C. serpens: *om.* L. meridiem: meridia C, *add.* ut F. iunctus: victus CM, iuctus (*literally* iuc'tus) D, ventus F, viris L, iunctus *or* vinctus PV.
4.   nigro: magnus F. niger: *literally* nig' C, iungetur NP. corvis: quorvis F, actionis L. In: et MNPV, a F.
5.   litteralibus: licteralibus F. succedet: succedit CDL, succedunt V. miser: *add.* et F.
6–7. destructor: destructio FV.
6.   urse: vite M. es: ex LMV, *om.* NP. esca: essca L. enim: est NP, *repeats* enim V.
7.   abhominabile: abominabile L. eorum: *add.* et C. oriente: *add.* .x. L, *add.* et M. turbabis: turbaris C, turbberis F, turbabas M, turbareris NP. et: *om.* L.
8.   civitatem: cacitatem L. tuam gemitum: getium tuum C, gemitum tuum D, et lumen gentium F, tuarum gentium M, tuam gentium LNP, tuam gencium V. meti: meri LP, *superscript* alias metus A.

Sententia iste igitur opinionis magis
tenebit hic rerum. Duplicium tercium et enim suis eques
cruciferi et eques et corniger sicut multi
uelor sic pronitus et Licinius principium ?
halens unitatem et finem unitati et duplici
et una ommus primo ununs recurrere figure nervor
accorum ficut in spe loin anni. Venit dies in qua te
nebit medietate figure multum magnis quintum rex
noluerint folus iste enim recipiens principium anteri
die in quo explebit cornuto diem mediante stella solit
nessere et pronitus ut multum et uelor eritens ad leila
properanis. O genus bigantin halens auditus nobis in
clinatos igni fine fremis. O amice, Deo ultima sillaba
nil lucrabitur te illon unignis propter spem cadent in te
principium et finis cor est

Picture III: MS Lunel, fol. 6ʳ

pope standing: *diaconus* [literally *ymago similis priori*] *cum corona sancti* A, on pedestal D, seated MPV. **bird (eagle) on head in profile:** frontal CDFM, *cum corona* A, with nimbus C, cross added to side D. **upraised hand:** holds staff with cross AD, at waist C, on book F, touches head of small figure P, holds book V. **hand with book:** *om.* A, *om.* book, hand upraised CDV, *om.* book, points to small figure M, at waist holding cloak P. **unicorn:** horn touches pope's eye FPV, paws touch pope CFMPV. **small figure:** boy A, adult, same size as pope F, kneeling M. **gestures, small figure:** *om.* A, one hand extended CD, hands extended to pope, one hand touching crown, the other pointing to pope's shoulder F, extended in supplication MP.

Vaticinium III

Penitencia.

Vestigia symonis magi tenebit.[a]

Duplum tercium. Et enim avis, eques, crucifera avis, et equus corniger,[b] sicut multum velox sicut promptus et lascivus. Principium habens
unitatem et finem. Unitati duplici vocationis, prime, unius, recurve figure,
numerorum extremum sicut in tempore[c] boni anni venit dies in qua tenebit medietatem crucite figure. Multum magnus quidem rex volucrum
solus. Iste enim recipiens principium a meridie in quo explebit cornuto
diem mediante stella poli vespere, et promptus ut multum et velox existens
ad bella preparatus. O genus Bizancii habens auditus nobis inclinatos et
ignis sine frenis. O amice sed ultima sillaba vel lucrabitur te in locis irriguis
propter spem cadens. In te enim principium et finis cornu est.

---

1. Penitencia: *Penite[n]cia* C.
2. Vestigia: *om.* P. magi: magy L, *add.* figuram P. tenebit: tenebre N, *add.* libe[r] tercius
    L.
3. Duplum: dupplicium L, supplicum M, duplicatum NP, *add.* est P, *add.* autem N.
    tercium: tren N, *add.* elementum NP. Et enim: *om.* DP, est N, *add.* est F. avis: *add.*
    et N. eques: *om.* F. crucifera: ancifera M. avis: *om.* L. et: *om.* V. equus: eques
    AFLMN, *add.* et L.
3–4. corniger: cor niger CV, cornuger D, cornipes F, cor iungetur NP.
4. sicut[2]: sic AF. promptus: prontus FL, promtus P. lascivus: lascivius F, lascivis V.
5. unitatem: veritatem F. finem: fraternitati N. unitati: unitatci *with* c *excised* C, *add.* et
    L, *om.* N. duplici: dupplicus A. vocationis: vaca omnis L. prime: primo L. unius: *om.*
    F. recurve: recreave F, recurrere L, roturne N. figure: figuras P.
6. numerorum: nervorum DLMV. extremum: accorium L, attractorum MV. sicut in
    tempore: in tempore sicut ACDF. boni: *om.* L. venit: veniet F, novit P.
6–7. tenebit: timebis D, timebit M.
7. medietatem: medietate L, *om.* NP. crucite: concite F, *om.* L, a note M, cuncte N.

magnus: magnum M. magnus quidem: quod [qd'] magnus V, quidem magnus FN.
rex: rep *corrected superscript* rex A.

8. enim: *om.* FMNP. recipiens principium: recipiet principium FM, principium
recipiens P. a: in V. explebit: implebit P, explebis V. cornuto: cor nuto C.

9. diem: die CNF. stella: stellam NP. poli: polit L. vespere: *om.* F. promptus: prontus
FL, proptus N, promtus P. et: *om.* F. existens: *add.* et ACDF.

10. preparatus: properans L, *add.* lu *but excised* C. genus: gentis CD, gens P. Bizancii:
Bizantii A, Bizanzii C, Bissanci D, Bisçancii F, bigantu L, Bicancii MV, bizancium N,
bisancium *P.* habens: habes D, *add.* autem CD. nobis: vobis CFV, nb' *for* nobis *but*
Daneu Lattanzi reads verbis P. inclinatos: inclinantes C, inquinatos P. et: *om.* FL.

11. ignis: igni ALNP, lignis F. sine: fruc C. frenis: fremis C, frenis? F. sed: sic A, et M.
ultima: ultimo V. sillaba: siba A, sill'a C, filabat NP. vel: vulnus F. lucrabitur: lucrabi-
t[ur]? C, lucrabatur NP. in locis: inllocis F, illoti L. cadens: *add.* ite C. irriguis: uriguis
L. propter: preter ACD.

12. In te: inter A, vite N. enim: *om.* FLMNP. principium: principatum MNPV. cornu:
eorum LM.

Picture IV: MS Lunel, fol. 6ᵛ

om. description A. CD combines images four and five. **middle vessel-like column:** *om.* CD. **tonsured head emerging from vessel:** head on serrated sickle CD, no tonsure, head surrounded by rays C, tonsure unclear D. **flying fish attacking crowned head:** *om.* CD, *om.*, handle-like extension curving over vessel F, *om.*, hand holds scimitar over tonsured head M. **column with crowned head atop:** *om.* CDF, two crowned heads within roundels to side CD, head of pope wearing mitre atop column M. **column with hand holding/touching fish:** *om.* CDF, hand holds scimitar M.

Vaticinium IV

Confusio.

Error concitabitur.[a]

Iste collateralis[b] quartus ab ursa currens gladiis et homo movens incisionem rose tamen siccabitur sicut rosa. Incidens rosam annis motus tribus
5 et enim tercia littera et tercium elementum significat manus et falx illa
prima littera incidet rosam la. M.[c] Miserum elementum illud videt, recipiens enim principium ut inciderem florem. Non miserebitur tui quamvis
in principatu maneas. Vide enim iste incipit colligere rosam autem ferens
in omnibus habens finem in quo letare multum frustra.

---

2. Error: amor V. concitabitur: *add.* liber quartus L.

3. collateralis: collis ACDL, collus MNPV. currens: carens FM, cusseris P. gladiis: gladius
CD. movens: manens D, monens M, moriens *N, add.* in CDN.

3–4. incisionem: incisione CV.

4. tamen: dum D. siccabitur: secabuntur F, insiccabitur N. sicut: sic F, *om.* L, satis P.
rosa: *om.* F, rosarus N. Incidens: inci[d]ens C. rosam: rosarii F. motus: motis F. et: ut P.

5. enim: *om.* N, est V. tercia littera: lictera tercia F. tercium: tercius F, iterum L. significat: signat N.

5–6. elementum . . . elementum: *eyeskip om.* F. *A follows the first* elementum *with* illud videt
recipiens enim principium, *then excises these words, correcting the eyeskip from* elementum
to elementum.

5. manus: magnus L. falx illa: falxs illa A, falcilla C, falx in illa D, falxilla M, fascilla P,
fals illa NV.

6. littera: litera CDLPV. incidet: incident M, incidunt LNP. rosam: rose P. la. M.: la.
M? Mt. C, *add.* im? D, la. et m [*or* in] L, lati Mat. M, l.a.m. NP, la. ma. V. Miserum:
Secundum CD, miserorum L, misera N. illud: *om.* DM. videt: invidet D.

6–7. recipiens: insipiens V.

7. enim: *om.* M. inciderem: incidentem AF, viderem *or* inderem *for* inciderem D,
incideret N. miserebitur: miserebit M.

8. maneas: manans P. Vide : Unde F. iste: *add.* enim A. incipit: incipiet e *excised* M.
autem ferens: anteferens FM, auferens N, autem feras P.

9. habens finem: habens furem A, finem habens M. letare: letorum P. frustra: frusta L.

Picture V: MS Lunel, fol. 8ʳ

sickle-bearer: *juvenis* A, wears simple, long, belted robe, no tonsure evident, barefoot C, wears simple, short, belted robe, no tonsure evident, barefoot D, wears simple robe and vestment, tonsured, barefoot F, robed tonsured monk with cowl, in profile M, tonsured monk P, wears simple robe and vestment, tonsured V. **maniple:** *om*. CDFMPV. **rose in left hand:** *om*. CD, branch with five flowers F. **angel, hands touching rose:** *om*. A, angel in figure's left hand CD, angel kneeling D, angel at pope's shoulder, hands extended F, bust of angel in corner M. [*add*. shackles to pope's right and leg? to pope's left P, signs of scraping and perhaps overpainting].

Vaticinium V

Elatio.[a]

Paupertas, obediencia, castitas, temperacio.
Castrimargie et ypocrisarum destructor.[b]

Vide iterum alienum existentis modum. Falcem magnam et rosam
quam fert tercium autem duplicatum primum elementum divisa sunt. Item
coniuncta falcifer quattuor mensium te scribo. Principatus autem omnes
quos consumpsisti gladio, templa ydolorum post paululum resuscitabis.[c]
Tres autem tres annos in mundo vivens senex, vade in infernum duabus
tribulationibus in medio.

2.   paupertas: paupertatis D. obediencia: obediencie D. castitas: castitatis DL. temperacio:
     temptator NP, temperator V.
3.   castrimargie: gule DL, castrimagie N, castrimeregie P. et: *om.* DL. ypocrisarum: ypo-
     critarum DL, ypocrisorum NP, ypocrisar V. destructor: destructo D, destructio LV,
     add. liber quintus L. In C *and* D, *texts four and five are run together, separated only by
     caption for text number five, for* C *the short form (line one), for* D *the long form (lines two and
     three of caption).*
4.   Vide: *om.* C. iterum: unum N. existentis modum: modum existentis F. existentis:
     existen V. Falcem: *om.* N. magnam: *om.* CN. rosam: rosa *add.* manu que est manna
     vel hec interpretatur idest quid est hec erit miraculum magnum F.
5.   quam: que? C, quid D. fert: defert L. autem: *om.* P. duplicatum: *om.* P. primum: *om.*
     P. divisa: *add.* autem CD, diversa N. Item: non D, in te L.
6.   coniuncta: coniuntam L. falcifer: falsifer A, falciferum CP, falcifere N. quattuor:
     quatuor LN. mensium: mencium V. te: *om.* L. scribo: reseri L, scuto N, *add.* in M.
     principatus: principaturus C, principatur N. autem: ante LM, in N. omnes: omnis F.
7.   quos: qui A, *om.* CD, quam L, quem FMV. consumpsisti: consumsisti L. Post: preter
     L. paululum: paulum P. resuscitabis: resuscitabo CLMNV.
8.   Tres autem tres annos: tres tres annos F, tres autem annos MPV, autem *followed by* os
     excised and lacuna *of two spaces* M. mundo: meto L, modo N, mondo P. vivens: vives
     FL. senex: senes AF. vade: valde AF, vadit L. medio: media A.

Picture VI: MS Lunel, fol. 8ᵛ

pope standing: *summi pontificis* A, on pedestal CD. **book in left hand:** *om.* ACDFMP, hand upraised CD, fingers pointing at animal F, hand extended downward MP. **right hand:** *om.* A, holds staff with cross atop CD, hand extended across chest F, fingers pointed to self M, hand upraised PV. **cow (*vacca*):** front legs not uplifted CF, sitting on haunches M. **crowned heads:** *om.* ACD (but *add.* in four/five CD), two mitred heads on horizontal bar of rectangular structure F, one head with secular headgear, on either side of pope, each facing the pope M.

Vaticinium VI

Incisio.

Ypocrisis in abhominatione erit.[a]

Vacca autem quintum,[b] et finis ursos pascentis.[c] Figura manifestat locum et modum. Unde adveniens solus manifestabit mihi amicus. Primus
5   enim habes virtutum aliorum plus, et dispensas circa amicos. Propterea invenisti dulcissimum finem. Solus sublimaberis a gloria. Et mortuus[d] relinques[e] potentissime potencias. Sicut enim ymbrem bene invenies potencias.[f]

---

1.   Incisio: *add.* et P.
2.   Ypocrisis: ypocrisie L, ypocris' N. abhominatione: abominatione L, habominatione P. erit: *add.* liber sextus L.
3.   Vacca: Vac M, Vacta N, Tacta P, Vaca V. autem: aut M. quintum: quictum *add.* filium F, quartum M. et: id est D. finis: filii L, filiis MNV. ursos: urse FMV, ursa LNP. Figura: signa F, *lacuna* figura *add. in margine* M, figuram: P. manifestat: manifestant F, manifesta L, manifestabat NP.
4.   locum et modum: modum et locum F. Unde: u unde L, ynde MV. adveniens: advens C, advincens V. manifestabit: manifestat ACD, manifestabimini F, manifestabat N. mihi: *om.* F, michi LMV. Primus: primax A, premas L, primas DNPV, plures F, p'm *for* primum, p'm *followed by* lacuna M.
5.   enim habes: enim habens DNP, habens enim F, habet L. virtutum: virtutes F, virtutem L. et: *om.* L. dispensas: dispendia N, dispensa LPV.
6.   dulcissimum finem: finem *lacuna* disanguibilium *add. in margine* M, dulcissimi *om.* finem N, finem dulcissimum LPV. Solus: *om.* M, *repeat* solus P. sublimaberis: sublimaveris A, subliberis *corrected in margin to* sublimaberis F, sublimaleris L, sublimaberis M, sublimabis N. a gloria: ad gloriam F, *add.* regnum CDNP. mortuus: mortuo A, mortuas C, mortuos *corrected in superscript to* mortuas D. relinques: relinquens ACFLNP.
7.   potencias: *om.* L. enim: *om.* L. ymbrem: imbrem N. Sicut . . . potencias: *om.* M. invenies: inveniens AN, invenias L.

Picture VII: MS Lunel, fol. 10[r]

pope standing: king A, figure wearing crown CD, on mound D. **gesture left hand:** *om.* A, not clearly pointing to animal C, index finger not shown F. **gesture right hand:** *om.* A, upraised DFPV, upraised, apparently holding cloak C, arm extended, finger pointing over head of animal M. **bear with two nursing cubs:** bear with four cubs A, bear with five nursing cubs CD, bear with one nursing cub F, bear with two cubs, one nursing P.

Vaticinium VII

Occasio.

Filii balax sectabuntur.[a]

Alia ursa secunda pascens catulos. Et in omnibus illa preterquam in
umbra tantum scripta. Natura temporum nativitas abortiva. In ultima enim
scribitur ultime subsolares, autem utrasque coronis[b] manifestant divisionem
totius potencie.

---

1.   Occisio: Ocasio L, Occasio N.
2.   balax: balaac D, *om.* L, balas N, balahe *possibly* balalx V. sectabuntur: sectabunt D,
   seccabitur L, seccabuntur N, letabuntur P, *add.* liber septimus L. L *repeats variant of
   caption within frame of picture*: occisio filii balas sociabuntur.
3.   secunda: *om.* V. et: *om.* L, se V. in: *om.* N.
4.   illa: illam F. tantum scripta: transcripta D. natura: patria F, *om.* L. temporum: templo-
   rum F.
5.   enim: vero NP. scribitur: scribuntur F, scribit V. ultime: ulitime P.
6.   subsolares: subssulares L. autem: et C. ante F, et ante M, aut V. utrasque: utrumque
   NP. coronas: coronis AFNP. manifestant: manifestat F, manifestent P. divisionem: di-
   visiones LMNP.
7.   totius: rotus L. potencie: penitencie AFNP.

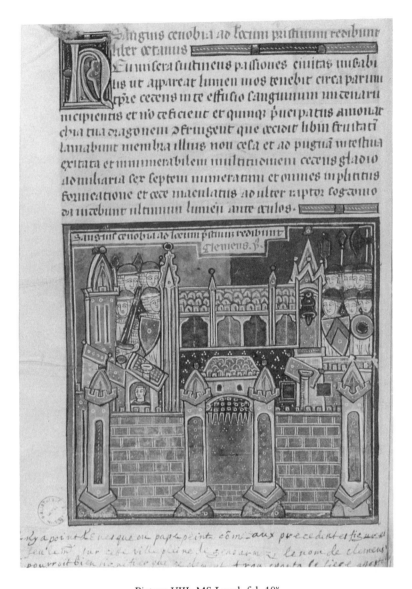

Picture VIII: MS Lunel, fol. 10ᵛ

fortification (fortified town) with gates closed: *una civitas* A, stylized building CD, three towers, but central tall tower, and with ecclesiastical overtones C, three towers of equal height D, *add.* below, head (as in vessel) with rays directed toward building CD, *add.* roughly drawn head with rays directed toward fortification superimposed on fortification at bottom of image F, *add.* pennant on central tower P, represented by three crenelated arches V. **soldiers:** *om.* ACDM, figures dropping stones from tower F, two soldiers with helmets, shields in first arch, two soldiers with helmets (visors up), shields, one soldier gesturing in second arch, a single larger soldier with visor covering his face and carrying shield in the third arch V.

Vaticinium VIII

Sanguis.

Cenobia ad locum pristinum redibunt.[a]

Heu, heu, misera sustinens passiones civitas miserabile ut appareat
lumen. Mox tenebit circa parvum tempus.[b] Cedes enim in te effusio sanguinum. Undenarii incipientes non deficient. Et quinque principatus a
monarchia tua draconem confringent que occidit libin. Frustratim lania-
bunt membra illius. Non cessa et ad pugnam intestina excitata. Et innumerabilem multitudinem cedent gladio ad miliaria sex septem numerata. Et
omnis implicitus fornicatione et cede. Maculatus adulter, raptor, iniustus
sodomita videbunt ultimum lumen ante oculos.[c]

---

1. Sanguis: Potestas V.

2. locum: loca? D. pristinum: pristima? D. redibunt: *add.* liber octavus L, L *duplicates caption within picture.*

3. heu: *om.* LMNPV. misera: miserima CD. sustinens: sustine M, *add.* dolores et F. civitas: civitatis M. miserabile: *om.* F, *add.* enim miserabile CD, miserabilis L. ut: *om.* N.

4. lumen: *om.* C. Mox: mos FL. *add.* te NP. tenebit: tenebre M. circa: arcana F. tempus:
tempore L. Cedes: cedens FMV, cedit N. enim: *om.* LNP. in te: *add.* et ACDF.

5. Undenarii: an dinarium F, ut denari M. incipientes: insipientis C, incipientis DL, *add.*
et LM. deficient: deficientes A, deficiet CF. Et: in F. monarchia: menarchia D.

6. draconem: dragonem L, drachonem V. confringent: constringent F. que: qui D.
occidit: cotidie N. libin: ibi libin [ibi *extends into margin*] M, libra N. Frustratim:
frustatim LP.

7. membra: menbra DF. illius: *om.* NF. cessa: occisa N. excitata: exitata L. et: *om.*
ACDF.

7–8. innumerabilem: innaturabilem V.

8. cedent: cedens LMNPV. ad miliaria: amililiaria F, ad miliciem N, ad miliciam P, ad
oriliariam ? V. numerata: numeratas: F, numeratum L, vulnerata N.

9. omnis: omnes L, *om.* M, homo V. implicitus: multiplicabitur F, implicit V. fornicatione: fornicationi F, fornicationum N. cede: cedet F. adulter: *add.* id est N, *add.* est
P. raptor: *add.* et F, id est raptor NP, *om.* M. iniustus: *om.* L.

10. sodomita: sogdomoda L. videbunt: videbit F.

Dcatio symonia cessabit liber nonus ·
Vulpinam figuratt amicitiam patienter censum
refrenans sicut multum senex et cautus habens
censum neniens inter simpliciter uoluciones
septies uolumtis conomisith ad   et effusiones
lisanguinum effuncas tu p victoriam expendith manu
bene graciose et brauium infine septri accepith

Picture IX: MS Lunel, fol. 12ʳ

no further evidence from A. **pope standing:** on pedestal D. **left hand:** holds scroll C, holds large seal? D, holds book? F, hand extended downward M. **right hand:** holds staff with cross CD, holds large key F, upraised and pointed to self M, upraised P. **animal (fox):** dog-like CD, upright F, leaping dog M, holds staff with cross in mouth P, donkey, one leg uplifted V. **three standards:** with unmarked pennants only CM, two with unmarked pennants only, one with spear top D, single pennant with cross on it, held by animal, *add.* large key atop animal's head F, two with unmarked pennants only, one staff with cross, *add.* small blue shield to right (decorated with horizontal wavy line and pattern of white dots) P, two topped with *fleurs de lis*, one with cross, no pennants V. *add.* two hands at pope's right, palms extended towards animal C, *add.* two hands at pope's left, palms extended towards inner margin D.

Vaticinium IX

Bona gratia.

Symonia cessabit.[a]

Vulpinam figurasti amicitiam paciencer, sensum refrenans, sicut multum
senex et canus habens sensum. Veniens autem dupliciter voluptiones sep-
5   ties, voluntas, condimisisti confringendas ad invicem et effusiones vali sanguinum effundendas. Tu pro victoria expandisti manus bene gratiose et
bravium accepisti in fine sceptri.

---

1.   Bona gratia: Ocasio L, Occisio NP.
2.   cessabit: *add.* liber nonus L, Occasio symonia cessbit *within picture* L *and on staff*
     vulpinam (*in smaller letters*) amicitiam simulastis? L.
3.   Vulpinam: Unde hominem C, Vulpum F, Vupinam V. figurasti: signasti F. amicitiam:
     add superscript A *and* amicitiam *completed in text in second hand* L. pacienter: patienter
     FNP, *add.* et CD. sensum: sensu FMNPV. refrenans: refrenam V. sicut: *add.* sicut P.
4.   senex: senes MN. et: ac V. canus: canum F, carius *L*, cans *s partially erased followed by*
     lacuna M. sensum: sensu F. autem: *om.* F, in te L. dupliciter: *literally* dup'lcr D,
     dupliciterater F. voluptiones: volupciones CV, volutiones F, voluciones LM, *add.* in
     te M, voluptaciones N.
5.   voluntas: voluptas DV. condimisisti: condimisti CP, a ? dimisti D, condimnisti N,
     cum dimisisti V. confringendas: *om.* LMV, confrigendos F, confringendos N, confrin-
     gendo P. ad invicem: ad *plus* lacuna (*sufficient for six letters*) L, aliud in vicem V. vali:
     vili? C, valli FV, li L, *om.* N, validas P.
5–6. sanguinum: sanguinem N.
6.   effundendas: effundas L, effudendas M. Tu: *add.* propter LMPN. pro: *om.* L. victoria:
     victoriam L. expandisti: expendisti L. bene: *add.* et F, huc N. gratiose: gloriose F,
     graciose L, *om.* NP. et: *om.* F.
7.   accepisti in fine sceptri: in fine sceptri accepisti L. sceptri: ceptri D.

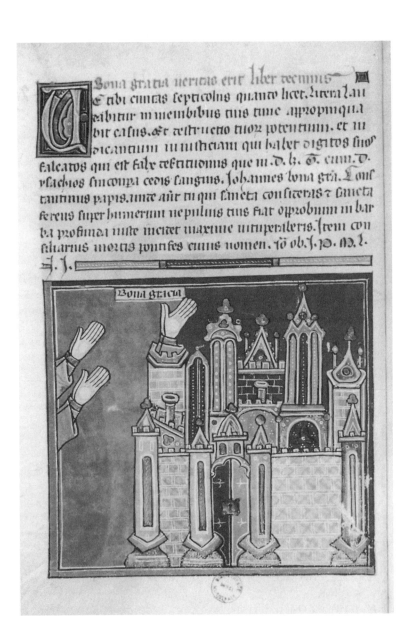

Picture X: MS Lunel, fol. 12ᵛ

fortified town: [considerable variety in details of town among FMPV], empty throne CD.
disembodied hands: single hand below throne CD, three single hands emerging from
shield F, three single hands M, two single hands V. **hand emerging from tower:** *om.*
CDFM, single hand behind tower P, single hand above tower V.

Vaticinium X

Potestas.

Unitas erit.[a]

Ve tibi civitas septicollis. Quin[b] *K* littera[c] laudabitur in menibus[d] tuis.
Tunc appropinquabit casus et destructio tuorum potentium et iudicancium
5 iniusticiam. Qui habet digitos suos falcatos. Qui est falx desertitudinis, et
in altissimo blasphemabit. Qui incipit [V. R. r. n^x m. v].[e] Ysachios sincopam cedis sanguinis, Iohannes bona gratia, Constantinus pauperis. Vide
autem tu qui sancta consideras et sancta ferens super humerum ne pulvis
tuus fiat obprobrium. In barba profunda iuste incidet.[f] Et maxime vitupe-
10 raberis ipse consiliarius mortis, pontifex cuius nomen I'o.[g]

---

1. Potestas: Rena gratia N, Bona gratia LP.
2. Unitas: Veritas DL. erit: *add.* alias laudabitur D, *add.* liber decimus L, *caption within picture* Bona gracia L.
3. septicollis: septicolliis L. Quin: quo F, quando L *add.* licet L, *om. sed add.* quando [qua] *in margine* M, q'n *for* quando N. *K: om.* LM, R FNV. littera: lictera F. laudabitur: *om.* CD, laudabiliter NPV. menibus: manibus CD, menibibus L. tuis: tuus C.
4. casus: casu F. potentium: potentum F.
5. iniusticiam: iniusticia C, iusticiam MNPV. habet: habent FNPV. falcatos: falcantes CD. falx: C ? *very faint,* fals MV, lalx N, falax P. desertitudinis: lacuna *add. in margine* M. et: *om.* L.
6. in: *om.* L. altissimo: altissimam C, *om.* L. blasphemabit: blasfemabit F, *om.* L, blasphemabitur N. qui: que FLMNV. incipit (*MHF*): 'm *for* incipit D, *om.* C, idest F, in. L, incepit M, in. N, in P, i V. [V.R. r. n^x m. v.]: *not in Leo Oracles, Lambecius version,* V. K. tt. E. . s.tt. C, vi K cci. G. ω D, cb.? R.G. cix. idest cb? F, V. K. ō. cum V. L, lacuna, *om. abbreviations* M, .V. R. r. n^x. m *or* in. v. N, io. K. t. en^x. m. cv. P, vo. K. ti. cum in. M. V. Ysachios: yaachios CD, ysathyos *add.* idest seperans in deum F, *lacuna* fluctuos *add. in margine* M.
6–7. sincopam: cincopam CD, syncopam F, sinconpera L. sanguinis: sanguis LMN. Iohannes: *add.* idest F. pauperis: papis. L. Vide: unde L.

8.   qui: *om.* F. consideras: *om. sed add. in margine* M. et sancta: *om. sed add. (with some erasure) in margine* M. ferens: fers FN.

9.   tuus: tuis CL. obprobrium: obproprium F, opprobrium LP. In barba: et bar*a*ram ? C, ut barobam D, et barba F. incidet: incides *FV.* Et: *om.* L. maxime: maximo D.

9–10. vituperaberis: vituperabilis CDN, *Daneu Lattanzi reads* nituperaberis P.

10.   ipse: *om.* CM, item *LPV,* vel N. consiliarius: conscilirius P. mortis: montis V. ipse . . . nomen: *om. but* quem consiliarius mortis pontifex cuius nomen *add. in lower margin* M. pontifex: pontifes L. cuius nomen: *om.* F. nomen: *add.* Imen. M. I'o *for* Johannes: I'o cc ? C, I'o obi D, io. ob^us. I. p. M.l.ii.I. F, Io ob. I. P. M. I.I.I. L, io. ob^us. lrl?.l. M. N. n. i.i. M, Jor'. cibus. y.p. M.L. n. J. N, Ior. ob^us. I. p. m. I. n. l. P, ior. ob'. ? . ii.p.M.l.ii.i. *add.* usque ad vesperam mane. Dies duo milia. CCC. et minabitur sacrificium (*cf.* Dan. *8:14*) V.

Picture XI: MS Lunel, fol. 14ʳ

half-naked figure seated on stones (or rock): figure on sarcophagus CD, fully naked emerging from cave F, on green mound M. **tonsure:** *om.* CDFMP. **beard:** *om.* MPV. **legs:** one as in motion F, crossed at knees M. **gestures:** one hand to head, the other extended downward on knee CD, arms awkwardly twisted, one hand extended as in blessing F, one hand to head, the other extended down M, hands upraised as in astonishment P, one hand upraised, the other extended V. **second figure:** in simple robe, hands crossed over chest CDP, standing on sarcophagus C, to one side of sarcophagus D, arms extended, gesturing towards figure emerging from cave F, small standing figure in robe, hands extended downward M, gesturing as in conversation V. **add.** to immediate right of half-naked figure, a rectangle, twice as long as it is wide, with a double-barred cross inside, six-pointed star above C, *add.* rectangle closer to square with double-barred cross inside, "star" with wavy arms D, *add.* six-pointed star above second figure and on same line as words *papa nudus* F.

Vaticinium XI

Bona honoracio.

Thesaurus pauperibus erogabitur.ᵃ

Et revelabitur virtusᵇ qui habet prenomen menachim.ᶜ Petram habitas.
Eya, veni, mihi aliene luctus.ᵈ Relinqueris et victum agrestem. Et vive
mortuus,ᵉ et gemebundus. Congregans bona dissipans ommne, bravium
iniquitatis iniustificatum. Quando maior stella apparebit nigra tibi. Nudus
itemᶠ vade in inferiora terre.ᵍ

---

1. Bona: bonus V. honeracio: oraco *or* Maco N, oratio LPV.

2. Thesaurus: thesaurum LNP, *add.* constantus D, Constantini L. erogabitur: erogabat N, erogabit LP, *add.* liber undecimus L, *add. caption in picture* Bona oratio thesaurus pauperibus erogabitur L.

3. Et: E [sic] Et F, *om.* N. revelabitur: elevabitur F. virtus: unctus C, untus F, unitus (*for* unitas) P, vinctus *or* iunctus NV. qui habet: qualiter M, qui habent V. prenomen: *om.* lacuna *of seven letters* L, pronomen N. menachim: monachim DL, menarchim F, me *followed by* lacuna menachim ? *add. in margine* M. habitas: *om.* L, habitans FMNPV.

4. Eya: *or* Exa N. veni: venit FLMNP. mihi: michi FMN, mihi ? V. luctus: *add.* aliene *but excised* C. Relinqueris: relinquens FLN. victum: vinctum F, Iuncum N, unicum P. agrestem: agustem V. vive: vue CNP, ne F.

5. mortuus: incentiuus FMNP, incencius L, incentuus V. et gemebundus: *om.* CD, *add.* g., *g excised* P. congregans: congregatus D. omne: omnen DF.

6. iniquitatis: *add.* Qui totus F, *add.* et L. iniustificatum: iustificatus F, iustificatum L, in iustificatum N. Quando: quam M. maior stella: stella maior F. tibi: *om.* FLMNPV apparebit: *add.* tibi CD. nudus: Nudus ? D.

7. item: idest M. vade: vadet F. terre: *add.* papa nudus *below in same hand* F. inferiora: iniferiora L.

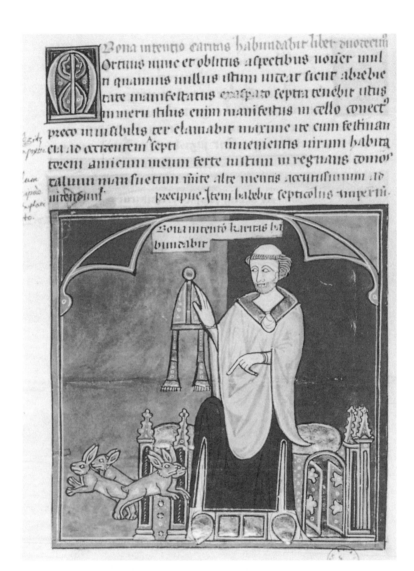

Picture XII: MS Lunel, fol. 14ᵛ

seated pope holding papal tiara over four rabbits: *om.* CDFMP, angel atop addorsed animals holds papal tiara in one hand, scroll in the other C, angel with nimbus seated on cloud above addorsed animals holds papal tiara in one hand, other hand extended down, *add.* eagle in flight above tiara D, angel with nimbus standing above two long arcs ending in animal heads holds papal tiara in one hand, the other broadly extended as in blessing F, figure with nimbus holds mitre over two dogs, other hand holds book M, figure with nimbus holds papal tiara over two bears, the other hand to body P. **rabbits:** addorsed bears, two dogs below CD, arcs ending in animal heads, mouths emitting rays, *add.* sarcophagus below arcs F, four dogs M, four bears P.

Vaticinium XII

Bona intencio.

Caritas habundabit.[a]

Mortuus nunc. Et oblitus aspectus. Noverunt multi, quamvis nullus
istum videat. Sicut ab ebrietate manifestatus, ex insperato sceptra tenebit
istius imperii. Stilus enim manifestus in celo connectus preco invisibilis ter
clamabit maxime: Ite cum festinancia ad occidentem septicollis. Invenietis
virum, habitatorem, amicum meum. Ferte istum in regias domos, calvum,
mansuetum, mitem, alte mentis, acutissimum ad videndum futurum precipue. Item habebit septicollis imperium.

1.　Bona intencio: *om.* C. intencio: interito P.
2.　habundabit: *add.* liber duodecimus L, *repeats caption in picture* Bona intentio karitas
　　habundabit L.
3.　Mortuus: *add.* et F. nunc: nunc? V. Et: *om.* F. aspectus: *add.* eius F, aspectibus LMV,
　　asptus P. Noverunt: venerunt D, novetur V. quamvis: quantus N.
4.　istum: istorum PV. ab ebrietate: adebrate F, abrebietate L, ebrietate *add.* et M, ab
　　ebritate P. manifestatus: manistatus F. ex: ab D. ex insperato: ex insperacio F,
　　ex[a]sperato L, ex inspirato N. sceptra: septra L. tenebit: *om.* M.
5.　istius: isti CN, istus L. imperii: in merii L, impii N. enim: *om.* F, enimque P. mani-
　　festus: manifestatus FV. connectus: congnectus F, connoctus N, convectus P, conectus
　　LV. invisibilis: invisibiliter F. ter: *om.* FV, terre NP.
6.　clamabit: declamabit V. maxime: *om.* M. maxime Ite: ite maxime V. festinancia:
　　festinacione C. septicollis: *add.* et F, septi lacuna *of five–six letters* L *add. superscript* A *in*
　　second hand. Invenietis: invenientis L.
7.　habitatorem: habitantem V. Ferte: fere N, forte V. istum: uste M, iustum LPNV.
　　regias: regnans L. calvum: talium? DL.
8.　mitem: mite L, mittem NP. mentis: montis N. futurum: fiturum C, acutum D, futu-
　　rarum F, *om.* lacuna *of six–seven letters* L.
8–9.　precipue: *add.* et CDF.
9.　Item: idem DM, in te F. habebit: habebis F. septicollis: septicoliis L. *add.* Papa cum
　　ovibus ante et cum metria in manu *in same hand* F.

Picture XIII: MS Lunel, fol. 17ʳ

standing pope: on low green mound D, kneeling F, seated V. **left hand holding book:** *om.* book CDFP, hand upraised CD, hands in prayer F, hands in *orans* gesture P. **right hand gesture:** holds staff surmounted by cross CD, hand upraised as in blessing M. **angel crowning pope:** holds staff with *fleur de lis* atop in left hand CD, other hand on pope's upper arm MV, one hand holds cloak P.

Vaticinium XIII

Prehonoracio.

Concordia erit.[a]

Ecce item homo de primo genere abscondito, intrantes simul numeri
annos. Nudus venit de petra tenebrosa et secundam splendentem incipit
5 vitam. Ymago secunde vite verissima, tantum solide solidus duplicatorum
annorum, intrabit[b] mortuus petram.[c]

---

2. erit: *add.* liber tresdicimus L, *duplication of caption in picture* L.
3. item: iste D, idem LMV. simul: similis DM, singuli F. numeri: numeros F.
4. de: *om. sed add. in margine* M. petra: *add.* te M. incipit: incepit V. vitam: vita F.
5. Ymago: inmago F. secunde: sedere F, sancte N. vite: vita M. tantum: tantu F. solide
    solidus: soli desolidus F, solidius N.
6. annorum: amorum L. intrabit: introit FLMPV, intrent N. petram: *add.* papa coronatus
    ab angelo *in same hand* F.

Picture XIV: MS Lunel, fol. 17ᵛ

seated pope: kneeling F, standing, face erased P. **holding book, one hand below, one above:** one hand upraised CMP, *om.* book, hands in prayer F. **angels standing on dais:** to each side CDF, standing above heads of two animals (addorsed, behind pope) P. **angels touching pope:** crowning pope FV, angel holds cross over shoulder F, with both hands V, angels holding arras behind pope CD, angels gesturing toward pope, arras behind M.

Vaticinium XIV

Bona occasio.

Vendencium sacra cessabunt.[a]

Recipe donum. Ne pigriteris, senex, sed recipiens potentissime, pensa
de fine. Et ad bonum dirige sceptrigeriam alia quidem non metuens
5   tempus. Et enim de super istum recepisti. Solum tribus auroris circumdati
anni, uno denario stelle complete, bene fini sacratum.[b] Quid admiraris
annunciacionem recipis? Reliquisti placite planta[c] habitacionem. Sequere
vocantem ad presentem gloriam. Bene finisti diem in principiis. Bono fine
comple universam creaturam. Et habitaciones ambula celestes. In te enim
10   principium bonorum et finis.

---

1.   Bona occasio: Occasio bona LNP.
2.   Vendencium: v[e]ndencium L, veniencium V. sacra: sacro L. cessabunt: cessabit DL,
      add. liber xiiii L.
3.   Ne: *om.* N. pigriteris: *add.* ut *in superscript* F, *om.* N. senex: senes FL, *add.* vendencium
      but crossed out N. sed: set CFLP, se M. potentissime: potissime F, potentissima N.
4.   fine: sine N. bonum: *om.* L. dirige: dinge L. sceptrigeriam: septrigeram D, sed trigena
      F, septrigenam L, septuariam P. septrigeria? V. alia quidem: aliquidem M.
5.   tempus: tempore DMN. istum: *add. but excises* de super C. recepisti: accepisti P. cir-
      cumdati: circondati N.
6.   anni: *om.* L, a M. uno denario: undenarii F, animo L, minimo denario M. complete:
      complere D, oblete L. bene: bone C. fini: fluisti M, sini N.
6–7. sacratum . . . annunciacionem: sacr *lacuna* ciacionem *corrected in margin to* sacratem quid
      admiraris annunciacionen M. sacratum: sacratu P, sacuratam V. Quid: quod F, quam
      L, pro N. ammirans F admiraris: admiratis N, amiraris LP, aminis V. annunciacionem:
      adnunciacionem D, ammirationem F, annunciatione L, annunciationem P.
7.   recipis: *add.* recipis N. placite: placuere D, placide FN, placita L. planta: *om.* L, plenta
      V. habitacionem: alucratione F, alterationis L, altercationis MV, alteracionem NP.
      Sequere: sequeretur V.

8.   vocantem: vocacio N. Bene: unde C. diem: dixit LPNV. principiis: principis C, principio L. Bono: bona DF, bone V. fine: fine ? C, fide D.

9.   comple: conple L. universam: inuniversa L, universa MPV, numerum N. creaturam: sacratum N. habitaciones: habitationem L. celestes: celeste LMNPV. In te enim: enim in te LMNV, enim iure P.

10.   finis: *add. somewhat apart from text* papa cum duobus angelis *in slightly smaller but same hand* F.

Picture XV: MS Lunel, fol. 19ʳ

pope standing holding tiara: on pedestal D, seated V, *add.* wearing mitre CDM, *add.* wearing tiara F, *add.* nimbus M. **book in left hand:** holds triple-barred cross F, holds book aloft M. *add.* beast with human face, headdress of horns or spikey feathers F.

Vaticinium XV

Reverencia.

Devocio augmentabitur.

Bonam vitam invenisti ab ingloriacione. A virtute autem accepisti plus-
quam a fortuna, sed nequaquam virtuose lucraberis gratiam. Invidia enim
5   contingens iudicia tibi nocenciam. Non privaberis a sorde de super.

2.   augmentabitur: au[g]m[en]tabitur L *add.* liber xi, *caption within picture* Reverencie
      devotio augmentabitur L, augumentabitur V.
3.   Bonam vitam: Ionam vita M, Bona vita PV. ingloriacione: ingeneratione F, gloria-
      tione L, ingeneracione M. virtute: viventute V. autem: *om.* L.
4.   a: *om.* F. fortuna: fortunam F. sed: set L. nequaquam virtuose: necquam virtuose C,
      om. lacuna *sed add. in [left] margine* nequam virtuosam ? M. virtose: virtuosam F.
      lucraberis gratiam: *om.* lacuna *sed add. in [right] margine* M. lucraberis: lucraboris N,
      luctaberis V. gratiam: gloriam L. Invidia: invidiam L, *om.* lacuna *sed add. in [right]*
      margine in ligna M. enim: *om. sed add. in [right] margine* M.
4–5. enim contingens iudicia: *om.* V. contingens: contingnens F. iudicia: iudica C, iudicabit
      D.
5.   nocenciam: nocentiam FLP, innocentia N. non: non? C, ire? M, ut LPNV. sorde:
      sorte FL. de: *om.* L. super: *add.* deo gratias amen F, *add. in same hand paragraph sign*
      papa cum libro in manu et cum metria F, *add.* Ve civitas sanguinum universa men-
      dacii dilaceratione plena non recedet a te rapina vox flagelli et vox impetus rote, et
      equi frementis (Nah. 3:1–2) PV, P *apparently in second hand*, V *in same hand as text.*
      Add. below image in red Explicit liber ymaginum papalium L. NP *add. as sixteenth text*
      verse from Dan. *4:13 with caption* Corona superbie, N *on same page as text fifteen,* P *on*
      following page: Cor eius ab humano commutetur, et cor fere detur ei et septem tem-
      pora mutentur super eum.

erit rumor in populo et diuiso uoces audient et time ag
nus timens in mansuetudine sua non erit ausus loq
nisi ue ciuitatis cui nomen irgilia cui vdir et agnos
cir locuto magnatis eius repleti uerecundia incipient
in uocare pacem et pax no erit amplius et remissis fje
lus fugient per diuersa coronabitur in die illa leo et tue
ursa egredietur de urisela et adurget catulo ueroni et
procreatis filius leonecp coronato et dragone deuicto era
tabir eos confr se et eius uictorie non erit finis. Egre
dietur in die illa agnus de ueroia et adiungef urse i
irgiliane et occurret leoni de tusela uemencia. et
eo deuicto spolus leonis gaudebit et continuo ex eo filios

Picture XVI: MS Lunel, fol. 22ᵛ

beast, crowned, with human face, bearded: *om.* CDFM, *om.* beard PV [note beast in picture fifteen F].

Vaticinium XVI

Corona superbie.[a]

Cor eius ab humano commutetur, et cor fere detur ei et septem tempora mutentur super eum.

1–3. Caption and text: *Only NP have caption or text.*
2–3. Cor . . . eum: Dan. *4:13.*

Notes to the Edition

VATICINIUM I

a.   *Prophecy number one, text and image*: Both the D and F scribes identify this pope as Nicholas III (1277–1280); the L illuminator includes the identification, "Nicholas tercius," within the frame of the image. Pipini, writing some time before 1317 (for date, see Lerner, "On the Origins," 620, n. 21), identifies the first pope of the prophecies as Nicholas III, Giovanni Gaetani Orsini (*Chronicon*, Cap. XX, cols. 724–725). As the commentary on the cardinal prophecies makes clear, the earliest version of the prophecies referred to Giovanni Gaetani Orsini as the first of five Orsini cardinals (see Rehberg, " 'Kardinalsorakel'," and Millet and Rigaux, "Aux origines," above). See also Dante, *Inferno*, 19: 61–120, in particular 69–72, as Nicholas III speaks, ". . . know that I was vested with the great mantle; and I was truly a son of the she-bear, so eager to advance the cubs that up there I pursued my gains . . ." Nicholas III made nine new cardinals, among them three relatives: Latino Malabranca, a nephew; Giordano Orsini, a brother; and James Colonna, a cousin. MS Yale, Marston 225 (M) shows three dogs instead of three bears, possibly a reference to dogs as persecutors of Christ (cf. Ps. 21:17); for a discussion of variants in the content of the pictures, here as elsewhere, see above, "Picture Tradition." For a detailed description of the miniatures in each manuscript, see above, "Descriptions of Manuscripts."

    In general, according to textual evidence, the nine MSS fall into two groups, ACD–F, which preserve the earlier of the versions, and LMNPV, which preserve a somewhat later version. The evidence of the captions provides the only substantial exception. F and M omit captions entirely; A and C record the short form (line one) as does the commentary on the cardinal prophecies; DLNPV record the long form (lines one and two combined). The Leo Oracles (Lambecius edition printed in Migne) have short captions but not always identical to those in A and C. Pipini does not quote all of the captions, long or short, but does include the long caption, for example, for prophecy number five, the one traditionally identified with Celestine V. Given the evidence of D, one must assume the longer form of the caption evolved very early on, certainly before 1317, at least for those long captions recorded by Pipini.

b. Given the testimony of the commentary on the cardinal prophecies (I:8), *filius* must have been the earliest reading, but curiously it is retained only by F and M.

c. *filios*: I have chosen *filios*, ACDF's reading rather than *oculos*, LMNP's reading (V omits) on the basis of sense. On the basis of textual evidence alone, either reading is defensible.

d. The commentary on the cardinal prophecies (Vat. lat. 3819) quotes "lugendum in altitudinem celi." The Arras copy (Bibliothèque Municipale MS 171, fol. 81^r) reads *latitudinem* for *altitudinem*.

e. The text to this point is not found in the Lambecius version of the Leo Oracles (although a variation is found in the sixteenth-century Barocci MS) and thus can be presumed to be an addition by the formulator of the *Genus nequam* prophecies with particular reference to Nicholas III. See also Rehberg, " 'Kardinalsorakel'," 51–52, 98–99, on this point.

f. LPV read *misera nequissima*, perhaps for added emphasis; the words have slightly different connotations.

g. *Imitata*: A case could be made as well for M's reading of *immutata*. No clear reading emerges from FLNPV.

h. N's reading, *convertis*, unique to it, makes good sense, but ACDFLM-PV read *converti*. Part one of the Regiselmo printed version (*Vaticinium XVI*) reads "Multos decipies nequissime sub aliena pelle immutata enim visum fallacem convertis in terra abscondens. ..." Version two in this printed edition reads "Multos decipis misera, nequissima sub aliena pelle unita: nam falcem convertis intra, abscondis. ...," with the variant, "Falcem converte intra, absconde. ..." recorded in the margin. The commentary on the cardinal prophecies makes no reference to this sentence, quoting only "multos decipis nequissima sub aliena pelle," picking up again at "abscondis deceptionem inimicos facientem" (I:24, 27).

i. The commentary on the cardinal prophecies reads *iustos* for *istos*.

j. *Christus*: A's scribe either knew both versions *tempus/Christus* or made an addition or interpolation. CD and the Lambecius edition of the Leo Oracles have *tempus*; A has *tempus* with superscription *alias Christus*. See also above, "Archetype and Copy Text: Text and Image," 23, and Daneu Lattanzi, " 'Vaticinia Pontificum'," 782, n. 2.

k. CD prophecy number one ends with this paragraph, apparently in error; yet note the Regiselmo printed edition of 1589 (*Vaticinium XVI*) prints two version of unit one, the first ending with "Multos decipies nequissime sub aliena pelle immutata enim visum fallacem convertis in terra abscondens, et deceptionem in multis faciens." The second version in the Regiselmo edition prints a slightly different version of the first and continues with "sic autem bene manes" to the end. Note also that Leo Oracle one is in two distinct parts and that the last reference to prophecy one in the cardinal or Orsini commentary is to the preceding sentence.

l. lines 12–13: M's reading here is unique and makes clear sense: "et manus expandis *ut servos Domini* pervertas" (emphasis mine).

m. Cf. Ps. 44 (45) 2: "Eructavit cor meum verbum bonum."

VATICINIUM II

a. *Prophecy number two, text and image*: The F scribe, the L illuminator, and Pipini (*Chronicon*, Cap. XXI, cols. 725–727) identify this pope as Martin IV (1281–1285), Simon de Brie. The text of prophecy number two roughly corresponds to part two of Leo Oracle one (PG 107:1129 B) with some rearrangement of lines. On *sanguis*, see commentary on cardinal prophecies II:33–36 (also Rehberg, " 'Kardinalsorakel'," 56) for play on the name of Cardinal Matteo Rosso Orsini.

The caption in its longer form may well refer to Martin IV's crusade tax, much of which went to funding Charles of Anjou's efforts to hold on to Sicily. On Easter Monday, 1282, in what has come to be known as the Sicilian Vespers, the Sicilians of Palermo violently attacked their Angevin occupiers. The uprising spread and the contest between Charles of Anjou and Peter of Aragon for control of Sicily intensified (Steven Runciman, *The Sicilian Vespers* [Cambridge, 1958], 201–241). If the winged beast in V and in the Regiselmo edition (*Vaticinium XVII*) is indeed a griffin (which I think unlikely), the word "griffon" referring to "Greek," as the "castle of Mategriffon," there is then the possiblity of a reference to Emperor Michael Palaeologus and the role he played in this contest.

b. The reading of the commentary on the cardinal prophecies, *se iunxit*, suggests *iunctus* rather than *vinctus*. ANPV read either *vinctus* (PV) or *iunctus* (AN); Daneu Lattanzi notes *vinctus* should be *tinctus* (" 'Vaticinia Pontificum'," 782, n. 10); L's reading of *viris* stands alone but could be related to the *victus* reading of C and M.

c. The commentary on the cardinal prophecies reads "et totus factus est niger" (II:40).

d. Translation: deprived of light *by* ravens or deprived of light *like* ravens (i.e., according to fable, ravens turned to black in punishment for treachery).

e. I have chosen *in*, ACDL's reading, over *et*, MNPV's reading, for reasons of syntax; the commentary on the cardinal prophecies omits, running the two sentences together.

f. Only A shares the reading *metus* (in superscript) of the commentary on the cardinal prophecies.

VATICINIUM III

a. *Prophecy number three, text and image*: The F scribe, L illuminator, and Pipini (*Chronicon*, Cap. XXII, col. 727) identify this pope as Honorius IV (1285–1287), Giacomo Savelli, as does the commentary on the cardinal prophecies, which identifies him as the third cub (see Rehberg, " 'Kardinalsorakel'," 68; Millet and Rigaux, "Aux origines," 144). The text of this prophecy corresponds to that of Leo Oracles two and three (PG 107:1129 C–1132 A), with considerable rearrangement of lines.

The gist of the oracles would seem to be an explanation of the opening words, *Ambiguum tercium*, and the number of emperors who will also bear the insignia of the bird bearing a cross. *Lines 1–2*: It is Martin IV who is called an heir of Simon Magus by contemporaries not Honorius IV (Nicholas of Bibra, cited in Horace K. Mann, *The Lives of the Popes in the Middle Ages* [London, 1932], vol. 16, 180); Honorius IV "shall follow the footsteps" of Martin IV and thus also those of Simon Magus.

b. *Et enim avis . . . corniger.* F's reading corresponds most closely to the image, i.e., a bird with cross, a knight (*eques*), and a unicorn. The second human figure elsewhere is small, hands in a gesture of supplication. The commentary on the cardinal prophecies reads "eques et corniger" (III:62). The repetition here apparently functions as a form of elaboration. In all the manuscripts except C and V, *corniger* is a single word.

c. The sense is unclear, but the word order in LMNPV seems marginally better. The commentary on the cardinal prophecies reads "extremus numerus in tempore unius prime figure" (III:66).

VATICINIUM IV

a. *Prophecy number four, text and image*: The F scribe, L illuminator, and Pipini (*Chronicon*, XXIII, cols. 727–728) identify this pope as Nicholas IV (1288–1292), the Franciscan Girolamo Masci; the cardinal or Orsini commentary identifies the fourth and fifth units with the fourth cub, Latino Malabranca (Rehberg, " 'Kardinalsorakel'," 56–57; Millet and Rigaux, "Aux origines," 146, 148; also Lerner, "Recent Work," 152–154). C and D combine texts four and five; in D's case, text five begins on a new line and is marked by rubrication. C runs the two texts together separated only by the one-word caption *Elatio*.

The text of prophecy four is drawn from Leo Oracles four and five (PG 107:1132 C-1133 AB) with the addition of several words and considerable rearrangement of lines, although unit five is drawn exclusively from Leo Oracle four.

b. F's reading, on the basis of sense; neither reading *collis* (ACDL) nor *collus* (MNPV) makes particular sense. The commentary on the cardinal prophecies also reads *collateralis*.

c. *la M.*: originally at least for Latino Malabranca (commentary on the cardinal prophecies IV:94–95); the commentary cites only *la.*, continuing *O miserum. . . .* (Rehberg, " 'Kardinalsorakel'," 110).

VATICINIUM V

a. *Prophecy number five, text and image*: The F scribe, L illuminator, and Pipini (*Chronicon*, Cap. XL, col. 736) identify this figure as Celestine V (5 July–13 Dec. 1294), Pietro del Morrone. Pipini notes his canonization in 1313 under Clement V. The text of this prophecy is drawn from Leo Oracle four (PG 107:1132 C-1133 A) with some rearrangement.

b. The long form of the caption shows considerable variation in syntax and in spelling; analysis of textual evidence provides no clear conclusions. DL have *gule* for *castrimargie*; DuCange gives *gulae concupiscentia* for *castrimargia*. Pipini omits the words *et ypocrisorum destructor*, but cites these same words as the caption in the description of Boniface VIII (*Chronicon*, Cap. XLII, col. 741).

c. Or *resuscitabo*; textual evidence is divided here. I chose *resuscitabis* to parallel the imperative *vade* in the next line, but it is clear there is considerable shifting back and forth between the grammatical points of view "I" and "you." No witness is entirely consistent.

VATICINIUM VI

a.   *Prophecy number six, text and image*: The F scribe (although the identification has been partially erased), L illuminator, and Pipini (*Chronicon*,
Cap. XLII, col. 741) identify this pope as Boniface VIII (1294–1303),
Benedetto Caetani of the Orsini family. Rehberg (" 'Kardinalsorakel',"
59–61) and Millet and Rigaux ("Aux origines," 144–145) argue that
the commentary on the cardinal prophecies refers to Giordano Orsini
(the fifth cub); Lerner ("Recent Work," 153–154) suggests this cub
might be Napoleone Orsini.

      The caption makes equal sense if lines one and two are run togeth-
er in a sentence; *ypocrisis* then is genitive not nominative case. I have
arranged the captions on the page as I have in order to give a clear
distinction between the short and the longer forms. Sometimes the
longer form of the caption is simply added to the short; in other instances a new sentence is formed incorporating both the long and
short forms. As noted above, Pipini gives a positive form of the caption. Otherwise it is the combination of caption, and possibly, iconography which points to negative qualities of Boniface VIII, not the
text itself, which follows fairly closely, with some rearrangement of
lines, that in Leo Oracle six (PG 107:1133 B).

b.   *Quintum*, I am assuming, refers to *genus* of prophecy one. F's reading
qui[n]tum filium must be close to the archetype.

c.   Thus, the sense of the line is "the end of the she-bear feeding on
bears." Other readings are possible since the textual evidence is divided between *finis* and *filiis/filii* and *ursos* and *ursa/urse*. The commentary
on the cardinal prophecies (VI:120–122) suggests that this "fifth son of
the bear" is at odds with the other "sons" and is "a friend to the
friends of the Church."

d.   Perfect participle, from *morior*, supported by A's reading. CD has
mortuas changing the sense of the phrase, i.e., *mortuas potencias*. The
commentary on the cardinal prophecies reads "eo mortuo relinquet
potentias" (VI:126–127).

e.   Or alternatively *relinquens*, then changing the period after *potencias* to
a comma.

f.   "Sicut enim ymbrem bene invenies potencias": Leslie S. B. MacCoull
suggests this sentence may be an allusion to Job 37:6. She notes there
is also perhaps an underlying reminiscence of the story of Gideon's
fleece in Judges 6 which is traditionally interpreted messianically, as a
prophecy of the virginal conception of Christ. Also cf. Deut. 32:2. I
am indebted to her for these references.

VATICINIUM VII

a. *Prophecy number seven, text and image*: The F scribe (although identification has been partially erased), L illuminator, and Pipini (*Chronicon*, Cap. XLVIII, cols. 745–757) identify this pope as Benedict XI (1303–1304), Niccolò Boccasino. In unit six it is the caption which points to Boniface VIII rather than the text. *Caption*: Pipini omits the caption entirely. *Balax*: for *Balac* or *Balak* (cf. Numbers, 22, 23, 24) and by extension Belial, i.e., "sons of iniquity" (*filii Belial* in Deut. 13:31, Judg. 19:22). Benedict XI was closely identified with his predecessor Boniface VIII, both popes supported by the Orsini rather than the Colonna families. Although Benedict pardoned all the French involved in Boniface VIII's capture at Anagni, with the exception of Nogaret, his encyclical of 6 November 1303 condemned those who participated in this uprising, calling them "sons of iniquity" (*Registres de Benoît XI*, ed. C. A. Grandjean [Paris, 1885], fasc. 3, #1099, 656–657, here 656).

b. If *ante utrasque coronas*, as M reads, the sense would be somewhat different.

VATICINIUM VIII

a. *Prophecy number eight, text and image*: Only the L illuminator identifies this prophecy with Clement V (1305–1314). F has the initials ɱ. .G. (M? V? for roman numeral V?) below the text and above the cityscape.

    The tone if not the language of this prophecy is similar to the lamentations of the prophet Jeremiah over the desolation of Jerusalem (Lamentations 1). The text follows closely that of Leo Oracle eight (PG 107:1136 AB), with some rearrangement of lines. The caption would seem to point to both the political disorder in Rome after Benedict's death and the hope for eventual renewal of the papacy in Rome.

b. This phrase, *circa parvum tempus*, might begin the next sentence.

c. Lines 11–14: Similar in tone to the language in Rom. 1:19, Luke 18:11, Apoc. 21:8.

VATICINIUM IX

a. *Prophecy number nine, text and image*: Although Pipini (*Chronicon*, Cap. XLVIIII, cols. 751–752) identifies this pope as Clement V (1305–1314), Bertrand de Got, there is little either in text or caption which points in particular to Clement. Clement was guilty of nepotism, and simony, rather than ceasing, would seem to have flourished (G. Mollat, *The Popes at Avignon 1305–1378* [London, 1949], 3–8). The text follows closely that of Leo Oracle nine (PG 107:1136 BC) with some alterations in the sentence beginning on line four of the pope prophecy text and the addition of the word *voluptiones*. Clement V was a sick man but there were, undoubtedly unfounded, rumors of voluptuous living (see the references to Villani and Mussato cited in Mollat, *Popes at Avignon*, 6, n. 2).

For the first line of the caption, only NP, each dependent on a common exemplar, give *Occisio* rather than *Bona gratia*. L reads *Occasio* (see Millet and Rigaux, "Aux origines," 138).

VATICINIUM X

a.   *Prophecy number ten, text and image*: The text is a lament for the city of Rome, although of course "the city of seven hills," line three, could refer as well to Constantinople, as it must have done in the corresponding Leo Oracles. (For similar language see Apoc. 18:2,10; 14:8; see also biblical references cited in the notes to prophecy 8.) V, alone of the early manuscripts, adds a text from Dan. 8:14: referring to the length of tribulations under the Antichrist: "Usque ad vesperam et mane, dies duo, millia trecenti; et *miniabitur sacrificium*" (emphasis mine). For the italicized words Daniel reads "mundabitur sanctuarium."

Prophecy ten corresponds to Leo Oracles ten and eleven (PG 107: 1136 D–1137 A) with the additions of the abbreviations in lines six and ten. The tone of the caption is at variance with that of the text, unless what is meant is that desolation must precede renewal as in Apocalypse 18. On the caption, see Millet and Rigaux, "Aux origines," 138.

b.   FLN's reading of *quando* for *quin*, which makes good sense, suggests different punctuation.

c.   Leo Oracle ten refers to the "20th letter," but the "Oraculorum Leonis Expositio" which follows the text glosses the 20th letter as Tau (the 20th letter if gamma and digamma are counted as separate letters), noting that this letter "est symbologica figura sanctissimae crucis" (PG 107:1165 B). Cf. Alexander, *Byzantine Apocalyptic Tradition*, 133, 152. The number "20" in Greek is represented by K; the Regiselmo edition (*Vaticinium XXV*) reads *K*, noting the alternative reading *R*. It is difficult to make absolute distinctions between *K* and *R* in the MSS, but given the length of the ascenders, CD and P have *K*. See Dan. 5:5, 24–25 for the handwriting on the wall. A reviewer of this book for MRTS notes that the 20th letter of the Latin alphabet is *X* and that "... in the *De seminibus scripturarum* X is the century during which Christ ... will reform the corrupt church. This century would begin about 1248 and run to 1348. The *De seminibus* was known to be used by both Roger Bacon and Arnau de Villanova who wrote a commentary about it." The letter does not seem to be an *X* in any of the MSS, but this reader's suggestion that the *De seminibus* might stand behind "this curious *vaticinium*" is an intriguing one.

d.   Either *manibus* or *menibus* makes sense. The Leo Oracle reads "wall"; the reader noted above prefers *manibus*; the Regiselmo edition gives *menibus*.

e.   As the textual notes show, there is a good deal of variation in this series of abbreviations; no two witnesses agree. I chose N's to print, for, relatively speaking, N's abbreviations were easier to read. Textual evidence makes the *Qui incipit* a likely reading rather than a certainty.

f.   I separated these last two sentences because of general textual agreement. Only V has a variant meaning, *incides*, but it is one which makes good sense.

g.   Leo Oracle eleven reads "his name is John (*Io.*)" (PG 107:1137 A).

VATICINIUM XI

a.   *Prophecy number eleven, text and image*: The text follows closely that of the last two lines of Leo Oracle eleven and all of Oracle twelve (PG 107:1137 A–1138 B). Of all the attributes an angelic pope might possess, it is worth noting that the caption calls attention to a redistribution of money. *Thesaurus* can also mean "treasury of prayers," but here that seems less likely. Note also the connection to caption number nine, "Simony will cease." As was also the case in captions five and ten, DL have an unusual correspondence, adding to the word "treasury," "of Constantine." The F scribe simply describes this pope as "papa nudus." In a much later manuscript, Vat. lat. 3816 (1448), the scribe adds a gloss "This is the Angelic Pope according to Joachim."

b.   *revelabitur virtus*: the reading of DLM. Only C's reading, *revelabitur unctus*, corresponds to the reading in Leo Oracle eleven (PG 107:1138 A); the Regiselmo printed edition gives *unctus* with the alternate reading *virtus*. An early manuscript of the *Liber de Flore* reads *virtus* (see above, "Relation of Manuscripts," 30–31 and n. 6); a fourteenth-century commentary by one "Rabanus" reads "Et revelabitur unctus a deo. . . ." (Carpentras, Bibliothèque Imguimbertine, MS 340, fol. 13ᵛ).

It is curious there should be such variation here, even if the differences among and between these four MSS (CDFM), while affecting sense, do not alter the larger meaning. The variations in NPV are all related, affect sense, and change the meaning somewhat. Except for F and P's readings, I do not see these variants as errors, but rather attempts to make the prophecy more specific or relevant. I suggest the following chronology: *unctus* was the archetype's reading, reflected in C, *virtus* became the vulgate reading, as reflected in DL, changed I would argue because the scribe wanted to distinguish between king and pope (both are of course anointed, but anointing is a sign of legitimacy for the king; see I Sam. 16:12,13, as the Lord directs Samuel to anoint David); the readings of NPV evolved as scribes attempted to differentiate the function and particular character of the angelic pope; *unctus* and *virtus* both survived as readings in late fourteenth and fifteenth-century versions (the Carpentras MS quoted above has *unctus* in the commentary, *virtus* in the text, Vatican Library, MS Vat. lat. 3816 [1448] reads *unctus*, Vatican Library, MS Vat. lat. 3818 [1410–1415] reads *virtus*).

c.   *menachim*: in the Leo Oracle this sentence is preceded by "his name is John [*Io*]" (cf. Luke 1:63 of John the Baptist, the forerunner of Christ); *menachim* is also a Jewish messianic name that appears in the Talmud.

d.   *habitas*: *habitans* is an equally plausible reading and makes for fewer shifts in point of view. McGinn suggests that the next few lines beginning with the verb *veni* are the words of the angelic pope, returning to "you" in the last line (*vade*) (*Visions of the End*, 195, n. 52). This often confusing shift in grammatical point of view is characteristic of the biblical prophetic books, as the Lord speaks through the prophet, and as the prophet speaks in his own voice.

e.   Although only CD read *mortuus*, I have chosen this reading on the basis of sense.

f.   FLP have a paragraph sign before *item*.

g.   *vade in inferiora terre*: cf. unit five, lines eight–nine.

VATICINIUM XII

a.   *Prophecy number twelve, text and image*: The text of the prophecy, based closely on that of Leo Oracle thirteen (PG 107:1137 BC) reinforces the emphasis of the images, suggesting both death and ascension, and the summoning of this "dead" figure to life (see above, "Picture Tradition"). In addition, the "Cento of the True Emperor," a Latin version of which is found in the Yale manuscript immediately following the *Genus nequam* prophecies, contains similar language, in both instances describing a messianic figure, a savior-emperor. It is tempting to see in the series of images and text, eleven through fifteen, at least in the earliest version, a narrative describing the calling forth of an "angelic pope," his being crowned by an angel, his reign, and its end (see Fleming, "Metaphors of Apocalypse," 136–137). It is clear, however, that in the *Liber de Flore*, and later, for Hugh of Novocastro, that units eleven through fifteen were read as a series of popes, the angelic pope and his three holy successors, and that prophecy twelve was read as a continution of prophecy eleven, describing the angelic pope (see McGinn, " 'Pastor Angelicus'," 239–246; Reeves, *Influence of Prophecy*, 325–331, 242–245, 370–372, 406).

Vaticinium XIII

a.   *Prophecy number thirteen, text and image*: The text corresponds quite closely to that in Leo Oracle fourteen (PG 107:1140 A).

b.   CD's reading on the basis of tense; later manuscripts read *introibit* rather than the *introit* of FLMPV (MS Vat. lat. 3816 [1448]).

c.   Note the allusions to the language of prophecy eleven, although the first sentence of this text is sufficiently ambiguous as to make it impossible to say with certainty whether the same or a different pope is being indicated. The F scribe is no help: although he adds at the end of this text the phrase "papa crowned by an angel," at the end of the next text he adds "papa with two angels," again not making it clear whether the "papa" is one and the same person.

Vaticinium XIV

a.   *Prophecy number fourteen, text and image*: The text is based on that of Leo Oracle fifteen (PG 107:1140 AB) with some confusion over the astrological reference in lines five–seven. The sense of line two of the caption is puzzling, as is the syntax.

b.   The astrological reference in lines five–seven is garbled in all witnesses.

c.   Except for L which omits it, *planta* is a consistent reading but makes no sense.

Vaticinium XVI

a.   *Prophecy number sixteen, text and image*: Daneu Lattanzi, " 'Vaticinia Pontificum'," 792, n. 6, calls attention to the similarity to the Tiburtine sibyl: " 'Hic (Antichristus) erit filius perditionis et caput superbiae'. "

Index

Abimelech, 64n
Acre, fall of, 102
Albert the Great, 47, 48n
Alexander VI, 81
Alexander the Minorite, 87
angelic pope
   absent from Cambridge, Corpus Christi College, MS 404 (Henry of Kirkestede), 47–48
   convergence with last world emperor, 15
   Genus nequam prophecies, 1
   identified as Celestine V, 37–38, 47, 60
   Horoscopus, 3, 3n
   iconography, 37–38, 60, 63
   Libellus of Telesphorus, 114
   Liber de Flore, 4, 114
   prophecy XI, 30, 30n, 63, 197–198
   prophecy XII, 199
   Yale, University Library, T. E. Marston MS 225, 15
angelic series, 21, 23, 72, 199. *See also* angelic pope
"Anonymous Paraphrase," 15, 70, 70n. *See also* "Cento of the True Emperor"
Anselm, Bishop of Marsico, 6n
Antichrist
   Ascende calve prophecies, 5
   Cambridge, Corpus Christi College, MS 404 (Henry of Kirkestede), 45, 48

Florence, Biblioteca Riccardiana, MS 1222B, 36, 60, 62, 111–112
   iconography, 36, 60, 62, 63, 67, 111–114
   illustrated Apocalypses, 48n, 60
   Lunel, Bibliothèque de Louis Médard à la Bibliothèque Municipale, MS 7, 63, 67
   predictions of its coming, 38, 38n, 66n, 73, 113–114, 114n
   three-headed, 64n
   Tibertine sibyl, 82n, 200
   Vatican Library, MS Vat. lat. 3819, 88–89, 196
Apocalypse, 5, 48, 105, 109
   illustrated, 48n, 60, 112–113
apotheosis, 109n, 110
Arnaude de Nogarède, 3, 64n
Arnold of Villanova (or, Arnau de), 3n, 75, 197
Ascende calve prophecies
   combined with *Genus nequam* prophecies, 5–6, 18
   fragment in Cambridge, Corpus Christi College, MS 404, 44, 46, 46n, 48
   history of, 5–6, 5n
   image of prisoner of Boniface VIII, 104n
   reference to Apocalypse, 48n

Bacon, Roger, 197
Bavaria, 71, 74

Benedict XI
    Florence, Biblioteca Riccardiana,
        MS 1222B, 14, 57, 58, 60, 195
    Genus nequam prophecies, 1, 1n
    iconography, 68, 105, 195
bestiary, 51n, 52, 52n, 53n
Boccasino, Niccolò. See Benedict XI
Boniface VIII
    Ascende calve prophecies, 104n
    Celestine V, 21, 34, 37n, 38n
        imprisonment of, 83n, 103–104
    controversy with Philip the Fair,
        37, 78, 79
    Florence, Biblioteca Riccardiana,
        MS 1222B, 58, 194
    Genus nequam prophecies, 1, 4,
        193–195
    iconography, 68, 104
    Yale, University Library, T. E.
        Marston MS 225, 72
Boniface XI, 4
Brie, Simon de. See Martin IV

Caetani, Benedetto. See Boniface VIII
Calixtus III, 81
"Cardinal Commentary," 19n. See
    also commentary on the cardi-
    nal prophecies and Orsini com-
    mentary
cardinal oracle(s), 20, 29, 96n. See also
    cardinal prophecies
cardinal prophecies, 6–9, 15n, 52n,
    60n. See also cardinal oracle(s)
    and commentary on the cardi-
    nal prophecies and Orsini com-
    mentary
Celestine V
    angelic pope, 37–38, 47, 60, 60n
    canonization, 79, 193
    commentary on the cardinal pro-
        phecies, 104

Florence, Biblioteca Riccardiana,
    MS 1222B, 34, 58n, 60, 193
Genus nequam prophecies, 1
iconography
    changes over time, 38, 95
    figure with sickle and rose, 34,
        42, 47, 48, 68
    identification by Henry of Kirke-
        stede, 47–48
    omitted from unit five in manu-
        scripts A–CD, 21–23, 94
    Oxford, Bodleian Library, MS
        Douce 88, 21–23, 54–55
    prophecy V, 35, 37n, 60, 60n,
        64n, 103n, 190, 193
    Latino Malabranca, 103
    Vatican Library, MS Vat. lat. 3819,
        90
    Yale, University Library, T. E.
        Marston MS 225, 72–73
    See also Boniface VIII and Celes-
        tine V
"Cento of the True Emperor," 15,
    30, 70–72, 70n, 75, 199
Charles of Anjou (Charles I, King of
    Sicily), 191
Charles V, 102
Charles d'Orléans, 80
Choniates, Nicetas, 5
Clement V
    canonized Celestine V, 193
    death, 79
    "Exivi de paradiso," 97, 97n
    Florence, Biblioteca Riccardiana,
        MS 1222B, 14, 57–59, 60n
    Francesco Pipini, 2, 106, 195
    iconography, 89n
    Monreale, Biblioteca Comunale,
        MS XXV.F.17, 83n
    Lunel, Bibliothèque de Louis Mé-
        dard à la Bibliothèque Munici-

pale, MS 7, 65, 68, 106n, 195
prophecy VIII, 195
prophecy IX, 106, 195
Vatican Library, MS Vat. lat. 3819,
89
Clement VI, 44, 48
Colonna
Giovanni, 90, 90n
James, 189
Columbinus Prophecy, 78n, 79
commentary on the cardinal prophecies
Cambridge, Corpus Christi College, MS 404, 47n, 49
captions, 10n, 24n, 27n, 189
controversy surrounding papacies of
Celestine V and Boniface VIII,
37n
description of, 7–8, 8n, 32n, 96n,
105n
Florence, Biblioteca Riccardiana,
MS 1222B, 58
iconographic evidence, 31–35, 96,
99–101, 104
interpretation of, 13n
omissions, 20n, 23, 29, 105
Oxford, Bodleian Library, MS
Douce 88, 53
prophecy I, 189–191
prophecy II, 191–192
prophecy III, 192
prophecy IV, 193
prophecy VI, 194
refers to first recension of Genus
nequam prophecies, 16, 19–20,
21n–22n
shows relationships between early
manuscripts (A–CD), 22, 28, 31
usage in this edition, 25, 31
Vatican Library, MS Vat. lat. 3819,
88–89

Vatican Library, MS Vat. lat. 3822,
41
Comnenus, Andronicus I, 103n
Cossa, Baldassare, 104n
Cotton, Bartholomew, 100
Council of Vienne, 37, 37n, 66n, 79
Curti, Raimond, 3
Cyril (the Carmelite), 3. See Oraculum
Cyrilli and Telesphorus' Libellus on

Dante (Alighieri), 95, 189
Dauphiné, 102
Délicieux, Bernard, 64n
owned "papalarius," 9, 66, 83n,
107, 107n
witness of pope prophecies, 2, 3,
3n, 19n, 24

Edward I, 102
"Exiit qui seminat," 97–98, 97n

Fiore, Joachim of. See Joachim of
Fiore
Franciscans, Italian Spirituals
adversaries, 75n
debate with papacy over poverty
and rule, 97, 98n
discourse, 97, 97n
iconography, 60
linked to pope prophecies, 1, 4–6,
9, 21
patrons, 65n, 74, 74n
resonance, 60, 60n, 95
views on Celestine V, 37–38, 37n,
60, 60n

Gentile of Foligno, 3, 3n, 19n
Giochimo, Abate. See Joachim of
Fiore
Got, Bertrand de. See Clement V
Gregorius, 108, 108n

Gregory IX, 4, 97n
Gregory XI, 45, 48

Henry de Carreto, 65n
Henry of Kirkestede, 21n,
    compilation of Cambridge, Corpus
        Christi College, MS 404, 44–
        45
Hildegard of Bingen, 3, 46, 66n
    anti-mendicant propaganda, 66,
        66n
    pseudo-Hildegard prophecy, 39,
        63, 66, 111
Honorius IV, 1, 21n, 33, 100, 192
    iconography, 67, 99, 103n
Horoscopus, 3, 19n
    commentary on, 3
    source for Yale, University Library,
        T. E. Marston MS 225, 75
Hugh of Novocastro
    identifies picture eleven as "papa
        nudus," 58, 108n
    reads last five prophecies as series
        of popes, 36n, 199
    refers to later manuscripts of *Genus
        nequam* prophecies, 19n
    describes last pope setting down his
        tiara, 114n
    witness of pope prophecies, 2, 2n

Innocent VI, 57

Jean de France, Duc de Berry, 80,
    113
Joachim, Abbot of S. Giovanni in
    Fiore
    Florence, Biblioteca Riccardiana,
        MS 1222B, ascribed to Abate
        Giochimo (Joachim), 57
    Lunel, Bibliothèque de Louis Mé-
        dard à la Bibliothèque Munici-

pale, MS 7, 39n, 63, 63n, 65n
    pope prophecies erroneously attrib-
        uted to, 1–4, 45, 46, 80
    prophecies of angelic pope, 108,
        197
    unicorn, 100
"Joachim super Apocalipsim," 87n
Joachite anthologies, 70
Joachite prophecies. *See* Joachim of
    Fiore
Joachite texts, 65n, 66, 111, 113n
Job, 108, 108n
John (King) of Bohemia, 90
John XXII
    confrontation with Franciscan or-
        der, 97–98, 98n
    elected pope, 79
    listed in Vatican Library, MS Vat.
        lat. 3819, 7, 89–91
    papal bulls, 75
    "Quia nonnunquam," 97n, 98
    "Quia vir reprobus," 98
    Yale, University Library, T. E.
        Marston MS 225, contempo-
        rary with pontificate of, 72, 74

last world emperor, 15
Leo Oracles
    "Anonymous   Paraphrase,"   or
        "Cento of the True Emperor,"
        70–71, 70n
    captions, 24, 53
    comparison with Regiselmo edi-
        tion, 22–23
    editions of, 5n, 18n, 102n
    Florence, Biblioteca Riccardiana,
        MS 1222B, 36, 59
    Greek texts, 15, 95
    iconography, 95–110
    influence on Cambridge, Corpus
        Christi College, MS 404, and

Oxford, Bodleian Library, MS Douce 88, 20, 20n, 47n, 49, 55, 96

inspiration for cardinal prophecies, 8, 19

interpretation of, 103n

items absent from Leo Oracles, 29, 32n, 41, 42, 83, 113

prophecy I, 95, 189–191

prophecy II, 98, 191

prophecy III, 99–100, 192

prophecy IV, 101, 193

prophecy V, 33, 103, 193

prophecy VI, 194

prophecy VII, 105

prophecy IX, 196

prophecy X, 106, 106n–107n, 196–197

prophecy XI, 30, 107–108, 197–198

prophecy XII, 109, 198

prophecy XIII, 110, 199

prophecy XIV, 199

source for *Genus nequam* prophecies, 5, 6, 9, 11, 13, 18, 34–35

Yale, University Library, T. E. Marston MS 225, 15, 70–72

Libellus of Telesphorus, 38n, 73, 73n, 88, 113–114, 114n

Liber de Flore

also known as *Liber de Flore sive de summis pontificibus,* 3–4

captions, 53

description of, 3–4

Herbert Grundmann's partial edition of, 4n, 38n

makes no reference to images in *Genus nequam* prophecies, 10n

prophecies of Last Things and Antichrist, 38n, 73, 73n, 113–114, 114n, 199

relation to later manuscripts of *Genus nequam* prophecies, 19n, 30, 30n, 31, 197

source for Yale, University Library, T. E. Marston MS 225, 75

Liber de magnis tribulationibus et de statu ecclesiae, 4n

Liber Ostensor. See Roquetaillade, John of

Louis (IV) of Bavaria, 72n, 74–75, 74n, 75n, 98

Louis XII, 80

Malabranca, Latino, 28–29, 33, 96n, 189, 193

in iconography, 101, 103, 103n

Mandeville's Travels, 113

Martin IV, 1, 10, 21n, 97, 191

heir of Simon Magus, 192

in iconography, 67, 98, 99

"man of blood," 4

Masci, Girolamo. *See* Nicholas IV

Merlin, 43, 43n

Michael of Cesena, 75n, 98

Morrone, Pietro del. *See* Celestine V

Nebuchadnezzar, 113, 113n

Nicholas of Bibra, 192

Nicholas III

beginning of *Ascende calve* prophecies, 5

beginning of *Genus nequam* prophecies, 1, 2, 4, 10, 46

beginning of the *Horoscopus,* 3

commentary on the cardinal prophecies, 7, 20, 96n

elected by Orsini party, 32, 100

iconography, 65

bear symbolism, 74, 95–96, 105

dogs, 74, 98

one of five bear cubs, 21n, 32, 32n

pope with bears, 53, 63, 67
identified as "Principium malo-
    rum" in the *Liber de Flore,* 4
made Latino Malabranca a cardinal,
    33, 189
papal bulls, 75
    "Exiit qui seminat," 97, 97n
prophecy I, 53, 189, 190
Nicholas IV, 1, 7, 29, 47, 193
iconography, 67, 102
Nicholas V, 90
Ninevah, 82, 88, 111
Nogaret, 79, 195

Oraculum Cyrilli, 87, 90
Orsini commentary, 8, 19n, 41, 49,
    193. *See also* commentary on
    the cardinal prophecies
Orsini
    Giordano
        cow symbolism, 105
        fifth bear cub, 34, 96n, 104, 194
        made a cardinal by Nicholas
            III, 189
        Giovanni Gaetano. *See* Nicholas III
    Matteo Rossi, 11, 21n, 32, 96n, 191
    Napoleone, 194

Palaeologus, Emperor Michael, 191
'Pastor Angelicus,' 4n
Peter of Aragon, 191
Philip IV the Fair, 37, 78, 79, 89, 102
Philip VI, 102
Philip of Majorca, 74
Physiologus, 100
Pierre des Vaux-de-Cernay, 78, 78n
Pierre d'Étampes, 78–79
Pipini, Francescon (*Chronicon*)
    references to images in the *Genus
        nequam* prophecies, 10–11,
        10n, 31, 31n

prophecy I, 96, 189, 190
prophecy II, 99, 191
prophecy III, 192
prophecy IV, 101, 101n, 193
prophecy V, 35, 103, 193
prophecy VI, 104, 194
prophecy VII, 105, 195
prophecy VIII, 106
prophecy IX, 195
references to the *Genus nequam*
    prophecies, 2, 2n, 19n, 24,
    53
propaganda, anti-mendicant, 66
"Prophecie Joachim." *See* Joachim of
    Fiore
pseudo-Hildegard. *See* Hildegard,
    pseudo-Hildegard prophecies
Pseudo-Methodian, 72

"Quia nonnunquam," 97n, 98
"Quia vir reprobus," 98

Rabanus Anglicus, 3, 198
Regiselmo, Pasqualino
    comparison with Leo Oracles, 22–
        23
    edition of pope prophecies, 5n–6n,
        30n
    iconography, 94, 102
    Monreale, Biblioteca Comunale,
        MS XXV.F.17, 81, 83
    prophecy I, 190, 191
    prophecy X, 196
    prophecy XI, 197
Robert of Naples, 74
Roquetaillade, John of (or, Jean de,
    or, John of Rupescissa)
    refers to later manuscripts of *Genus
        nequam,* 19n
    quotes "Cento of the True Emper-
        or," 30, 30n, 71

quotes *Liber de Flore* and *Genus ne-quam*, 3, 3n
sources, 75, 75n
Salimbene, 103
Savelli, Jacopo (or, Giacomo). *See* Honorius IV
savior-emperor, 5, 15, 70, 72, 74, 199
Sicilian Vespers, 191
Sicily, 70, 191
history, 72
Simon Magus, 192
Spirituals, Franciscan. *See* Franciscans, Italian Spirituals

Telesphorus (of Cosenza). See *Libellus* of, and *Liber de magnis tribula-tionibus et de statu ecclesiae*
Templars, 37n, 64n, 79
Tibertine Oracle (or, Tibertine pro-phecy) 70–72, 82n, 200
Tibertine sibyl. *See* Tibertine Oracle

Tractatus de Victoria Christi contra Anti-christum. See Hugh of Novo-castro
Tripoli prophecy, 70, 70n, 71

Urban V, 90n
Urbanus VI, 45, 47, 48

Vaticinia de summis pontificibus, 4, 6
Vaticinia sive Prophetiae Abbatis Joachimi et Anselmi Episcopi Marsciani. See Regiselmo, Pasqualino
Visio Fratris Johannis
contains other prophecies of holy popes, 30n
establishes date of first eight pope prophecies (1292), 6n, 7, 8n, 16, 34–35
makes no reference to the captions, 53

William of St. Amour School, 66n

MRTS

MEDIEVAL AND RENAISSANCE TEXTS AND STUDIES
is the major publishing program of the
Arizona Center for Medieval and Renaissance Studies
at Arizona State University, Tempe, Arizona.

MRTS emphasizes books that are needed —
texts, translations, and major research tools.

MRTS aims to publish the highest quality scholarship
in attractive and durable format at modest cost.